INDIA

Northern, Northeastern and Central India

Second Edition
completely revised
1994

TABLE OF CONTENTS

WHERE FANTASY REIGNED

SPECIAL INTERESTS

FEATURES

GUIDELINES

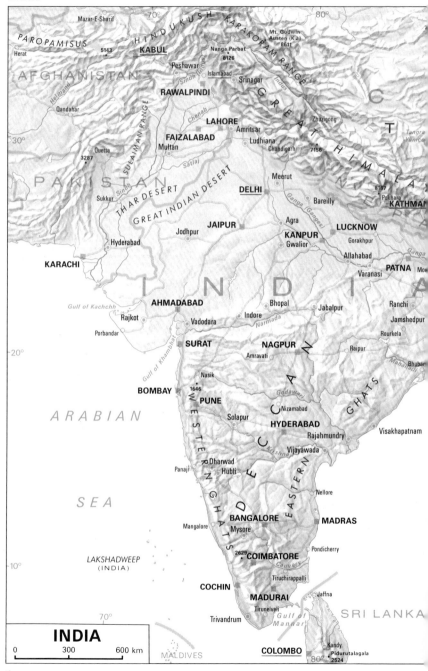

INDIA

0   300   600 km

LIST OF MAPS

Please note: in some cases the spelling of the place names on the maps is not the same as in the text, because the spelling on the maps is according to UN guidelines, whereas the usual English spelling is used in the text.

Nelles Guides

... get you going.

AVAIABLE TITLES

Australia
Bali - Lombok
Berlin
 and Potsdam
Brittany
California
 Las Vegas, Reno, Baja California
Caribbean
 The Greater Antilles, Bermuda,
 Bahamas
Caribbean
 The Lesser Antilles
Crete
Cyprus
Egypt
Florida
Hawaii
Hungary
India
 Northern, Northeastern
 and Central India
India
 Southern India
Indonesia *West*
Kenya
Mexico
Morocco

Munich
 and Surroundings
Nepal
New York
 City and State
New Zealand
Paris
Philippines
Provence
Spain
 North
Spain
 South
Thailand
Turkey

IN PREPARATION

Cambodia - Laos
Canada
 East
China
Malaysia
Moscow - St. Petersburg
Rome

INDIA - Northern, Northeastern
 and Central India
© Nelles Verlag GmbH, D-80935 München
 All rights reserved

2. Edition completely revised 1994

ISBN 3-88618-404-8
Printed in Slovenia

Publisher:	Günter Nelles	**Cartography:**	Nelles Verlag
		Color	
Chief Editor:	Dr. Heinz Vestner	**Separation:**	Priegnitz, München
Project Editor:	Shalini Saran	**Printed by:**	Gorenjski Tisk

- 04 -

12

AN INVITATION TO INDIA

"India is like an ancient palimpsest on which layer upon layer of thought and reverie has been inscribed. This is the complex and mysterious personality of India. ... About her is the elusive quality of a legend long ago; some enchantment seems to have held her mind. She is a myth and an idea, a dream and a vision, and yet very real and present and pervasive."

- Jawaharlal Nehru -

Indophiles are unable to define the true essence of India, but all agree that there are certain characteristics which yield a glimpse of it. India's infinite variety, clichéd as it has begun to sound, is one of these features which frequently overwhelm even the experienced Indian traveler.

This variety has arisen, to a large extent, from the assimilation of alien influences into the Indian mainstream throughout the course of history. While some of these influences underwent further change, geographical factors and the sheer size of the country prevented their simultaneous and even impact.

Before the advent of British rule in the 19th century, political unity had been experienced only in the 3rd century B.C. While, in the span of 2000 years and more, highly evolved and sophisticated achievements occured at the many centers of religion and power, there were – and still are – vast areas where folk and tribal cultures remained virtually untouched.

Preceding pages: The Raja of Bundi, Rajasthan (19th century). The cowdust hour. 18th-century miniature painting from Kishangarh. Scenic valley near Lamayoro, Ladakh. Candlelight at Diwali festival. Left: Dandiya dancer, Rajasthan.

This diversity is increased by the coexistence of ancient and contemporary beliefs and ideas, occupations and lifestyles and differing modes of creative expression. It accounts for India's contradictions, and for quaint, and sometimes startling, juxtapositions; but it also lends an extraordinary vitality and texture to life. It allows for a lively range of possibilities, and reveals the astonishing ability of the Indians to take the most incongruous situations in their stride.

As unique and deep-seated as this diversity is the unmistakable presence of a deeply unifying factor, an "Indianness" as it were, which is pervasive, vital and enduring. Even today, in the face of rapid industrialization and change, and in the midst of poverty and hardship, there is a certain poetry to life in India. It is not merely the poetry of the picturesque, and less still of the legendary erotica often associated with India, but a far more profound poetry, integral to a world-view that is not entirely materialistic. It manifests itself through inspiration rather than design, and at many levels – in the brilliant marigolds that the wayside vendor scatters upon his heap of purple berries; in the reverence with which hill folk regard the majestic Himalaya; in the full-throated song of the desert dweller; in the sublime ecstasy of classical art; in the beauty of symbolic expression.

You will experience this poetry if you can look beyond the crowds and the confusion; if your vision is not clouded by preconceived – and often, misconceived – ideas; and if you do not try to resist the Indian pace of life. It can move you to question much that you have always taken for granted. And it can touch you so deeply as to remain more than a memory when you return home.

Today, India has emerged as the world's largest democracy and the phase of transition into a modern society, though not without its traumas, is a dynamic one. It is as necessary to respond to this as to the splendors of the past, if you wish to understand India. We hope that this Nelles Guide will be a helpful and inspiring companion on your journey through India.

India has been covered in two books – **Northern India** and **Southern India**. They are complementary; although to encapsulate the exuberance, complexity and diversity of a country such as India within even two books is a task both challenging and frustrating.

The challenge has been admirably met by a team of knowledgeable and experienced writers, most of whom are Indian. What you read, therefore, is valuable information combined with the insights of Indians into their own country; insights that have evolved and matured through years of work related to a specific region or interest, and also through having lived or traveled extensively in a particular area. The text is supplemented by wonderfully evocative photographs. There are also over 30 historical and city maps throughout the text.

Northern India begins with "A Profile of Indian Civilization," written by a leading social historian. It gives you a background – historical, social and religious – to north India in particular. This introduction attempts to pinpoint those factors that have shaped the course of India's historical and cultural evolution over the last 3500 years. At the same time, it establishes the tenacious links between the past and present-day India. This introduction will help you to place in context much of what you see in the course of your journey.

The main travel section **Northern India** covers Delhi, Haryana and Punjab, and the plains of Uttar Pradesh; the Himalayan regions of Jammu and Kashmir, Himachal Pradesh and the hills of Uttar Pradesh; Bihar, Calcutta and West Bengal; Sikkim and the Northeastern States; and Rajasthan, Gujarat and Madhya Pradesh. The aim throughout this section

is to bring to life these states and cities so that you may have some idea of what to expect, and, once there, some understanding of what you see. Each state is supplemented by a *Guidepost* which lists details of accommodation, restaurants, tourist offices, museums and festivals, and in the case of the Northeastern States, details about entry permits as well.

The next part of the book focuses on special interests. These are arranged as six itineraries, each of which concentrates on a single interest. They include trekking in the Himalaya; a taste of princely and British India; India's Buddhist heritage; Hinduism's seven sacred cities; and a choice of national parks.

In the features section, which follows, further insight is given through brief texts on six aspects of India which you may be confronted with, read about in newspapers and magazines, or which may perplex you. The subjects range from urban migration and communal strife to the pantheon of Hindu gods and the reasons why the cow is revered in India.

The next part, *Guidelines*, deals with traveling in India, and is a comprehensive list containing, among other details, information on arrival formalities, currency and exchange, health regulations and precautions as well as special schemes offered by airlines and the railways in India. The addresses of airline offices in Delhi and Calcutta, of embassies, high commissions and consulates in India, and of tourist offices abroad have also been included for your convenience.

Some Hindi phrases, which you may like to use more out of fun than necessity, have also been included in *Guidelines*.

The credits acknowledge the work of the writers and photographers. They are among several people who made a valuable contribution to the creation of this book, and who, together, invite you to share the beauty of India.

- Shalini Saran -

A PROFILE OF
INDIAN CIVILIZATION

India is a civilization of classical dignity and antiquity and at the same time it is a young and vibrant nation. Over the span of five millennia and more, the people of India have developed a rare material and moral culture. They have accomplished this through harsh physical toil and incessant labor, through intellectual reflection and artistic exploration.

India's development is characterized by great durability and resilience as well as by a colorful vitality and striking exuberance which is overwhelming in its momentum. The epic scale of Indian civilization merits favorable comparison with some of the greatest civilizations known to history, such as those of Europe or China. Yet it is unique in its lasting fusion of the old with the new; in its ability to merge ancient moral values, social institutions and ways of working with a modern vision and a contemporary industrial culture; and finally, in its capacity to weave a variety of classes and communities into one cohesive social fabric. Moreover, India possesses the ability to retain its distinctive characteristics in the midst of the rapid social transformation that alters other civilizations. One decisive factor in shaping the material culture, the social and political institutions, the artistic output and the spiritual outlook of the people of India is the ecology of the subcontinent. A brief account of the geographical characteristics of India will shed considerable light upon the history as well as the culture of her people.

The northern boundary of the land mass of India is set by the majestic,

Preceding pages: The Taj Mahal at sunset. Left: The quiet rapture of divine lovers, Khajuraho.

snow-clad peaks of the Himalayas, which are, geologically speaking, one of the youngest mountain formations on the face of the earth.

The relatively young age of the Himalayas is reflected as much in the towering height of its peaks as in the characteristics of soil and climate which the mountains bestow upon the great alluvial plain to the south. Towards the northwest, the Himalayas merge into a series of lesser mountain ranges that lack the features of height and gradient which characterize the parent range itself. Furthermore, these lesser ranges of the northwest curve in a southernly direction, to create a junction, through smaller and smaller spurs, with the Arabian Sea, strechung across an axis that marks the western boundary of India.

Through alluvial action over a considerable span of geological time, the lofty ranges of the Himalayas and its related offshoots in the northwest have generated the plains of the Indus and the Ganga (more familiar in the west as the Ganges), which make up a very important segment of the subcontinent. This has been accomplished through thousands of years of ecological action by a massive and intricate network of major and minor rivers, whose capacity to carry water and silt is probably still unrivaled on the face of the earth.

Lifelines of India

The three principal rivers associated with the Himalayas - the Indus, the Ganga and the Brahmaputra, all originate in the central region of this mountain range. However, these mighty rivers, which nourish and sustain both the physical and the spiritual culture of India, all pursue very different terrestrial careers in their passage to the Arabian Sea or to the Bay of Bengal.

The Indus river flows in a westerly direction for quite some distance before it makes a sharp turn, to flow through the fertile alluvial plain that it has created in association with its tributaries, the Jhelum, the Chenab, the Ravi, the Beas, and the Sutlej.

The alluvial plain created by the Indus and its tributaries is, in certain crucial respects, rather different from the one created by the Ganga and the Brahmaputra. Although the Indus plain is also one of the central points of Indian civilization, it lacks the generous rainfall, as well as the fertility of soil, that has made the valley of the Ganga a densely populated region and one of the most vibrant centers of human activity for thousands of years.

The Ganga and the Brahmaputra both originate in the central region of the Himalayas, at a point not far removed from the source of the Indus. Very close to its source, the Ganga descends in a southeasterly direction to the northern tip of its alluvial plain.

Thereafter, it flows eastwards, for 1000 km (620 mi) and more to end its journey in the Bay of Bengal. The Ganga is fed by a network of tributaries, prominent among which are the Yamuna, the Gomti, the Sone, and the Rapti.

Before it turns south for the last leg of its journey, the Ganga is joined by the great flood-tide of the Brahmaputra, a river that is monumental in the sheer volume of water that it carries down from the Himalayas to the plains, and also monumental in the fertility as well as the occasional destruction that it bestows upon the valley through which it flows to meet its junction with the Ganga.

The great alluvial plain of the Ganga and its tributaries constitutes the heartland of the civilization of India. Here, in a compact segment of the subcontinent – barely 400 km (249 mi) along its north to south axis, and not more than 1,200 km (746 mi) along its east to west axis – has

lies a land mass that, over the ages, has harbored a mass of humanity greater than any other comparable region on earth. Here, over many centuries, if not millennia, the people of India have developed a distinctive material culture, social order, spiritual and moral outlook that have collectively sustained them as an individual civilization.

The valley of the Ganga has been the epicenter for people and society in India since the very dawn of history. The river itself has always featured prominently in the myths, dreams, hopes and aspirations of the common people, just as it has always been vital in the organization of the agricultural activity that supports and feeds them.

In the words of Jawaharlal Nehru, a distinguished Indian of the 20th century, the people of India are tied to this great river by an umbilical cord which only the total destruction of their culture could sever:

The Ganga, especially, is the river of India, beloved of her people, round which are intertwined her racial memories, her hopes and fears, her songs of triumph, her victories and her defeats. She has been a symbol of India's age-long culture and civilization, ever-changing, ever-flowing, and yet ever the same Ganga. She reminds me of the snow-covered peaks and the deep valleys of the Himalayas, which I have loved so much, and of the rich and vast plains below, where my life and work have been cast. Smiling and dancing in the morning sunlight, and dark and gloomy and full of mystery as the evening shadows fall, a narrow, slow and graceful stream in winter, and a vast roaring thing during the monsoon, broad-bosomed almost as the sea, and with something of the sea's power to destroy, the Ganga has been to me a symbol and a memory of the past of India, running into

Right: The Alaknanda and Bhagirathi rivers mingle at Deoprayag, to form the Ganga.

the present and flowing on to the great ocean of the future.

The people of India believe that there is no river comparable to the Ganga on the face of the earth and the civilization that it has sustained over the centuries, as well as the multitude of life and the moral outlook that it sustains even today. The Ganga is symbolic of the human toil and spiritual striving that is the life force of India which combines in the creative spirit of man.

A crucial factor in shaping the climate of north India, and indeed, of the subcontinent as a whole, is the seasonal rainfall also known as the monsoon. This rainfall originates in moisture-bearing winds that blow in a northeasterly direction across the land mass of India, from the Arabian Sea and the Bay of Bengal during the months of summer.

As the monsoon crooses the alluvial plain of the Ganga – and to a lesser extent, the valley of the Indus – it provides vital water for crops and thus shapes the cycle of agricultural production. Like the mountains and the rivers, the monsoon is another crucial constituent of the ecological cycle of India. And also like the mountains and the rivers, the monsoon features centrally in the religious life and the artistic creation of the people of the subcontinent. Although the valleys of the Indus and the Ganga form two of the core regions of India, there are other important ecological and cultural characteristics to consider.

To the south of these valleys stands a formidable range of mountains called the Vindhya, which separate the alluvial plains of north India from the rest of the subcontinent. The peninsular land mass south of the Vindhya is characterized by a number of substantial rivers, most of which originate in the mountain ranges parallel to the western coast of the subcontinent (called the Western Ghats) and thereafter flow eastwards to the Bay of Bengal. The rivers south of the Vindhya – the Mahanadi, the Godavari, the Krishna and the Kaveri – do not rival the rivers of north India, neither in the vol-

21

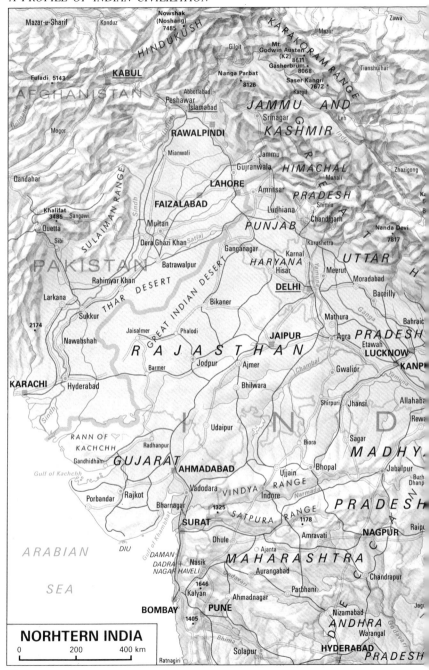

NORHTERN INDIA

0   200   400 km

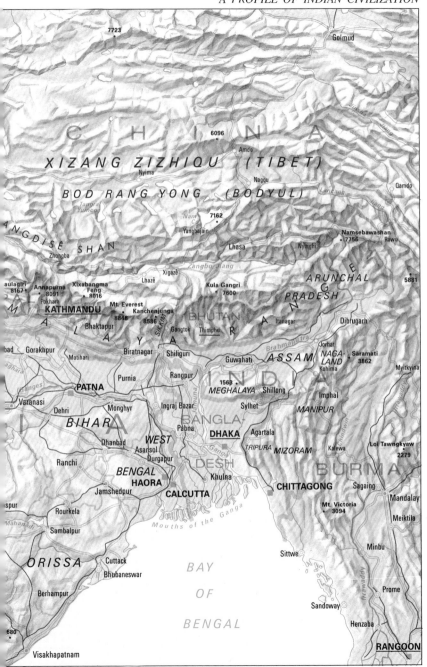

ume of water they discharge into the seas, nor in the scale and magnitude of the alluvial plains that they have created over millenia of geological time. Nevertheless, the river valleys of the south are significant as centers of agricultural activity and cultural creativity. In these regions, too, over the course of time agricultural communities grew up which evolved a material and moral culture that is comparable to those of similar communities in the north, and integral to the composite civilization of India.

The Indus Civilization

Although the culture and artifacts attributed to prehistoric man in India are very old indeed, it is only with the emergence of the Indus Valley civilization in the third millennium B.C. that we witness

Above: The city of Mohenjodaro as visualized by an artist (Mohenjodaro Museum).
Right: Remnant of a vanished civilization: A steatite seal from Mohenjodaro.

for the first time a great flowering of human activity in the subcontinent. This civilization flourished principally in the region of India that now constitutes the sovereign state of Pakistan. Its geographical expansion ranged from Lothal in Gujarat, on the western seacoast of India, through Rajasthan, to sites like Ropar in the Punjab, in the foothills of the Himalayas.

The flourishing cities, towns and ports that characterized the Indus civilization were sustained by an agrarian economy relying on wheat as the principal crop. It is likely that the climate of the Indus valley was different from its climate today, as fossil remains of the flora and fauna of the region in the third millennium B.C. suggest a heavier rainfall than that experienced today.

It would be appropriate to mention briefly some of the important features of this civilization, because of its great influence on the culture of India, historically as well as contemporaneously. It is important to remember that the settle-

ments, whether large or small, of the Indus people were not without their own pre-history. Archaeological evidence points to a long era of gradual development of small human settlements, partly pastoral and partly agricultural, which preceded the amazing emergence of one of the greatest proto-historical cultures known to human history. However, in the ancient twin cities of Mohenjodaro and Harappa, which were once located on the banks of the Indus, at a distance of 600 km (313 mi) apart, this culture achieved its loftiest expression.

The social and cultural activity of the people of the Indus has been reconstructed through the remains of their cities, or through the artifacts – particularly ceramic wares of exquisite quality and design – that were a common part of their daily life.

The cities of Mohenjodaro and Harappa were large and well planned in their social organization. The layout of the cities was probably unequalled in the subcontinent until the late medieval centuries. There is clear evidence of orderly civic institutions which organized the basic amenities of life, like the supply and drainage of water. They carefully husbanded all the resources necessary to sustain a collective social existence, material and spiritual, through the provision of public granaries, places of worship, or as in the port of Lothal, facilities for the anchorage of ships which sailed across the seas to conduct trade with the contemporary cultures of West Asia.

Perhaps the most striking legacy of the Indus civilization is the very large number of seals that it has bequeathed to posterity. These seals were made of steatite and other materials, and, sculpted in bold relief, they depict a variety of gods, goddesses, sacred animals, totemic designs, folk emblems, or scenes of solemn ritual or secular activities. The seals also contain as yet unsatisfactorily deciphered inscriptions. As a result our knowledge of life in the Indus civilization still remains somewhat incompletes. Indeed, the decipherment of the Indus script would reveal many details about the ethnic character of the people and their relationship with subsequent folk migrations to India.

Just as striking as the seals are some of the sculptures – a bronze dancing girl; a torso with a missing head; the head of a priest or a warrior – all relics of the Indus civilization. Finally, no account of the artistic activity of this civilization would be complete without reference to the terracotta "Mother-Goddess" figurines that are found in great profusion in the settlements of this epoch. In total, therefore, some of the distinctive features of the people of the Indus have, over the centuries, become integral parts of Indian civilization as a whole and have given the inhabitants of the subcontinent much of the poise and sense of continuity that have been needed during eras of traumatic social transformation and challenges of history.

The Aryans

The reasons behind the decay of the Indus civilisation are not fully known. One possible reason was the arrival in north India of a new group of pastoral folk, who referred to themselves as "Aryans". These new arrivals produced a substantial amount of literature, partly religous and partly social in Character, which not only relates to their arrival in India around 1500 B.C. but also draws upon their memory of an earlier home outside of the subcontinent. The origin of the Aryans, who were at one time considered an indigenous people, is somewhat shrouded in mystery. However, there is reason to believe that the Aryan tribes hailed from the Caspian region, or from the southern steppes of Russia, and moved in a southeasterly direction from their original homeland during first half

Right: A Bengali bride and groom exchange garlands; the first ritual of a Hindu wedding ceremony.

of the second millennium B.C. some reaching the regions of Asia Minor, some migrating to modern Iran, and some finally crossing the mountainous belt that surrounds northwestern India to descend upon the great alluvial plain of the Indus and its tributaries.

The relationship between the pastoral Aryans and the earlier communities of northwestern India, whether they belonged to the Indus civilization or to less sophisticated cultures, is difficult to establish with any measure of certainty. However, in the literature created by the Aryans, there is a folk memory of their tribal leaders, often protrayed as gods such as Indra, destroying fortified settlements, called *purs*, that had been built by communities which were, in all probability, sections of the Indus civilization. There are also references to conflict with communities living in the forests and surviving through food-gathering and hunting. It is clear that as the Aryans journeyed into northern India, they established numerous settlements along the rivers, first of all along the Indus and its tributaries then in the Gangetic basin. Over and above this, the Aryans gradually adapted to the business of agriculture, but without wholly abandoning their traditional pastoral way of life.

The gradual settlement of the Aryan tribes into the northwest, and then the north, of India is vividly reflected in the prolific literature that they have bequeathed to posterity under the collective name of the Vedas. The Vedas are four in number - the *Rig Veda*, the *Sama Veda*, the *Yajur Veda*, and the *Atharva Veda*. They were composed in Sanskrit, the language of the Aryans. They also formed part of an oral tradition, which was transmitted down the centuries by generations of religious specialists, whose members memorized segments of the Vedas for recitation on sacred occasions. While it is difficult to ascribe a precise date to this massive body of Indian writing, it is very

likely that the earliest segment of this ancient literature, partly reflected in the compilation of the *Rig* and partly also in that of the *Atharva Veda*, dates back to the closing centuries of the second millennium B.C.

The Vedas consist of an enormous collection of verses created by the shamans and priests of the Aryan tribes, and they embody the thinking of these men of religion as they attempted to incorporate into the world-view of their tribal communities the sacred and profane experiences of life. Some of the poetical compositions of the Vedas touched upon the phenomena of nature which the Aryans discovered with a dramatic intensity in their new homeland. Others dwell upon the birth of the universe and the appearance of people, as well as of their social orders. Others, again, draw upon folk myth and sympathetic magic and are inspired by the belief that the power of speech had a potency which conferred upon people control over the elements and, indeed, over one's social destiny.

Collectively, the Vedas refer to a variety of gods – Varuna, Rudra or Shiva, Agni, Prajapati and Vishnu, to mention only a few - whom we shall encounter later within the fully established pantheon of Hinduism.

The literature produced by the Aryan seers was by no means exclusively sacred in character. It also provides evidence, indirect rather than direct, about social organization and political structure. When the Aryans arrived in India with their pastoral wealth and their superior military prowess, they were already differentiated into chiefs and horse-riding warriors, on the one hand, and the common run of tribal folk, whose skills and labor underpinned the social existence of the community as a whole, on the other. An equally significant figure within each tribe was the religious leader, a priest or a shaman, whose store of wisdom and knowledge of ritual provided the little community with the moral armory necessary for sustenance and survival. Needless to say, the wisdom and the

magical power of the priests were a crucial constituent of the collective wisdom and power of the tribe, and provided the chief and the warrior elite with the courage and skills necessary for overwhelming the indigenous people, for warfare with other competing Aryan tribes, and for establishing themselves in a new world. The rites of passage that were devised by the priests at this juncture became so deeply entrenched in the sacred lifestyle of the Aryans that even today across the span of three millennia, they determine the ritual life of orthodox Hindus.

The Vedas provide us with a fascinating picture of the settlements, increasingly agricultural in character, that the Aryan tribes created for themselves in their new homeland. The flocks of cattle which the Aryans brought with them still

Above: This south Indian woman fulfills her dream of bathing in the Ganga at Varanasi. Right: A Brahmin worshipping at the sacred river Ganga at sunrise.

constituted an important, though secondary, source of wealth for the tribe, but the agricultural activity that they initiated, soon became their primary source of sustenance. Moreover, as they moved into the more fertile valley of the Ganga, they turned increasingly from the cultivation of wheat to the cultivation of rice. Each homestead in an Aryan village, often a settlement strategically located on a river bank, was presided over by the elder of the family. The voice of this elder was an important force in resolving the affairs of his family, at the same time as it featured decisively in the village council, which resolved the affairs of the rural community as a whole.

A powerful lineage of elders in a settlement, or a group of settlements, provided the warrior elite of the tribe, and this lineage was quite clearly differentiated from other members of the tribe through the designation of Kshatriya. The warrior elite often elected one from among them as a lineage head, and as the chief of the tribal settlements as a whole. The politi-

cal power and military skills of the Kshatriya elite were counterpoised as well as supported by the spiritual power and ritualistic skills of the priestly leaders, who soon came to be designated as Brahmins. These Brahmins – or the truly inspired men among them – were the creators of the great body of poetical compositions which constitute the Vedas. The relationship between the Kshatriya and the Brahmin thus reflected a relationship of tension and balance between the wielders of political power and spiritual authority within a community.

Below the warrior and priestly elite stood the bulk of the tribal folk, who were engaged in agricultural and pastoral activity and who were designated as the Vis, later changed into the Vaishya.

There is a clear hint in the Vedas that the aboriginal folk of the forests and marginal lands were drawn into the rural settlements as an inferior social class upon whom many of the more burdensome tasks of cultivation and cattle rearing were heaped. The members of this inferior class were designated as Sudra and the Vedas unambiguously suggest that the Sudras were a lowly folk, non-Aryan in origin, whose dark complexions and snub noses differentiated them from the high born Aryans, Kshatriyas and Brahmins alike, who were their conquerors and subjugators.

Perhaps the origin of the caste system within Hindu society rests upon the social formations that resulted from the migration of the pastoral Aryan tribes into the plains of north and northwestern India; their transformation into sedentary tribal communities engaged in wheat- or rice-based agriculture; and their interaction with indigenous folk, who originally sustained themselves through hunting and food-gathering. These people were drawn into the activities of the new settlers and into the fabric of their new society, as the most underprivileged class. The Vedas throw very little direct light upon the fate of the people who had created the highly urbanized Indus civilization. Yet archaeological evidence relat-

ing to protohistorical and classical India corroborates fairly positively the tentative clues provided by the literary texts of the period that have survived into our own times.

We have more than abundant evidence of the decay of the cities of the Indus Valley, and their eventual destruction, either through the havoc wrought by floods, or through the devastation engineered by the warring Aryan tribes. Yet the Vedic compositions speak just as much of conflict between different Aryan tribes as they do of conflict between the incoming Aryans and the indigenous communities of the subcontinent.

The intertribal warfare, in which the members of the Kshatriya groups took part under the leadership of their Rajanya (later Rajas), or elected chiefs, clearly reflects a point at which the Aryan tribes had completed the first stage of settlement in their new homeland, and had, thereafter, turned to the business of consolidating their hold over their newly acquired lands. During this phase there was bitter squabbling between rival tribes and even rival lineages for control of the more fertile territories.

Mahabharata and Ramayana

It would be untrue to suggest that each phase in the history of Indian civilization is characterized by a distinctive literature, reflecting the changes in the life of the people. Nevertheless, it is true that the epic literature of the Hindus, comprising the *Mahabharata* and the *Ramayana*, carries the story of the initial migration and settlement within the subcontinent of the Aryan communities to a stage beyond the arrival of the Aryans, told above. From all accounts, the *Mahabharata* is the older of the two, and it deals with the

Left: The rice-paste symbol on her forehead reveals that this Bengali lady is a Vaishnavite.

lifestyles and struggles of the Aryan tribes after they had settled in the region of the upper valley of the Ganga and the Yamuna, around Delhi. It was originally composed by the sage Vyasa, around the beginning of the first millennium B.C. although the text has numerous later interpolations.

The *Mahabharata* revolves around a fratricidal war between two groups of cousins, the Kauravas and the Pandavas, who had a common ancestor in their grandfather, Vichitravirya. As the Kauravas had a blind father, Dhritrashtra, who could not rule because of his infirmity, the responsibility of ruling over Hastinapur, the center of their kingdom, was passed on to his younger brother, Pandu. However, when the Kaurava princes came of age, they asserted their right to rule over Hastinapur through the eldest brother, Duryodhana, who was a formidable warrior and a man of insatiable ambition. The Pandavas were then given a piece of territory adjoining Hastinapur and, in Indraprastha, a site within the modern city of Delhi, they built for themselves a new capital for the domain allocated to them.

Although the ancestral domain of their forefathers had been divided between the Kauravas and the Pandavas, the partition of these territories did not bring about peace between the cousins. The conflict between them resulted in a major war, characterized by much bloodshed, during the course of which the Pandavas defeated the Kauravas and won for themselves a primary position in the affairs of the region. A crucial part was played in these events by the semi-divine hero, Krishna, who ruled over the Yadavas - a pastoral community living around the ancient city of Mathura, near Delhi. With the help of Krishna, the Pandavas were able to defeat their cousins and establish their hold over north India.

As a result of later interpolations, the *Mahabharata* serves as a veritable ency-

clopedia of the life and vision, the politics and society of the Aryan communities at a very significant phase of their existence. At the center of the epic is a long philosophical composition – the *Bhagavata Gita* – which sets out a dialogue between Krishna and the Pandu warrior, Arjuna, on the eve of the Great War. It is difficult to explain the panorama of social and reflective issues spelt out in the *Mahabharata*, which is the largest epic known to history. This great work not only provides a fascinating glimpse into the life and times of the people of north India during the first half of the first millennium B.C., it also draws into its composition the full range of philosophical thought that was available to man at this juncture.

The *Ramayana*, which was composed by the poet Valmiki, relates to a slightly later phase of the Aryan settlement within India. The *Ramayana* details the

Above: An offering of vermilion suffuses this ancient weather-worn image with beauty.

Aryan tribes and their politics in the central regions of the Gangetic valley, around the modern city of Ayodhya. It deals with the history of the royal house of the Raghus, whose political power was based upon control of the agricultural community in this location. The ruler of Ayodhya, Dasaratha, was obliged to send his eldest son, Prince Rama, into exile in order to atone for a folly committed by him in his youth. The consequent wanderings of Rama took him into hitherto unexplored regions beyond the Vindhya, which constituted the southern boundary of the Gangetic plain.

It is clear that the journeys of Rama represent the first Aryan penetration into a region which, so the epic suggests, was inhabited by tribes who lived by hunting and food-gathering. The exiled prince was drawn into the fierce factionalism of the tribes beyond the Aryan pale, and at the same time his consort was abducted by one of the tribal chiefs. Rama was able to vanquish his aboriginal enemy through the assistance of some friendly tribes, and, in the process, he carried "Aryanization" to the indigenous communities in a hitherto unexplored part of the subcontinent. Subsequent workings of the *Ramayana* not only elevate Prince Rama into a god incarnate, they also greatly extend the geographical horizons of the setting in which the story was enacted.

Just as the conflict between the Kauravas and the Pandavas, in the *Mahabharata,* was elevated into an Armageddon in which all the rulers of north and northeast India were drawn, the glosses put on the *Ramayana* by later authors transformed it into an account of the Aryan penetration of south India and Sri Lanka.

Nevertheless, even if we strip the two epics of later embellishments, it is clear that they mark a crucial stage in the moral and material consolidation of the Aryan communities in the subcontinent and the consequent evolution of Indian civilization. Indeed, even in our own times, the profound impact of the *Mahabharata* and the *Ramayana* is still powerfully reflected in the classical, no less than in the popular, culture of India.

Hinduism and Buddhism

The end of this epic era dates the Aryan colonization of the Gangetic valley to about 500 B.C. The consolidation of the social hierarchy and the political order which took place at this juncture are reflected in the literature and in the archaeological remains of the period. Throughout the valley of the Ganga, there exist a large number of sites whose earlier history is characterized by a distinctive early ceramic industry, called painted grey ware. This phase coincides with the centuries that witnessed the social turmoil reflected in the epic literature.

The level of material culture of this period was, to start with, relatively modest. However, the increasing differentiation of society brought about by the growth of agriculture is reflected in the emergence of a new ceramic industry – northern black polished ware. It is likely that the social classes who utilized this aristocratic ceramic ware were in possession of both wealth and leisure.

Yet another striking development of this period was the discovery of extensive deposits of iron, particularly in the region around the present-day Patna, called Magadha. The location of substantial iron deposits and the development of an iron technology triggered off a crucial transformation in the valley of the Ganga. For the first time, the use of iron implements facilitated the clearance of dense forests on an unprecedented scale; simultaneously, the iron tipped plow enabled the cultivators to turn the thick alluvial soil of the Gangetic plain more effectively, and thereby greatly extended the horizons of Indian agriculture.

The Kshatriya warriors could also now arm themselves with weapons of iron, rather than weapons of copper or bronze, and thus gain a technical advantage over their opponents. Indeed, this was a period in which conflict between local and regional powers acquired an intensity that had been absent in earlier times. The advantage in this conflict between the powers, big and small, lay with the regional state of Magadha, which had a prosperous agricultural hinterland, which controlled the rich iron ores located in its proximity, and which, through its capital city of Pataliputra (the original name of Patna), also controlled the riverine trade along the lower Gangetic Valley.

The emerging political scene in north India can be graphically reconstructed from contemporary literary texts. There were about 12 or more major states in this region in the 6th century B.C., which stretched out in the shape of a great arc, with its northwestern arm resting upon the Indus and its tributaries, and its south-

eastern arm resting upon the delta of the Ganga. The region thus constituted the social and political axis of north India, a position it still occupies today, even after an interval of 2,500 years. Some of the states referred to above had emerged through conflict between local polities, and were presided over by Kshatriya lineages which often elected one from among them as a chief or a *rajanya*. Others were organized in the form of republican states, in which authority was vested collectively in the dominant Kshatriya communities, rather than in a *rajanya*, or a tribal chief.

Monarchical polities were more often than not located in the most fertile zones of the valley of the Ganga, where substantial agrarian surpluses had stimulated the accumulation of wealth and the concentration of authority in the hands of rulers, whose office gradually came to be transmitted from father to son. Precisely

for the same reason, the republican states were located in the sub-Himalayans and semi-arid regions, where the soil did not yield substantial surpluses. Some of the most prominent states of the 6th century B.C. were those of Gandhara, Kuru, Panchala, Matsya, Kosala, Kashi, Magadha and Anga. Of these states, Magadha was destined to eclipse all others and emerge as the first pan-Indian state in the history of the whole subcontinent.

The growth of the agrarian economy and the development of the regional states was accompanied by changes in the moral outlook of the people of the region. The later Vedas, reflecting a change in social, political and economic conditions, speak clearly of a more complex and differentiated society. Indeed, some of the verses of the Vedas seek divine sanction for the hierarchical orders that characterized society in this period.

Moreover, the profound philosophical reflections of the Brahmins now went considerably beyond the relatively simple concepts about life in this world and

Above: A gathering of village elders whose opinions still hold considerable weight.

beyond, formulated by their forefathers. These reflections are embodied in a new corpus of literature, called the Brahmanas and the Upanishads.

Hindu Philosophy

These two texts set out the six most important formal schools of Hindu philosophy, namely Nyaya, Vaisesika, Samkhya, Yoga, Purvamimamsa and Vedanta. Whatever the distinctive characteristics of these formal schools of philosophy might be, they all arrived at one common discourse, and revolved around concepts which, in their essence, formed the basis of Hinduism as it still exists today in the late 20th century.

The far-reaching ideas triggered off in the Brahmanas and the Upanishads, particularly the latter, were those of *Brahman*, *Atman*, *Moksha*, *Dharma*, *Samsara* and *Karma*. *Brahman* constituted the essential reality behind the ephemeral phenomenal world as well as the Absolute. *Atman* was the projection of this reality into the consciousness of the individual. *Moksha* referred to the liberation of man from the world through the realization that *Atman* was identical with *Brahman*. *Dharma* was the moral law which guided man through the sacred, no less than through the profane, world.

Samsara denoted the circle of birth and rebirth from which the individual sought *Moksha* or liberation through the observance of the moral law of *Dharma*. Last but not least, *Karma* denoted the social action of man which determined the place he would occupy on his rebirth in the world of *Samsara*. The endless cycles of birth and rebirth constituted the meshes of *Samsara* from which man sought *Moksha* or liberation, through the observance of *Dharma* acquiring a true awareness of his identity and, finally, through the realization that his *Atman* was identical, he would finally merge into *Brahman*.

Diversity of Religious Beliefs

Perhaps it would be appropriate here briefly to compare the ideological structure of Hinduism with that of Semitic religions like Judaism and Christianity. Unlike the latter, Hinduism is characterized by a wide range of philosophical beliefs and a great diversity of social communities organized into distinctive cults, sects and denominations. Indeed, the sacred no less than the profane world of Hinduism can be understood much better through a comparison with the pagan culture of classical Greece, or the religious outlook of the Scandinavian communities before they were drawn into the moral vision of Christianity.

While the formal schools of Hinduism, drawing upon a common moral discourse, reflected speculation and debate among the warrior and priestly elites, there also existed robust undercurrents of belief, thought and practice, wholly at variance with these schools, among the lowly farming classes, or among the food-gathering and hunting communities located on the margins of a civilized society. The lowly Aryan classes, as well as the pre-Aryan aborigines who had been drawn into Indian civilization, brought with them a conceptual order resting upon tribal gods and goddesses and totemic beliefs, which brought to the contemporary spiritual situation a great diversity of religious belief and spiritual outlook.

Some of the deities of the lowly classes were merged with Aryan gods in a bid to provide an ideological basis for a more cohesive social order. Thus the semi-divine hero Krishna, who featured so prominently in the *Mahabharata*, became the center of a new cult, whereby a large number of tribes whose members worshiped mother goddesses were integrated into a larger collectivity. This social process was reflected in the religious domain in the sacred love-play between

Krishna and his *gopis* or milkmaids. However, much more significant than the various steps of integration mentioned above, which moved along parallel lines in the secular and spiritual domain, were the forms of folk belief covered by the generic term *Lokayata*, or the "Way of the People". The *Lokayata* did not correspond to the spectrum of views contained within the moral discourse of the Vedas, the Brahmanas and the Upanishads. The formulators of the *Lokayata* looked askance at the transcendent concepts which formed the bases of the formal schools of Hindu philosophy. Instead, they subscribed to very matter-of-fact views regarding earthly existence and life beyond.

To describe the world-view set out in the *Lokayata* as materialistic, in contrast to the idealism of the elite texts, would, perhaps, be to give too formal a definition to beliefs whose articulation was loose and amorphous rather than structured and rigorous in character. Nevertheless, the down-to-earth concerns of the lowly classes within or outside the Aryan fold were completely at variance with the lofty concerns of salvation (*Moksha*), and union of the individual soul (*Atman*) with the universal (*Brahman*) voiced in the Brahmanas and the Upanishads with such philosophical felicity and logical rigor.

The Age of the Buddha

In the middle of the first millennium B.C, yet another eloquent voice within Indian civilization was that of the Sakyan prince Siddhartha, better known to the world as the Buddha, or the Enlightened One. The Buddha, who was born in 566 B.C., appeared at a time when the differentiation of society in India and its spiritual development within a certain

Right: The Buddha preaching his First Sermon at Sarnath (Sarnath Museum).

framework had already attained an advanced level.

The Brahminical world-view, with its division of the social order into different castes and its emphasis upon ritual and sacrifice, upheld the secular power of the kingly rulers and Kshatriya warrior elites at the same time as it upheld the spiritual power of the priestly specialists. Yet this established world-view, as the *Lokayata* suggests, did not satisfy individuals or social classes who were uneasy with the amoral manner in which the Kshatriya elites and the priestly intelligentsia lived off the labor of others. It is relevant that the Sakyan community into which Siddhartha was born was a republican, and not a monarchical, polity.

The record of the times suggests that as the young Prince Siddhartha journeyed through the valley of the Ganga, in search of a new moral order, he came across many individuals who were engaged in a similar spiritual enterprise. As is also well known, while reflecting upon the human condition at Bodh Gaya, in modern Bihar, the Buddha attained Enlightenment, and thereafter held out to mankind a new path for its salvation.

The wheel of *Dharma*, or the moral law, which the Buddha set in motion through a sermon he addressed to a small group of disciples at Sarnath, rested upon a few seminal principles.

The Buddha looked upon desire and covetousness as the source of all human misery and suffering. He further believed that the annihilation of the desire to control and to possess, through the exercise of constraint and self-discipline, would enable men to acquire for themselves a state of perfect harmony. Thus, rightful conduct rather than regard for ritual, or acquiescence in social hierarchy, opened the path to the attainment of salvation or *Moksha*, which enabled man to escape the endless cycle of birth and rebirth.

Over and above this, the Buddha refused to voice any opinion regarding the

existence or non-existence of God. Instead, the most striking quality of the phenomenal world, as he saw it, was the unquestionable fact that it was in a state of permanent flux.

The Buddha was not only the founder of a new moral discourse. He also provided an institutional support for his ideas. In the *Sangha*, or the monastic order, he devised, for the first time in the history of world religions, a base for his followers who could lead a pure life at the same time as they disseminated the views of their mentor to the people.

The Buddha, along with a few of his chosen disciples, spent a great portion of his life in propagating the new message among the people who resided in the heartland of the Gangetic Valley. By the time he attained *nirvana* in 483 B.C. he had already brought about a dramatic

Above: Jain nuns renounce wordly pleasures to follow a path of severe austerity. Right: The sunlight pours into the sparse, makeshift shrine of this sadhu.

transformation in the moral climate of this region.

A contemporary of the Buddha, who expressed the disquiet of this period with similar eloquence, was Mahavira. He founded the puritanical sect of the Jains. Mahavira, who was born in 540 B.C., also wandered around the valley of the Ganga in search of spiritual understanding before enlightenment came to him, as it came to the Buddha. The ideas upon which Mahavira founded his sect were in circulation before him, but he organized these ideas into a coherent shape. He believed that the universe functioned according to an eternal law whereby it went through cosmic phases of progress and decline.

Every living being had a soul whose purification and consequent transference to a state of perennial bliss was the objective of all true knowledge. The purification of the soul, so Mahavira believed, was further possible only through strict non-violence and the adoption of a lifestyle so austere that it could be pursued

only by men of religion. Jainism never acquired the popularity of Buddhism. But the message of Mahavira spread from the valley of the Ganga to western India and to the south. Furthermore, the philosophy of Jainism deeply influenced art and culture in later centuries and this influence is reflected in the architecture and sculpture of India as well as in paintings in illustrated manuscripts.

Asoka and the Mauryan Empire

To regard the Brahminical and the Buddhist world-views as antagonistic is seriously to misread the moral culture of Indian civilization in the middle of the first millennium B.C. During past centuries as well as today, the content of this civilization was richly plural and characterized by a variety of speculative visions. The differences between the Brahminical and the Buddhist standpoints can legitimately be regarded as the complementary outlooks of a society in which the formation of a profound agricultural revolution, and the consequent differentiation of society and institutionalization of politics, had created the need for a new outlook on sacred and profane phenomena. The Buddha sought to give dignity and knowledge to men trapped in an era of dramatic social change, at the same time as he drew upon the tremendous freedom given to the ascetic, or the *sannyasin*, within caste society to create a cadre of activists who would offer ethical teaching about social order. It is difficult to assess the degree of success that the Buddha achieved in his own times. However, later accounts of his dialogues with men of substance, princes and merchants, as well as with ordinary men in contemporary society, speak of the profound influence he exercised during his lifetime. Indeed, the Buddha's personal stature, no less than his influence upon the spiritual history of mankind, mark him out as the greatest son of India.

The social and political conflict of this period provided a particularly poignant setting for the ethical values that characterized the Buddha's message to rich and poor alike. Small wonder, then, that somewhat later, in the 3rd century B.C. when the Emperor Asoka was able to consolidate the entire subcontinent into a vast pan-Indian state, he discerned in the *Dharma*, or the moral law of the Buddha, an admirable basis for promoting social peace in his domain.

Asoka was drawn to the teachings of the Buddha early in his imperial career. As a result of this influence, he set out a code of behavior for his subjects – who were divided into diverse regional cultures, into warring sects and denominations, and, finally, into different communities of caste and tribe – which sought to teach social tolerance and religious catholicity to them in their relations with each other.

This code was inscribed on stone pillars and rocks placed throughout the four corners of the empire, in market centers, at crossroads and thoroughfares, and in the cities, large and small, where the people could read it and be influenced by it. In these inscriptions, Asoka defined social tolerance and spiritual generosity as the true basis of the good society, particularly necessary in a country so highly differentiated in its culture and social organization as India.

Perhaps one facet of the achievement of Asoka needs to be emphasized. It was stressed earlier that the pastoral Aryan tribes probably destroyed the urban settlements created by the Indus civilization. A second cycle of urbanization manifested itself around 500 B.C. and various archaeological sites mark this phase. However, it appears that the creative spirit of the Aryans – so far as it pertained to religious or secular architecture – manifested itself principally in perishable materials which have left no permanent record. As a result of this, we have no

Right: The Buddha at Kusinagar, revered as the place where he attained nirvana.

architectural remains of any kind for over 1,000 years. But Persian influence persuaded Asoka to commission sculpture in stone which still speaks across the centuries of the lofty idealism and the truly liberal ethos of his imperial state.

Some of the edicts of Asoka were inscribed on highly polished pillars which were topped by sculptures of imperial emblems, like the lion or the bull. The Persian influence on these capitals is obvious. At the same time, they reflect an esthetic quality which also draws heavily upon indigenous traditions.

Asoka also commissioned a great number of *stupas*, or memorials to the Buddha, consisting of hemispherical mounds of burnt brick, surrounded by circular railings of stone, which are carved with the most exquisite designs, depicting episodes drawn from the life of the Enlightened One or from the round of contemporary social life.

The carved railings around the *stupas* are quite different in quality to the sculpted capitals of the stone pillars mentioned earlier, and they reflect a purely indigenous tradition of artistic creativity which had earlier expressed itself in less durable materials such as wood, bone or ivory. Perhaps the place occupied by the Great Emperor and the Enlightened One, his mentor, in the historical tradition of India is most eloquently reflected in the fact that the *Dharma Chakra*, or the Wheel of the Sacred Law, which was set in motion by the Buddha, and featured prominently in some of the Asokan pillars, featured equally prominently in the national flag adopted by the Republic of India in 1950. Also, the Lion Capital of the Asokan pillar is the emblem of the Government of India.

Transformation of Classical Heritage

Much attention has been focused on developments in the second half of the first millennium B.C., largely because

they provided a base for the structure of society and the political economy, on the one hand, and for spiritual culture and artistic endeavor on the other, which thereafter remained "frozen" in an almost unbroken frame for 1000 years and more.

However, before we trace succeeding phases of Indian civilization, one of its outstanding features needs to be stressed. In the past, the creative genius of the people of India found much better expression in religious reflection and social creativity than in political experimentation and technical innovation. Polities on a sub-continental scale, like the Asokan empire, were not a lasting feature of the history of the subcontinent. Instead, the regional states, which embraced relatively compact areas held together by language and culture, were the more durable institutions. Below the regional states stood local polities, diminutive in scale, often resting upon landed communities whose members were bound to each other through ties of kinship as well as interest. The break-up of empires into constituent regional states was a phenomenon that occurred repeatedly in the political history of the subcontinent. At the same time the restlessness of the local polities, which underpinned the regional states, was often discernible in the internal politics of the regional states.

It would be appropriate to focus attention upon yet another factor which gave shape to the changing character of Indian civilization, namely, that the Aryan migration was by no means the only or the last migration into the basins of the Indus and the Ganga to have important consequences. The demographic pressures in Central Asia, and elsewhere, constantly resulted in massive folk movements into the alluvial plains of the Indian subcontinent, more particularly to its northern segment, because of the fertility of this region and its consequent capacity to sustain a large population. An overview of the history of India reveals that the culture and values of the people were constantly shaped and reshaped by the inflow of new communities, which contributed substantially to the evolution of Indian civilization.

The centuries following the dissolution of the Asokan empire clearly illustrate both these facets of the history of India. In the period that followed, there was something akin to a Brahminical revival in north India. Yet, politically speaking, the rulers who followed the imperial Mauryas, whatever their religious persuasion, were only able to weld the northern region of the subcontinent into a single state.

It was a fresh migration of warrior communities from Central Asia, who feature in the history of India as the Yuehchi people, that triggered off political consolidation in north India. Like Asoka, the Kushan rulers, who presided over this community, looked upon Buddhism as the valid basis of a substantial polity and thus pursued the Asokan ideal. The Kushan rulers also gradually drew vast sectors of Central Asia into their political system.

The Kushan empire was controlled from the twin centers of Peshawar, in modern Pakistan, and Mathura, an important center in the upper Gangetic Valley associated with the epic hero and god, Krishna. Among the notable contributions of this empire was the evolution of a style of sculpture called the Gandhara School. It owed its genesis to a synthesis between Indian artistic traditions, and Greek esthetic norms as they flourished in West Asia. The Buddha, as visualized by the Gandhara School, bore a close resemblance to the god Apollo as conceived by Greek artists and this marriage between two high cultures produced art of a quality that bears favorable comparison with the highest achievements of some of the most outstanding civilizations known to mankind.

Right: Tibetan devotees praying before the Dhamek Stupa at Sarnath.

If the crystallization of the Kushan Empire reveals the important contribution of migrating communities to the history and culture of India, then its breakup, in the 3rd century A.D. substantiates the view that in ancient India large political institutions had a relatively limited life span. This dissolution was followed by a phase in which the political history of north India presented a picture of some disorder. However, the life of the common people, who were primarily engaged in agriculture, continued unaffected during this period. So did commercial and cultural activity, mainly resting upon merchants and artisans.

The Gupta Empire

Once again, in the 4th century A.D. a hitherto obscure dynasty of the Gangetic valley was able to create an empire.

The Gupta Emperors, who presided over north India from the 4th to the 6th centuries A.D., cannot be looked upon as imperial rulers of the same scale as the Mauryas of the 3rd century B.C. Yet the territorial consolidation which they gradually achieved was rather impressive and bears testimony to the military and political skills of individual emperors - like Samudragupta and Chandragupta Vikramaditya - in controlling the empire efficiently.

Unlike their predecessors, the Guptas were inclined to support Brahminical values rather than the austere world-view of the Buddha. Indeed, during the Gupta rule, the Brahminical revival was also reflected in a resurgence of the classical language of India, namely Sanskrit. Some of the literary compositions of this period are held to be masterpieces of medieval Hindu culture.

Nevertheless, the plurality that had characterized the religious scene earlier, continued during the Gupta era. A tangible manifestation of this plurality was a flourishing school of sculpture located at

Mathura, which created widely acclaimed statues of the Buddha which can be ranked among the greatest sculptures known to man. Visitors to Sarnath, the site near Varanasi where the Buddha preached his first sermon after receiving Enlightenment, can, even today, see the visible proof of this catholicity in an inscription which commemorates generous donations by a Gupta queen of a later period for the maintenance of Buddhist monasteries.

The centuries following the break-up of the Gupta empire, which was partially the result of Hun incursions into India, are conventionally referred to as the "dark ages" of Indian civilization, because political consolidation of any scale did not feature at all in this period. Instead, the available evidence suggests that during these centuries much conflict

characterized political life in the valley of the Ganga. But there is no reason to believe that the fields of creative art or religious speculation remained sterile. Indeed throughout this period the sustained efforts of the religious intelligentsia created, in the Puranas, a substantial body of texts, partly historical and mythical in character, and partly devoted to an elaboration of the metaphysical framework of Hinduism as it had crystallized earlier. Similarly, the architectural and esthetic knowledge of Indian civilization was incorporated into religious texts in this period, and provided the basis for a great flowering of religious architecture as well as of artistic creativity in the following period.

Religious Architecture

The noblest example of Indian art and architecture in the first millennium A.D., falls outside the limits of any survey of Indian civilization confined to the north. But we must touch upon this esthetic

Above: This fresco from the Ajanta caves is more than one thousand years old. Right: The fullness of the artistic imagination at play. Temple façade, Khajuraho.

achievement briefly, to convey some idea of its content and range. At the evocative site of Ajanta, 100 km (62 mi) from Aurangabad, in forbidding mountainous terrain, stands a magnificent series of rock-cut caves of Buddhist inspiration. These caves house *chaityas* or prayer halls, and monasteries which were excavated over a long period of time, stretching from the 2nd century B.C. to the 7th century A.D.

The interior architecture of these caves, which captures the profound understanding and the deep compassion of the Buddha with rare sensitivity, is important in itself. But even more striking are the murals, probably executed by artists who were Buddhist monks, in celebration of life, both sacred and profane. Some of these murals are veritable commentaries on the social history of late classical Indian society. Others reflect the development of Buddhist metaphysics and theology. The most striking feature of the murals is the vivid use of line and color to impart spiritual depth and beauty to the artistic execution. Perhaps the most

eloquent expression of all is to be found in the beautiful murals depicting the *Bodhisattvas* (spiritually gifted members of the holy order) Padmapani and Avalokitesvara.

However, the domain of religious architecture in the first millennium A.D. was by no means confined to the work of Buddhist patrons. The Gupta era also witnessed the foundation of Hindu temple architecture. The immediate impetus behind such a development was provided by the depiction of gods and goddesses in anthropomorphic form. From this to the provision of "houses" for the gods was a short and logical step.

Commencing from modest beginnings, as reflected in the simple stone structures of the 5th century A.D., temple architecture underwent a dramatic phase of development during the second half of the first millennium A.D. Two basic variations are reflected in the styles of north and south India. The most celebrated examples of the north Indian style are to be found in the states of Madhya Pradesh and Orissa. As for the temples located within Madhya Pradesh, the complex at Khajuraho, particularly the Kandariya Mahadev temple dating from the 10th century A.D. is still world famous. Similarly, Bhubaneswar, today the capital of Orissa, houses a beautiful complex of temples, while, not far from Bhubaneswar, there is the famous solar shrine of Konark. The temples of Madhya Pradesh or Orissa are distinguished by the perfect proportions of their architecture and the superb artistry of their sculptures. Finally, there is reason to believe that the valley of the Ganga also contained magnificent examples of temple architecture which have been lost to posterity through the vicissitudes of history.

Perhaps one final feature of the first millennium A.D. needs to be highlighted before we proceed any further. Some scholars believe that the break-up of the Gupta Empire was somewhat different from earlier dissolutions of the many empires within the subcontinent. While the earlier breakdowns had a repetitive character about them, developments from the 8th to the 10th centuries A.D. or even slightly later, led to an altogether different political scenario. The later Guptas could survive only by parceling out sovereignty to landed magnates and tribal chiefs in their empire, who, as a result, exercised considerable power over distinct localities and regions.

In this manner, a process comparable to the emergence of a feudal society in western Europe was initiated within India. This growth of a feudal society was further stimulated by the incursions of the Huns and other communities, which took place from the 7th century onwards. For the first time in the history of India, we encounter petty rulers called Rajputs who represented the social class

responsible for the growth of feudalism in India. These Rajput chiefs presided over powerful clans, which were distributed as land-owning communities over distinct localities in the north. The development of Indian feudalism represented the growth of Rajput chiefs in a style that made the emergence of cohesive empires difficult for a long period of time.

Hinduism and Islam

The interaction between the followers of Islam and the elite as well as the popular classes of the subcontinent, which commenced with the second millennium A.D. was one of the most creative encounters in the history of Indian civilization. As a result of this interaction, profound changes took place within society in the social, political and economic domains. Further, the material aspects of Indian civilization, as well as its spiritual outlook, underwent a basic transformation, which contributed greatly to the stimulation of creativity in various areas of human endeavor.

It would be appropriate here to say a few words about the ideological identity of Islam in the West Asian context. In its classical formulation, the religion of Islam called upon its followers to acknowledge an all powerful and transcendent god called Allah. The Koran was the word of Allah as it was revealed to the Prophet Mohammed and the Koran provided a corpus of ideas designed to guide all true believers in their journey through this world as well as beyond it. Over and above the Koran, there existed a body of prescriptive texts termed the *Sunna,* which was available to all true believers as an integral part of the prescriptive order of Islam. Last but not least, the pronouncements of the Prophet, under the title of the *Hadis,* were also available to Muslims as guidelines for social and moral duty. Taken altogether, therefore,

Right: The 12th-century Qutb Minar in Delhi, built by Qutbuddin Aibak.

the Koran, the *Sunna* and the *Hadis* constituted the *Shariat*, or religious law, which shaped the lifestyle of the followers of Islam.

Most of the the warrior communities of Islam, which descended upon the plains of the Indus and the Ganga during the 12th century, were initially involved in long and bloody warfare with individual Rajput rulers or with confederacies of Rajput chiefs in northern India. However, as in the earlier centuries, it soon became clear that the migrating communities possessed a military technology and a capacity for martial organization superior to that of the Rajput chiefs. This superiority was clearly reflected in the repeated military victories that the leaders of the Islamic hordes scored over the Rajput rulers of north India. The leaders of the Islamic war bands also possessed a politi-

cal culture based upon a more cohesive view of the state, and a more forceful articulation of its authority over its subjects. Not surprisingly, these leaders tried to create a substantial state from a base in the imperial city of Delhi, which initially controlled the resources of the fertile basins of the Indus and Ganga and thereafter reached out to the subcontinent as a whole. The political history of north India during the 13th and 14th centuries reflects this trend when, from the epicenter of Delhi, successive Islamic rulers first consolidated their rule over the provinces of north India, and then ventured out to the south. The most successful phase of this venture came about under a ruling dynasty called the Khiljis, one of whom, Alauddin Khilji, was able to achieve a very substantial imperial consolidation within the subcontinent.

The Mughal Dynasty

The most creative phase of Islamic interaction with Indian civilization came

Above: Cloisters of the Quwwatu'l Islam, the earliest extant mosque in India. Qutb, Delhi. Right: A Muslim fakir who spends his life wandering from shrine to shrine.

somewhat later, in the 16th century, when a war band from Central Asia (to be precise, from the modern Republic of Uzbekistan in the former Soviet Union) under a very distinguished young leader called Babur, finally defeated the ruler of Delhi, Ibrahim Lodi, and established a dynasty called the Mughal dynasty, whose heroic role in the medieval centuries approximated to the role of the Mauryas in the classical centuries.

Despite the initial conquest of Babur, the real establishment of the Mughal Empire over India was the achievement of his grandson, Akbar, who ruled from 1556 to 1605. The first decade of Akbar's tenure as a ruler was largely devoted to the task of consolidating the Mughal Empire in north India. His skills as a military tactician and strategist of some genius were fully reflected in this phase of his career. By the middle of the 16th century, however, the task of consolidation being completed, Akbar took up the crucial business of building a political, economic and moral infrastructure for the vast em-

pire which he had conjured into existence. Within his domain Akbar created a ruling class of noblemen called the *mansabdars* which was drawn from chiefs who hailed from Central Asia or Persia and the indigenous landed aristocracy, Hindu and Muslim. Indeed, the shrewdest stroke of policy executed by Akbar lay in drawing into the *mansabdari* order those Rajput aristocrats whose social dominance had marked the political scene in north India during the centuries of feudalism.

Akbar also instituted a massive reorganization of the fiscal resources of the state through a detailed survey of all landholdings, large and small, over the length and breadth of the Mughal Empire. The economy of the Mughal state rested upon a scaled land tax, which the Emperors appropriated for their own use as well as for the use of the *mansabdars*. Through establishing a fiscal link with the small landholders in the villages of the basins of the Indus and the Ganga, the Mughal state created for itself a resource base whose richness was unequaled in the medieval ages anywhere else in the world. Although the political achievements of Akbar were impressive, it is his catholicity in the fields of culture and religion that marks him out as a truly distinguished ruler in the tradition of the Em-peror Asoka. However, before we dwell upon this facet of medieval India, a brief introduction to the cultural history of Indian civilization is necessary.

The Indian tradition of cultural plurality greatly eased and aided coexistence as well as a creative interaction between Hinduism and Islam. Both of these religions, however, needed subtle alteration in their ideological content before their influence on the popular classes - artisans, peasants and members of tribal communities - could be truly significant. The classical formulation of Hinduism was reinforced towards the end of the first millennium B.C. by the distinguished philosopher Shankara, who hailed from Kerala. Shankara's principal achievement was clarifying the metaphysical armory of Hinduism in its dialogue with Buddhism.

However, the monastic world-view of Shankara was too lofty a concept to influence the common people, or their outlook and behavior. Slightly later, another philosopher from the south called Ramanuja initiated another philosophical movement that had a profound implication on the values of the lower classes. Shankara interpreted the sacred texts of Hinduism, namely, the Upanishads, the *Bhagavad Gita* and the Vedanta Sutras, as signifying the oneness of *Atman* and *Brahman*, or the individual soul and the reality behind the universe as a whole. Ramanuja, however, saw a distinction between the individual soul and the universal principle embodied in the *Brahman* and he proceeded to identify the latter with theism. No less significant than this was Ramanuja's fundamental belief that man could only gain a pro-found understanding of God through personal devotion or *bhakti*. Indeed, the Supreme Being of Ramanuja was a compassionate God, immanent in the rich diversity of life, and all too ready to bestow his divine grace on all those, rich or poor, high or low, who approached him as his *bhaktas* or devotees.

The possibility of salvation through devotion, which was thrown open by Ramanuja, offered a sharp contrast to the *Gyana Marga* or the Path of Knowledge, advocated by Shankara. The immanent God of Ramanuja could reach out to the individual, and sustain him in his journey through *samsara* in a manner that was altogether impossible through the path advocated by Shankara. Small wonder, then, that Ramanuja was able to attract numerous followers in his lifetime, particularly from the lowly classes, who looked upon his teachings as the means of their salvation.

Ramanuja, therefore, occupies a central position within Hinduism because of the profound impact of his ideas upon the rank and file of his community. Indeed, he was the first of a long line of popular religious figures who transcended the distinction between the superior and the lowly classes within the Hindu social order. The disciples of Ra-manuja played an equally crucial role in disseminating Hinduism among the common folk of medieval India. The most outstanding of these disciples was Ramananda, who lived for a large part of the 15th century in Varanasi, the spiritual hub of Hinduism, and soon became a key figure in the *bhakti* movement in north India.

Religious Leaders

The two most significant figures in the *bhakti* movement in north India, after Ramananda, were undoubtedly Tulsidas and Kabir. The religious literature generated by these two saintly figures exercised a profound influence over the popu-

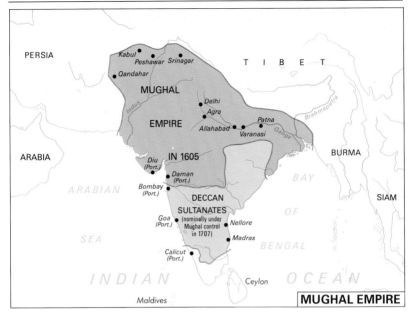

MUGHAL EMPIRE

lar classes in the valley of the Ganga. Both of these saintly figures drew inspiration from Ramananda, and subscribed to the view that the way to salvation, or *moksha*, lay through *bhakti* or the devotional worship of God. Beyond this common belief, however, Tulsidas and Kabir advocated slightly different notions of an immanent God.

For Tulsidas, God was manifest in the person of the semi-divine hero, the Lord Rama. The epic poem, called the *Ramacharitmanas*, that he wrote in Avadhi, the folk dialect of the middle Gangetic Valley, was a composition of great lyrical beauty and spiritual power, which exercised over rich and poor, high and low, a profound influence that remains potent even today, across the span of 500 years and more. Tulsidas was certainly no social rebel. Instead, he accepted the institutions of caste and the hierarchy of society without questioning their moral legitimacy. In contrast, the saintly weaver Kabir of Varanasi was something of a rebel, whose particular brand of devo-

tional theism was designed to restructure the secular institutions of society and rid them of their exploitative character. Besides challenging the social and the sacred order, Kabir, probably because of the influence of *sufi* Islam, imagined God very differently to Tulsi. Kabir's Supreme Being was devoid of anthropomorphic form and he could be understood only through abstract language.

A near contemporary of Kabir was the founder of Sikhism, Nanak. Born a Hindu, Nanak was influenced by Islam, but the path to salvation he held out to his followers in the *Adi Grantha*, the sacred book of the Sikhs, rejected the cant and ritual that characterized both of these religions. The strict monotheism of Nanak sought a religious community in which spiritual equality would hold together men and women of all ranks in allegiance to a common God. Not surprisingly, therefore, even during his lifetime, Nanak attracted a substantial following among from the peasantry of north India. However, the doctrines of Sikhism were

51

given a more militant form by one of his later followers, Govind Singh, in the late 17th century. Govind Singh was engaged in the process of carving out for himself a theocratic state in the Punjab. The social temper of Sikhism, as it exists nowadays, draws heavily upon the militancy given to it by Govind Singh.

The popular Hinduism of the *bhakti* saints found an equally powerful and morally potent counterpart within Islam in India. The transformation of the transcendent God conceived by the Prophet Mohammed, into a compassionate and immanent God, who in his infinite capacity for love reached out to all those who accepted Islam as a noble way of life, was achieved by a group of divines called the *sufis*. The growth of *sufism* had a profound impact upon the destiny of Islam

Above: Precursor of the Taj Mahal, the tomb of the Mughal Emperor Humayun (d. 1556), Delhi. Right: A Kabirpanthi singing a devotional composition of the saintly weaver, Kabir.

within India. The saints of the *sufi* movement, unlike the *ulema* of Islam, were able to reach out to the lowly and the humble. The *sufis* spoke of a God who bestowed his love on men irrespective of their status in society.

When the Emperor Akbar was consolidating his empire, the ideas of the folk saints of Hinduism and Islam had already effected a spiritual rapprochement between the rank and file of the two communities. The sharing of common values by men of diverse religions offered an ideal setting for the pursuit of an imperial policy which sought to reinforce the ties of cordiality between different communities in the subcontinent. The catholicity of Akbar's stance in politics was just as forcefully reflected in his religious policy. In the course of his reign, the Emperor issued a rescript proclaiming the formula "Peace to All" which in an manner reminiscent of the inscriptions of the Asoka of the 3rd century B.C., exhorted diverse religious communities to live in peace and harmony with each other. Per-

haps the dissemination of almost identical notions of social tolerance and religious harmony by Asoka and Akbar was not wholly fortuitous. The social and religious diversity of India required her rulers to advocate such tolerance as the only valid basis for keeping peace and order within the subcontinent. Within the charmed circle of his court, however, Akbar went considerably beyond his illustrious Mauryan predecessor. In the *Din-i-Illahi*, or the Faith of God, he propounded a new spiritual doctrine which sought to draw noblemen of goodwill and distinction into allegiance to a God who had chosen the Mughal Emperor as his special instrument. The *Din-i-Illahi*, however, was a movement confined only to an elite circle within the court.

No account of the flowering of Indian civilization in north India in the medieval centuries can be complete without mentioning the amazing architectural and artistic achievements. The opening centuries of the second millennium A.D. constituted a period in which Hindu temple architecture attained a distinction it rarely achieved afterwards. The engineering skills that the rulers of Islam brought with them to north India were of an altogether different quality. The dome as a graceful and esthetic means of bridging space was well known in West Asia, and the Muslim rulers brought this technology with them to India. The cities of north India – imperial capitals like Delhi and Agra, or provincial capitals like Allahabad or Patna – contain many religious or secular monuments that demonstrate the architectural achievement of this period. Apart from magnificent palaces and awe-inspiring fortifications built around cities, or formidable fortresses located at strategic points, the architectural glory of the medieval centuries is reflected in a large number of mosques and mausoleums which are scattered throughout north India.

Broadly speaking, these monuments can be stylistically divided into two distinct phases: pre- and post-Mughal. The city of Delhi contains distinguished

examples of both styles. The Qutb Minar and the Lodi Tombs are exquisite gems that reflect the austere sensibility of the pre-Mughal rulers of the region just as the tomb of Humayun, the Red Fort, the Jama Masjid Mosque reflect the imperial taste of the Mughal rulers. However, for a sight of the finest architectural achievements of the Mughal era, one must visit the city of Agra, 200 km (124 mi) from Delhi. Here, in the 17th century, in the memory of his wife, Mumtaz Mahal, Shah Jahan created a mausoleum famous throughout the world as the Taj Mahal which embodies in its flawless perfection and grandeur the greatest architectural achievement of Indian civilization.

Miniature Paintings

The patronage that the Mughal Emperors extended to art and artists was extremely fruitful in its results. We referred

Above: First landing of the British at Surat, historic etching (1671).

earlier to the Buddhist craftsmen of the first millennium A.D. who created murals of superb quality at Ajanta. There is little reason to believe that this tradition came to an abrupt end. However, the Mughals brought with them a new Persian tradition of delicate miniature painting, which was then firmly grafted onto the existing artistic traditions of India.

Under Akbar and his son Jehangir, imperial patronage to artists resulted in the creation of a tradition of artistic activity that flowed from a merging of indigenous and Persian styles. Nor did the miniature art of this period remain confined to the imperial court at Delhi or Agra.

The great Rajput nobles, who had been drawn into the Mughal *imperium,* emulated the example of their suzerain. As a result of this, the art of miniature painting also thrived at the provincial courts in Rajasthan and in the hills of the Punjab. There is no fundamental difference, stylistically speaking, between Mughal and Rajput miniatures, as these two schools are termed.

However, the artists in the imperial court concentrated on portraiture and regal life while their peers in Rajasthan, or in the Punjab hills, utilized the new art form to depict the epics or to illustrate the harmony and sentiment embodied in music, over and above any visualization of courtly themes. The creative energy that the Mughal Emperors released within Indian society through astute political management was equally forceful in the economic domain. Agriculture was the mainstay of the economy in this period, as it was in earlier times.

The Mughal peace ensured that new technologies and a widening of the base of agriculture greatly stimulated rural productivity. At the same time, the immense wealth of the imperial court at Agra or Delhi, or the lesser courts of the provincial governors scattered throughout the empire, gave a great impetus to artisan and mercantile activity.

From all accounts, at the height of Mughal power in the 17th century, the region of north India constituted one of the most prosperous and best developed centers of economic activity in the world. Indeed, taken in conjunction with the fusion of popular religious sensibility reflected in the *bhakti* and the *sufi* movements, the Mughal era constitutes a phase of Indian civilization comparable in its glory and greatness to the Mauryan era of the classical centuries B.C.

Colonial Interlude

Despite its remarkable achievements, the Mughal state was underminded by tensions in the formal structure of politics as well as in the informal system of governance which caused a great weakening of the polity in the first quarter of the 18th century.

The burden of taxation which the Mughal Emperor and the ruling class jointly imposed on the peasants triggered off a series of agrarian uprisings which finally resulted in a breakdown of the system as a whole.

Fifty years after the death of the Emperor Aurangzeb in 1707, generally regarded as the last, and one of the greatest Mughals, the great empire created by Akbar had given way to a dozen regional states whose rulers paid only lip service to the imperial authority of his descendants. The break-up of the Mughal empire coincided with the invasion of European commercial corporations into India. These corporations came with the objective of purchasing the artisanal and agricultural products of India, which commanded a very high price in the markets of Europe.

The European trading companies - the most significant among them being the British East India Company - initially established themselves on the western, the southern and eastern coasts of India, creating in the process new port-cities like Bombay, Madras and Calcutta. From the bridgeheads that they conjured into existence on the coast, and because of their strength on the high seas, the European companies – most particularly, the British East India Company – were able to make inroads into the interior and thus establish themselves as political and economic powers of considerable weight on the subcontinent.

Although it was the French and the Dutch who pioneered the commercial exploitation and political penetration of India, it was the British who finally deployed their superior naval and mercantile strength in the east to the greatest possible effect in the 18th century.

By the end of the 18th century the British had acquired vast possessions in northeastern, southern and western India, mainly through defeating the regional powers that had emerged after the breakdown of the Mughal polity. By the first quarter of the 19th century, the conquest of India by the British was more or less complete, although the northwest still remained to be vanquished. There were also vast regions within the subcontinent where the native princes, as they were called, were permitted to survive as clients of the British *imperium*.

The system of government that the British established over India was in some ways a unique experience for the people of the subcontinent. Never before had the different regions and localities of India been so closely integrated, administratively and politically, as they were under British rule during the 19th century. The colonial government, with its apex manned by a Viceroy and Governor-General located in Calcutta (after 1911, in Delhi), consisted of an enormous bu-reaucratic system which operated through its Provincial Governors and District Officers throughout the whole length and breadth of the land.

This formal system of administration was supported by informal alliances with important sections of Indian society. These included the rulers of the Princely States, the great territorial aristocrats, whose holdings were affirmed by the colonial government, and a newly emergent bourgeoisie which, until the third quarter of the 19th century, looked to the British for the furtherance of its eco-nomic interests at the same time as it absorbed new ideas through the education which it received under the colonial dispensation.

While the British rulers created an administrative unity within India which had not existed before, their role in the transformation of the political economy, or the social culture, of the subcontinent was a regressive one. The initial conquest of India was motivated by the search for profits through trade in Indian goods by the British East India Company.

However, as the industrial revolution gathered force within Great Britain in the mid-19th century, her economic relationship with India underwent a complete change. The colony still remained a supplier of cereals to Great Britain. But in-stead of buying the products of Indian craftsmen, Great Britain now dumped her industrial produce, at her terms, in the markets of the subcontinent. The sale of textile goods set the pace for this system of exchange but it was soon extended to a whole range of goods.

For the first time in her long history India was reduced to a vast market for an overseas producer of material values. Her indigenous craftsmanship suffered grievously and there was, over the course of the 19th century and part of 20th, a great flow of wealth, through unequal exchange, from the subcontinent to Great Britain.

The Rise of Indian Nationalism

Perhaps the lasting contribution of the long British domination over India lay in the generation of new ideas and new principles of political organization. To promote the socialization of the intelligentsia under the British dispensation, the colonial authorities created a system of education which drew extensively upon the scientific and humanistic knowledge available in Europe. As a result of this exposure to Western thinking, there grew up, in the first half of the 19th century, a class of Indians who were fully committed to the values of the Enlightenment, and sought to bring about dramatic changes within the whole of the Indian society. An outstanding member of this class was Raja Rammohun Roy, who came from a middle-class background in Bengal, and who initiated change in social, religious and cultural domains which has rightly earned him the title of "Father of the Indian Renaissance".

The educated classes who came into existence under colonial aegis, first in the port-cities of Bombay, Madras and Calcutta, and later in the cities of the interior, did not take long to outgrow the constraints imposed upon them by their British mentors.

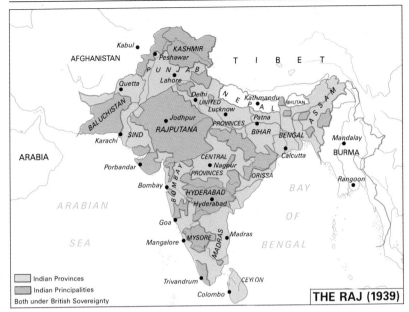

THE RAJ (1939)

Indian Provinces
Indian Principalities
Both under British Sovereignty

Well before the 19th century drew to a close, a few political leaders, drawn from these classes, voiced the growing aspiration for Indian independence, to enable the people to express themselves in the generation of material wealth no less than in the generation of a new culture. To rid themselves of the British yoke, the educated classes organized themselves into local and regional associations which came together in 1885 to give birth to a pan-Indian political organization called the Indian National Congress.

The values of the Enlightenment, which the British disseminated in India, did not extend to social classes below the new middle classes. But the effects of the aquisition of material wealth throughout India by the British, were much more profound in their consequences.

The role in which India was cast, as a vast market for the industrial produce of Great Britain, and as a supplier of cheap cereals for those who toiled in British factories, caused widespread impoverishment in the subcontinent and created a great surge of anti-imperialism among peasants, workers, artisans, tribesmen and other sections of the social order.

To a considerable extent, the Great Uprising (known in the west as the Sepoy Mutiny) which took place in 1857 demonstrated the growing anger of these lower classes, who found in the declining nobility and aristocracy of the old order, their natural leaders against the British *imperium*. Although the Uprising of 1857 was suppressed with great ferocity and ruthlessness, the dispossessed classes remained hostile to the British presence in the subcontinent.

The task of welding the nationalism of the middle classes with the anger of the poor and the deprived, was accomplished with great subtlety by Mahatma Gandhi. For this reason the Mahatma, literally meaning "Great Soul", is fondly remembered by the people of India as the "Father of the Nation".

During his sojourn of 15 years in South Africa, where he fought against racial oppression, Gandhi developed a technique of political action, termed *satyagraha*, which looked upon moral persuasion as the only legitimate mode of political force. The Mahatma thus reactivated a tradition of moral radicalism in Indian civilization which had been reflected earlier in the thought and action of figures like the Buddha. In this way, he united the rich and the poor in a mighty movement of protest against the British Government.

The mobilization of the people, which took place under the aegis of Mahatma Gandhi in the decades between the two world wars, was without equal in the 20th century. Eventually, Gandhi's movements were to be responsible for the liberation of India from British Rule in 1947. Moreover, their final success in liberating India created for the Mahatma a place in the hearts of his countrymen which had been occupied only once before during the long history of Indian civilization – by the Buddha.

The Contemporary Transformation of Indian Civilization

We now come to the last phase of our overview of Indian civilization. The decades since 1947 have witnessed profound social transformation in a partially completed industrial revolution; a unique attempt to create liberal political institutions in a Third World society; and a flowering of modern scientific innovation and artistic creativity - which is comparable in its sweep and significance to the agricultural revolution which swept ancient India and changed the subcontinent during the middle of the first millennium B.C.

Indeed, at the present time the people of India are undergoing so dramatic a change in their material and cultural lifestyle, that historical wisdom and the les-

Right: The Battle of Khanua (from the Baburnama, 1598). National Museum, Delhi.

sons of past experience have little to offer them by way of guidance as they advance towards a new century.

The Struggle for Freedom

No satisfactory assessment of the period beginning in 1947 can be made without touching briefly upon the struggle for freedom which enabled the people of India to defeat the greatest imperial power that has been known to history. This struggle was destined to transform Indian society radically. At the political level, the leaders of the struggle, most prominent among them being Mahatma Gandhi, were able to create a great alliance of all classes and communities in India – Hindus, Muslims, and Sikhs, the rich and the poor, industrialists, merchants and professionals, peas-ants, artisans and tribesmen – against the imperial presence in their midst. Yet the struggle for freedom was not confined to political objectives. Over and above such an ambition, it sought to transform a civilization of antiquity into a modern nation-state; to create an industrial order in place of an agricultural one and last, but not least, to stimulate the cultural creativity of the people.

Partition

While 15 August, 1947 marked a great triumph for the people, this triumph was not without its tragic aspect. The partition of British India and the emergence of Pakistan were major failures of the national movement, which throughout the struggle for freedom had attempted to keep the country united at all costs. Indeed, the consequences of this failure are felt even today in the internal politics of India and in relations between the different nations of South Asia. Independent India was immediately confronted with problems of formidable proportions. The communal disorders of 1946-7, and the

birth of Pakistan, resulted in one of the most massive migrations in history. No less serious was the issue of the Princely States, which covered approximately 40 percent of the territory and ruled 20 percent of the population of the subcontinent. It took statesmanship of the highest order to accomplish their fusion with the new Indian State.

The Indian Constitution

Another important problem awaiting resolution was the framing of a constitution which would provide the ground rules for politics within the new state. That such a document could be devised within a span of four years was a remarkable achievement and spoke well of the maturity of the leadership at the helm of affairs at that time.

This constitution sought to combine and unite the different linguistic regions and religious communities of India into a cohesive nation-state, at the same time conferring substantial autonomy upon the diverse provinces of the Indian Union, and safeguarding the interests of minorities and deprived social classes. The extraordinary political courage that was needed to introduce adult suffrage in a society with a modest level of social development is something that needs to be stressed.

The architects of liberal theory in the west had advocated a link between the popular vote and the level of social and economic development in a society. But with unflinching confidence in the good sense of the people, the founding fathers of the Indian Constitution based the governance of the country upon the free choice of hundreds upon millions of its citizens.

Perhaps it was their confidence in the maturity of the tradition of oral culture

Right: Mahatma Gandhi. Detail from the Gandhi Memorial at Kanniya Kumari.

within India, as distinct from formal literacy, that encouraged them to take this step. The difficult and lengthy translation of liberal principles into democratic practice raises numerous problems and calls for delicate handling. The leadership of India at that time was able to resolve these problems with outstanding success. Here, it is only appropriate to refer to the contribution of the post-1947 leaders, most prominent of them all being Jawaharlal Nehru, in nurturing the institutions as well as the values of liberal democracy in this huge country.

Within only a decade and a half of independence, the rural aristocracies which had dominated the riverine plains of India were largely divested of their landed wealth, although their social influence was by no means wholly undermined. Similarly, by the late 1950s, a system of planning had been devised that sought to create a public sector to preside over heavy industries, at the same time as it provided incentives to the private entrepreneur and stimulated the productivity of artisans and craftsmen, thus giving employment to millions of people with only modest capital outlays.

The Post-Nehru Period

If our survey conveys the impression that during the first decade and a half after 1947 every attempt at social engineering was fully successful in attaining its objectives, then nothing would be farther from the truth. Indeed, when Nehru departed from the political scene in 1964, he bequeathed a wide range of unresolved problems to his successors. While feudalism as a dominant social system had been largely undermined by the 1960s, the former landed classes still wielded considerable power in rural society, particularly because of the absence of organization among the lower classes. More importantly, although the abolition of the landed estates was supported

by various programs of community development, agrarian production did not increase as fast as was anticipated or desirable. Nor was the industrial scene any more buoyant than the rural scene.

After some initial enthusiasm, the growth of the industrial sector ran into heavy weather, partly due at least to failures in foreign policy which necessitated a substantial diversion of resources for the purposes of defense. The task of facing the challenges which beset India after Nehru's demise in 1964 fell, after a brief respite, upon Indira Gandhi.

These challenges were apparent in many theaters of national life. There was an acute crisis in agricultural production and prophets of doom were casting doubts upon the ability of the nation to feed its growing population. The initial thrust of industrialization had petered out and there was a marked slowing down on this front.

The stagnation of the economy triggered off considerable discontent among different classes and communities which was also reflected in factional and ideological conflict within the arena of politics.

The regime of Indira Gandhi finally decided to reaffirm the strategy of Jawaharlal Nehru on a more radical note, focusing upon the task of eradicating poverty under the slogan of *Garibi Hatao* (eliminate poverty).

True, the slogan of *Garibi Hatao* was in some respects only an emotive phrase, lacking in concrete content. Yet in the stimulus which it provided to agriculture through the so-called "green revolution", or in the manner in which banking institutions were nationalized and the vestiges of princely privilege eliminated, this radical trend brought about many of significant changes in the political and economic climate of the country.

Perhaps the most significant change concerned the agricultural scene where, within a decade, a country that had suffered chronic deficits was able to feed its vast population and even generate modest surpluses in cereal crops.

61

By the time the 1970s drew to a close, the great experiment in social transformation, which had been initiated in the 1950s, had attained a substantial measure of succes. At the very core of this experiment lay the objective of creating a massive industrial society, shaped by the political will of hundreds upon millions of citizens, and seeking to combine the strengths of a liberal with those of a social democracy.

Perhaps the crucial factor in this truly epic venture, was the "face in the crowd" – the man behind the plow or the workbench – whose choices and ambitions were shaped as much by the social context in which he was placed as by the overall interests of the nation. Again and again, during this period, the aggregate political behavior of the citizen demonstrated his ability to look upon social and economic issues with great clarity and foresight. Indeed, as elections in India

have repeatedly demonstrated, no polity can seek a better guarantee of its stability, in the midst of radical transformation, than the institutions of popular democracy among citizens with a fully awakened sensibility.

Perhaps the awakened sensibility of the people of India in the decades since 1947, is best reflected in a social and cultural transformation for which there is no parallel in the history of the subcontinent prior to the 20th century. The roots of this transformation go back to the struggle for national liberation, which was not only a political phenomenon but also extended to many varied spheres of economic and cultural activity.

The Ferment of Regional Cultures

At the very outset, the closing decades of the 19th and the opening decades of the 20th centuries witnessed great literary ferment in the dozen or more regional cultures of the subcontinent. This ferment focused upon the creation of a mod-

Above: Pageantry marks the annual Republic Day Parade in Delhi.

ern literature in languages like Hindi, Bengali, Urdu, Gujarati and Punjabi, to mention only a few.

The literary revival of this period - which was influenced by contemporary western ideas at the same time as it drew inspiration from past Indian traditions - was, in many instances, anchored to the social and political issues that were an integral part of the nationalist struggle.

In other instances, it took on the elusive task of forging a new identity for the people. Perhaps the outstanding figure of this phase was the Bengali writer Rabindranath Tagore, whose prolific work has not only shaped the sensibility of modern Bengal but also earned him the Nobel Prize for literature. But men like Premchand, Muhammad Iqbal, K.M. Munshi, Maithili Saran Gupta or Vir Singh were no less distinguished in the fields of prose or poetry which drew on the agony and the aspirations of the people as they strove to reshape their lives in a new world that combined material dignity with cultural creativity.

There was an equally noticeable revival, prior to 1947, in the spheres of art and architecture. Behind these cultural and artistic achievements lay the emergence of a new social class, whose consciousness was shaped through exposure to western literature and art forms. It was a product of British imperialism and its attitudes were shaped in the institutions of higher education, particularly the universities of Bombay, Madras and Calcutta, which were created in the 1850s.

While it is true that the British objective behind the creation of these institutions was the socialization of a professional class within the empire, once this class discovered the scientific and humanistic knowledge of the west, it not only organized a powerful national movement, but it also created for itself a literary and artistic culture which drew on contemporary western forms at the same time as it sought to reinforce itself

through the legacy of the classical as well as of the medieval centuries.

The Rise of the Middle Class

The decades after 1947 have witnessed an explosive growth in the range, diversity and quality of social and cultural activity within India. At the heart of this activity lies a great expansion of the middle class (whose emergence underpinned the nationalist movement), as well as its involvement in various fields of creative endeavor.

The growing urbanization of the subcontinent has resulted in the emergence of large metropolitan cities like Calcutta, Bombay and Delhi. Within these cities are found cosmopolitan elites - drawn from the artistic vocations or from business and enterprise - who straddle the meeting point of the industrial communities of contemporary India, on the one hand, and the post-industrial societies of the west, on the other.

As we proceed from these massive urban conurbations to the capitals of the diverse states of the Indian Republic - cities like Lucknow, Patna, Ahmedabad, or Jaipur - we encounter a vigorous regional elite, which links the world of the me-tropolitan cities to the popular classes and rural cultures that characterize the coun-tryside. These regional elites, whose numbers are growing rapidly, have become an increasingly visible presence through their control over the mechanisms of political power no less than through the cultural influence that they exercise over the rural hinterlands.

Beyond these elites lie the mass of the rural classes and tribal communities, roughly 600 million out of a total population of 800 million, who have been drawn into the 20th century through media and market influences. Yet large sections of them still do not share the prosperity flowing from the industrial revolution in India.

The cultural scene in India today has been deeply influenced by all the social changes that have taken place over the past few decades. For instance, there has been a tremendous burst of creative activity in the sphere of painting.

The country can boast of artists whose work reflects a contemporary sensibility, seeking to interpret the identity of a rapidly transforming society at the same time as it seeks to express the burdens as well as the strengths of the past. Not surprisingly, however, the outstanding work of such sophisticated artists does not extend beyond the charmed circle of the cosmopolitan elite. The restricted audience for the cultural artifacts of modern India applies equally to "art cinema", in which figures like the late Satyajit Ray and Ritwik Ghatak, to mention only two outstanding names, produce films internationally renowned for their quality.

The more esthetic world of the elites who reside in the provincial cities, small towns and rural settlements, or that of the small middle classes and the proletariat of the metropolitan centers, is powerfully reflected in popular cinema and in television. The films created for popular consumption perhaps constitute the most powerful influence in shaping the attitudes and lifestyles of the overwhelming majority of the men and women living in cities and towns, as well as for substantial segments of the rural population. Such films are the handiwork of directors whose talents lie in their appreciation of a mass market rather than in the creation of works of art. A particularly well-known creator of this genre of cinema was the late Raj Kapoor, whose work dominated the popular screen from the 1950s until his death in 1988.

Over the past decade or so, however, the emergence of television has threatened to displace popular cinema from the central place which it has occupied in the cultural life of millions of Indians. The content of television programs has had such an overwhelming impact upon popular values and sensibilities, and even more particularly among the young, that it is not possible to ignore the emergence of this powerful new medium of mass entertainment and visual "education". With suitable modifications, the themes utilized by the creators of popular movies, are frequently reproduced in the entertainment that is offered through television. However, one striking feature of television has been the creation of serials which narrate the great epics to audiences of tens of millions. Thus the *Ramayana* and the *Mahabharata* still offer, even in the midst of the traumatic industrial transformation of the 20th century, a moral outlook based on the firm foundations of the past as well as a new moral order for today.

As India undergoes its industrial revolution, there is a noticeable and powerful reiteration of classical values in the face of the sweeping changes that are transforming both elite and popular lifestyles throughout the land. At the root of these changes lies a new means of generating wealth, which greatly increases the amount of material goods available for consumption, at the same time as it reorders the distribution of affluence and poverty, and reshapes relations between individuals as well as different classes and communities within the country.

That a certain amount of social disorder and moral disruption flowing from this transformation should be visible to even the casual observer should cause no surprise. What is no less striking, however, is the evidence of social growth and cultural creativity, seen in various walks of human life, as men and women strive to create for themselves a life of dignity and cultural richness, which is slowly but surely transforming the nation into a modern industrial society.

Right: A modern Indian woman in her traditional finery.

1	Arunchal Pradesh	7	Assam
2	West Bengal	8	Nagaland
3	Himachal Pradesh	9	Meghalaya
4	Punjab	10	Manipur
5	Haryana	11	Tripura
6	Sikkim	12	Mizoram

THE FERTILE PLAINS OF THE NORTH

DELHI
HARYANA AND PUNJAB
THE PLAINS OF UTTAR PRADESH

DELHI

Delhi, India's capital city, is growing at a breathless pace, beyond the scattered citadels of former dynasties and far beyond the expectations of colonial and latter-day town planners. Such pressures notwithstanding, it remains a modern and convenient gateway to India. Reminders of the past and its pace-setting ambitions also make the city a fitting introduction to the often bewildering aspects of an ancient civilization now absorbing contemporary values.

Delhi has been a center of power almost continuously since the 13th century. As a result there are innumerable medieval monuments (the Archeological Survey lists over 1300) which survive cheek-by-jowl with high-rise, residential localities and crowded commercial complexes. The huge city is divided into Old and New Delhi; the former also comprises the "seventh" city, Shahjahanabad, and the areas further north; the latter has as its core the plan of the capital created by the British in 1911. New Delhi has some of the finest museums in the country. Its boutiques and shopping arcades are showrooms of the skills of

Preceding pages: Old Delhi seen from the Jama Masjid. Left: Winnowing grain.

traditional craftsmen all over the country. It has enough restaurants to keep a gourmet in good spirits; soothing gardens and parks; and, in the winter months particularly, a plethora of important cultural and international events. It is a stronghold of bureaucrats and red-tape, of ambitious politicians and immense political pressures, of high-level commerce and a burgeoning *nouveau riche*. New Delhi is a world away from its older counterpart. Old Delhi has much the richer and more colorful character, resulting from its organic growth over several centuries and its still somewhat medieval ambience.

Ancient Prelude to Medieval Splendor

From the 13th to the 17th centuries, the rulers of successive dynasties established seven "cities" in different parts of Delhi. However, the span of the city's eventful life harks even further back in time, for, in 1955, accidental excavations at the Purana Qila revealed that this area, on the banks of the Yamuna river, was inhabited more than 3000 years ago. Fine earthenware pottery, known as Painted Grey Ware and dated to 1000 B.C., confirmed this as yet another site associated with the epic *Mahabharata*; and Indraprastha, the capital of the Pandavas, has been identified with Delhi.

69

A clearer picture emerges from the end of the 10th century when the Tomar Rajputs established themselves in the Aravalli hills south of Delhi. The isolated rocky outcrop served as a safe shelter for a royal resort, which the Tomars called Dhilli, or Dhillika. The core of the first of the seven cities was created by Anangpal when he raised the defenses of Lal Kot. The Chauhan Rajputs later captured Delhi from the Tomars. Prithviraj III, also known as Rai Pithora, and famous for giving battle to the Muslim invaders, extended Lal Kot with massive ramparts and gates; Qila Rai Pithora became the first city of Delhi and is known to have had several Hindu and Jain temples.

Prithviraj was ruling when Muhammad of Ghor invaded India, and he died at the second battle in 1192. Ghur returned to his native land, leaving as viceroy his slave Qutbuddin Aibak, who, in 1206, crowned himself the first Sultan of Delhi. Delhi became the capital of the Slave or Mamluk dynasty, the first Muslim dynasty to rule over north India.

One of the most obvious manifestations of Muslim rule was in architecture. The Islamic emphasis on congregational prayer necessitated a place of worship quite different from the Hindu temple. The mosque, therefore, has a spacious courtyard with a large prayer hall, its orientation naturally towards Mecca (in India, westwards). The *mihrab*, a recessed alcove in the prayer hall, indicates the direction (*qibla*). The courtyard often has a tank for ablutions, and may be surrounded by cloisters. The tall tower or *minar*, used for calling the faithful to prayer is integral to mosque architecture. The burial of the dead, as opposed to cremation, introduced the tomb, which essentially comprised a domed chamber with a cenotaph in its center, a *mihrab* in its western wall and a real grave in the

Right: Capital splendor - New Delhi's South Block, which is the seat of power.

underground chamber (or *maqbara*). The structure was more complex in the tombs of important personages.

The earliest Islamic structures can be seen in Qila Rai Pithora, which Qutbuddin occupied. Iconoclastic zeal provided ready availability of building material. This, coupled with the need to use Hindu craftsmen, made improvization the order of the day. Before he crowned himself Sultan, Qutbuddin built the **Quwwat-ul Islam mosque** (which, except for pre-Sultanate monuments in Kutch district, is the earliest extant mosque in India), using pieces of destroyed temples to build the cloisters. Within the spacious courtyard, he retained the **Iron Pillar** which was a 4th-century standard of Vishnu.

In 1199, Qutbuddin laid the foundation of the **Qutb Minar**, still one of Delhi's landmarks today. It is likely that he meant it to be both a symbol of victory and a minaret for the adjoining mosque. From a base of 14.32 m (47 ft) it rises 72.5 m (238 ft), tapering at its height to 2.75 m (9 ft). It is the tallest stone tower in India, a perfect example of a minar, and one of the finest Islamic monuments ever to be raised. It was completed by Qutbuddin's son-in-law and successor, Iltutmish. The other monuments in this area belong to a slightly later date, but will be discussed here for the sake of convenience. Northwest of the mosque is the **tomb of Iltutmish**, built by the ruler himself in 1235. The dome has not survived, but its interior is decorated with profuse ornamentation.

The Quwwat-ul Islam mosque was extended twice, and when Alauddin Khilji ordered renovations in the year 1311, he also built the impressive **Alai Darwaza**, which forms the southern gateway to this complex. It is the first building employing wholly Islamic principles of construction and ornamentation, including a pointed horse-shoe arch. Alauddin also nursed ambitions to build a tower twice as large as the Qutb Minar, but he died

soon after the work began and it remains in an unfinished state.

The Khiljis came to power in 1290, and Alauddin established the second city of Delhi, called Siri. Except for the remnants of embattlements, very little of Siri survives. Contemporary historians record that at this time Delhi was the "envy of Baghdad, the rival of Cairo and the equal of Constantinople." Alauddin also dug a vast reservoir at **Hauz Khas**, to meet the needs of the citizens of Siri. The reservoir lies near Sri Aurobindo Marg, by a tranquil deer park. Hauz Khas was extensively renovated by Firuz Shah Tughlaq, a later sultan, who added a two-storied college for religious instruction as well as a mosque. His own tomb is also found there. In recent times exclusive and expensive boutiques have opened in some *havelis* (traditional houses built around a central courtyard) in Hauz Khas village. This novel location has proved to be as much of a draw as the items for sale.

The year 1321 saw the Tughlaqs on the throne. Ghiyasuddin, the first Sultan,

added a new capital, **Tughlaqabad** (8 km or 5 mi from the Qutb Minar), Delhi's third city. He built it mainly to guard against Mongol invasions and it does, indeed, have a rather grim and forbidding character. **Ghiyasuddin's tomb** lies to the south of the deserted fort and is a fine example of Tughlaq architecture with its squat dome rising above sloping walls. Known as Darul Aman – the abode of peace – the tomb originally stood within a vast reservoir and was connected to the fort by a causeway.

Muhammad bin Tughlaq, his successor, built Delhi's fourth city, Jahanpanah, which largely comprised a walled enclosure between Siri and Qila Rai Pithora.

Firuz Shah Tughlaq created the fifth city, Firuzabad, today known as **Firuz Shah Kotla**. It lies off Bahadur Shah Zafar Marg; the few surviving buildings at this citadel include a mosque where Timur once prayed. Of greater interest is an **Asokan pillar**. Firuz Shah discovered two pillars, at Ambala and Meerut, and contemporary historians describe their transportation to Delhi. The Sultan had one placed in his capital, and the other near his hunting lodge, Pir Ghaib. The Asokan edicts on the former were the first to be deciphered in 1837 by James Princep, yielding the key to the Brahmi script.

The instability that followed Firuz Shah's death was accentuated by the invasion of Timur (1398) who ruthlessly plundered and devastated Delhi. The growth of Delhi remained static during the reign of the Sayyids and the Lodis. Nothing new was built, and significant architecture was confined to tombs. The best of these are to be seen at the **Lodi Gardens**, Delhi's green area, formerly known as Lady Willingdon Park.

The undulating gardens were graciously landscaped around the **tomb of Muhammad Shah**, the **Bara Gumbad** (large domed) **tomb**, and the adjoining mosque. **Sikandar Lodi's tomb** lies in the northeast corner, surrounded by high walls. To the east of this lies a quaint bridge, raised at the time of the Mughals.

In 1526, the last Lodi ruler, Ibrahim, was overthrown by Babur who founded the Mughal empire. The next century was to witness the extraordinary culmination of Indo-Islamic traditions, energized as much by new blood as the personal interest of the first six Mughal emperors.

The **Purana Qila** is Delhi's sixth city, the combined effort of Humayun, Babur's son, and of the Afghan Sher Shah Sur, who temporarily deposed him. Within this fort, which rises off the busy Mathura Road, are two important buildings which anticipate the characteristics of Mughal architecture – the **Qalai Kunha Mosque** raised by Sher Shah in 1541; and the **Sher Mandal**. The purpose of this latter two-storied, octagonal structure is not known. It may have been a pleasure resort; it may also have housed Humayun's library of manuscripts. He died here, falling down the stairs as he turned to answer the call to prayer. The

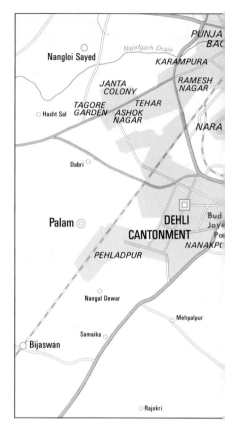

Purana Qila overlooks the **Zoo**, and affords a fine view of Delhi across the river. To its north is the **Pragati Maidan** where excellent exhibitions are regularly held. Within the Pragati Maidan is the excellent **Crafts Museum** and the **Rural India Complex**, where craftsmen work in simulated rural surroundings.

About 2 km (1.25 mi) south of Purana Qila is **Humayun's Tomb**. It is the first, and one of the finest, examples of the type of garden tomb that was to be perfected in the Taj Mahal. Its high arches, its double dome and its restrained grandeur are characteristic of Mughal architecture. It was begun in 1564 by his widow, Haji Begum, nine years after his death, and designed by a Persian architect

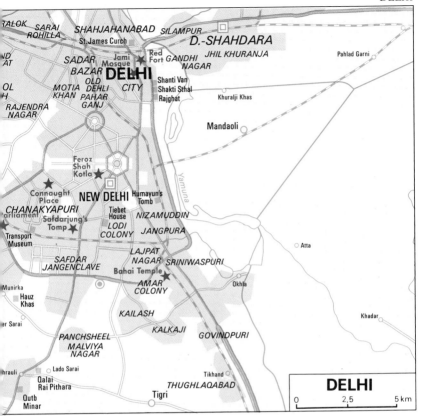

Misak Mirza Ghiyas. The wives of Humayun, Shah Jahan's son Dara Shikoh, and later Mughals are also buried here. The last Mughal emperor, Bahadur Shah Zafar, who was exiled to Burma by the British after the mutiny, took refuge here along with his three sons, but was captured by Lt. Hodson.

Just across the busy highway is one of the oldest, continuously inhabited localities of Delhi, closely associated with the Sufi saint Nizamuddin Auliya (d. 1325). This much loved saint is buried here. Apart from people whose families have lived here for several generations, the shrine also draws pilgrims from all corners of the Islamic world. Buried near the saint is his beloved disciple Amir Khusrau, a man of letters, a courtier, and a poet *par excellence*.

Shahjahanabad

While the first four Mughal emperors had their capital at Agra, Shah Jahan decided to move to Delhi even as the Taj Mahal was being completed. On 16 April 1639 the foundations were laid for Delhi's seventh city, which took nine years to build. It epitomized the grandeur associated with the Mughal empire; two and a half centuries later Shahjahanabad was all that remained of it. Yet, despite devastation, upheaval and the onslaught of alien influences it was never deserted. Today it is one of the most densely popu-

lated localities in the world; 90 percent of Delhi's Muslims live here, and in the cool secluded *havelis* which lie off the bustling roads and lanes, there are people who proudly claim to be descendants of the Mughals or those who served the Mughals. A certain vitality, which gives it its main charm, transcends the congestion and the chaos.

Shah Jahan's imposing citadel, the **Red Fort**, was built at the eastern extremity of the walled city, along the river front. Entrance to the fort is through the imposing Lahori Gate which leads to a roofed passage called **Chatta Chowk**, now lined with antiques shops. The Chatta Chowk ends at the **Naqqar Khana** (drum house) which marks the entrance to the royal enclosure. Five times a day, at the auspicious hours, musicians played upon a range of instruments here. The War Memorial is presently housed in the upper story.

Above: The Bahai Temple - New Delhi's spectacular modern landmark.

A wide open space leads to the **Diwan-i-Am** (the hall of public audience). Even though the Red Fort is comparatively well preserved it requires either a deep familiarity with miniature paintings or a vivid imagination to picture the palaces as they must have been when the emperor lived there.

The pillars and ceilings of this hall were richly ornamented with gilded stucco; heavy brocaded drapes enclosed it and exquisite carpets covered the floors; there was no furniture. The richly carved marble structure inlaid with semi-precious stones is where the emperor's throne was placed, and the ornate panel behind it is said to have been worked by a Florentine named Austin de Bordeaux.

The six main palaces (one of which has disappeared) were built right behind the Diwan-i-Am, and through these palaces once flowed the Nahr-i-Bihisht, the Stream of Paradise. Starting at the southern end, is the Mumtaz Mahal which was part of the imperial seraglio. Today it houses the **Delhi Museum of Archaeo-**

logy, with primarily Mughal exhibits. The **Rang Mahal**, the palace of colors, also part of the seraglio, was pillaged by troops when the British garrisoned the fort. It consists of six apartments, including the glass studded **Shish Mahal**. The **Khas Mahal** (private palace) consists of three parts - the Tasbih Khana, the chamber for telling beads, used by the emperor for his private worship; the Khwabgah, the chamber of dreams; and the Baithak, or sitting room, a long hall to the south with finely worked walls and ceilings. The Khas Mahal also has a beautiful marble lattice screen, impressively depicting the Scales of Justice. It is from here that the emperor and his queens witnessed elephant fights and were entertained by jugglers and acrobats down below on the banks of the river which then flowed by the fort. The semi-octagonal tower called the **Muthamman Burj** is where the emperor appeared briefly each day for the benefit of his subjects. A balcony was added later and is where, in 1911, King George V and Queen Mary appeared before the citizens of Delhi.

The **Diwan-i-Khas**, the hall of private audience, was used by the emperor for meetings with chosen courtiers and visitors. The legendary jewel-studded Peacock Throne was placed on the marble dais; but a century later, Nadir Shah, the Persian invader took the throne home as part of his loot. The Diwan-i-Khas retains some of its exquisite inlay work, and restoration work continues. On the gilded ceiling, retouched in 1911, is a couplet which reads: "If there be a paradise on earth, it is this, it is this, it is this... ." The **Hammams**, or royal baths, are in a much better state of repair and the inlay work is almost entirely preserved; even the floors are covered with this "stone embroidery." It is closed to visitors but a glimpse can be had of it through the windows.

West of these royal apartments is the **Pearl Mosque** built entirely of marble by Aurangzeb for his private worship. North of this mosque is the Hayat Baksh (life-bestowing) garden. Except for the monsoon months, a *son et lumière* performance is held every evening at the fort.

The other grand monument of Old Delhi, the **Jama Masjid**, was also raised by Shah Jahan. It is the largest mosque in India; its proportions are perfect and its tranquil interior is conducive to contemplation. The mosque is separated from the congested arterial road by a sprawling esplanade, which, in the evening, is the scene of many fascinating activities. If the mosque is the nerve center of Old Delhi, this is its leisure ground. It has wayside food-stalls; bazaars catering to the needs of pilgrims; ear-cleaners with red turbans; a pigeon market (pigeon flying is still a popular sport in the old city); "computer" astrologers; masseurs; chess players; a wrestling arena; *bhishtis*, who carry water in goatskins; aphrodisiac sellers; roadside dentists; acrobats; vendors of talismans and "corrective" semiprecious stones. According to contemporary records, the scene was much the same two centuries ago.

For the intrepid explorer, there is still more. **Chandni Chowk** pierces the very heart of Old Delhi. Here the roar of traffic mingles with the echoes of worship, the animated talk of businessmen, the cries of vying hawkers, the curses of rickshaw pullers and the persistent promises of conmen and touts. This largest trading center in north India was once a quiet road, shaded by banyans, with a canal flowing along its entire length. Jahanara, Shah Jahan's daughter, had a square built on this road and in its center a pool fed by the canal. On a clear night the water reflected the light of the moon; so it came to be known as Chandni Chowk, the moonlit square. The nobility built mansions here, shops sprang up along the street, and Chandni Chowk became the most fashionable place in the empire. In 1837, Emma Roberts, an Englishwoman, recorded in her diary that the streets often

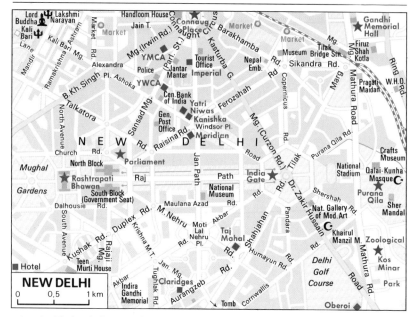

echoed with the shrill roar of caged cheetahs and hooded hunting leopards being
hawked. The titles of great men were
shouted by their followers. There were
Persian cats and greyhounds for sale,
while the trumpeting of elephants mingled with the sounds of cartwheels and
itinerant musicians. "The business, as
usual," she wrote, "carried on...amidst
the bustle and confusion of the streets... ."
The last holds good today, even though
Emma Roberts would not recognize
her Chandni Chowk and the cheetah, long
extinct, has been replaced by consumer
goods. But Ghantewala, the sweetmeat
store, established in 1740, and Gulab
Chand perfumers, established in 1860,
are still there.

The **Gurudwara Sis Ganj** commemorates the spot where Aurangzeb had the
ninth Sikh Guru Tegh Bahadur beheaded.
The 3rd British column led its assault
along this street, and a few decades later
Lord Curzon rode in procession here.
The new rulers built a Baptist church,
filled up the canal and Jahanara's pool

and built a clock tower which came
crashing down in the late 40s. During the
freedom struggle, bonfires of foreign
goods were lit along the street. The
stories are endless ...

The lanes that lead off Chandni Chowk
are as fascinating: **Khari Baoli**, the spice
market; **Dariba**, the silver street; **Para-
thewali Gali**, where you can still eat the
best *parathas* in town; **Kinari Bazaar**,
known for its tinsel and trimmings are
among those easier to find.

Imperial Delhi

It is hard to believe that barely 3 km
(1.5 mi) away, lie the wide tree-lined
avenues of New Delhi. At an imperial
durbar held for King George V and
Queen Mary on 12 December 1911 it was
announced that the British would finally
move their administrative center from
Calcutta to Delhi.

New Delhi was to be "conceived with
spaciousness and care so that the new
creation would be in every way worthy of

this ancient and beautiful city." The task of designing it fell upon Edwin Lutyens and Herbert Baker, who traveled through India for years studying ancient architecture.

The 340-roomed Viceregal lodge was raised on Raisina Hill and is today the **Rashtrapati Bhawan**, where the President of India lives. The strength of this building is accentuated by the Rajpath axis, and the symmetrical location of the **India Gate**, the World War I memorial arch. Rashtrapati Bhawan is flanked by the North and South Blocks, which house government offices. Nearby, is the circular, collonaded **Parliament House**. Rajpath is the scene of pageantry during the annual Republic Day Parade. As it leads to the portals of power, it is also the point where demonstrators converge to voice their protests.

Around the India Gate area are two fine museums: the **National Museum** on Janpath is the premier museum in the country, with a superb collection of antiquities. Adjacent to this museum, within the premises of the Archaeological Survey of India, is the **Auriel Stein Gallery** of Central Asian Art. The **National Archives** are also on Janpath. The other important museum is the **National Gallery of Modern Art**. It exhibits contemporary Indian art, and also has a fine selection of the paintings of Amrita Sher-Gil, Rabindranath Tagore and Jamini Roy, as well as 19th-century art.

Connaught Circus, planned as part of imperial Delhi, is the prime commercial center. Of particular interest to travelers would be the wayside stalls and Tibetan market on **Janpath**, where there is also the **Central Cottage Industries Emporium**. On **Baba Kharak Singh Marg** are emporiums that sell textiles and handicrafts from each state in the country. In the midst of all this, off Parliament Street, is the **Jantar Mantar**, an early 18th-century masonry observatory built by Raja Jai Singh II of Jaipur.

Other Places of Interest

At the junction of Lodi Road and Sri Aurobindo Marg is the **tomb of Safdarjang**, who was Viceroy of Awadh under Muhammad Shah (1719-48) and later his prime minister. It is also a garden tomb, but its weakness of proportions is evident; it has been aptly described as the "last flicker in the lamp of Mughal architecture in Delhi."

Not far from here, on Safdarjang Road is the **Indira Gandhi Memorial**, where the late prime minister lived and was assassinated. Close by is the **Teen Murti House**, the gracious residence of Jawaharlal Nehru. It has been converted into a museum and the life of that era is recreated in a *son et lumière* show. The **Planetarium** is within the precincts, too. The open air **Rail Museum** is in Chanakyapuri, the posh diplomatic enclave of the capital. Its fascinating collection, which includes a steam engine (1855) in working order, will delight the railway buff. The **Tibet House** on Lodi Road has a museum which houses ceremonial objects brought from Tibet by the followers of the Dalai Lama. About 8 km (5 mi) away, near the concrete jungle of Nehru Place, is the lotus-petaled, hemispherical **Temple of the Bahai**, a tolerant Islamic sect founded in Iran in 1836 by Bahaullah. It is one of the architectural landmarks of modern Delhi.

The **International Dolls Museum**, housing some 6000 dolls from 85 countries, is on Bahadur Shah Zafar Marg. Further north, beyond Shahjahanabad, are remnants of the pre-1857 British era, including **St. James Church** (1824) and the **Flagstaff Tower**, at the crest of the northern ridge, which commemorates the site where British women and children gathered on 11 May 1857 during the Revolt. On Ring Road, are **Rajghat**, **Shanti Van** and **Shakti Sthal**, memorials to Mahatma Gandhi, Jawaharlal Nehru and Indira Gandhi, respectively.

DELHI
Accommodation

LUXURY: **Ashok**, 50 B Chanakyapuri, Tel: 600121. **Best Western Surya**, New Friends Colony, Tel: 6835070. **Centaur**, Delhi Airport, Gurgaon Road, Tel: 5452223. **Claridges**, 12 Aurangzeb Road, Tel: 3010211. **Holiday Inn Crowne Plaza**, Barakhamba Avenue, Connaught Place, Tel: 3320101. **Hyatt Regency Delhi**, Bhikaji Cama Place, Tel: 6881234. **Imperial**, Janpath, Tel: 3325332. **Kanishka**, 19 Ashok Road, Tel:-3324422. **Le Meridien**, Windsor Place, Tel: 3710101. **Oberoi Maidens**, 7 Sham Nath Marg, Tel: 2525464. **The Oberoi**, Dr. Zakir Hussain Marg, Tel: 4363030. **Qutab**, Off Aurobindo Marg, Tel: 660060.**Taj Mahal**, 1 Man Singh Rd., Tel: 3016162. **Welcomgroup Maurya Sheraton**, Sardar Patel Marg, Diplomatic Enclave, Tel: 3010101.

MODERATE: **Broadway**, 4/15 Asaf Ali Rd. Tel: 3273821. **Diplomat**, 9 Sardar Patel Marg, Tel: 3010204 **Jukaso Inn**, 50 Sundar Nagar, Tel: 690309. **Kailash Inn**, 10 Sunder Nagar, Tel: 4625047. **Lodhi**, Lala Lajpat Rai Marg, Tel: 4362422. **Marina**, G 59 Connaught Cicus, Tel: 3324658. **Metro**, N 49 Connaught Circus, Janpath, Tel: 43805/56/41**. Nirula's**, L-Block, Connaught Circus, Tel: 3322419. **Vikram**, Lajpat Nagar III, Tel: 6436451.

BUDGET: **Country Castle**, E-58 Greater Kailash, Tel: 6416228. **India International Centre**, 40 Lodi Estate, Tel: 619431. **Maharani Guest House**, 3 Sunder Nagar, Tel: 693128. **Panchsheel Inn**, C-4 Panchsheel Enclave, Tel: 6433874. **Samrat Inn**, C/29 South Extension-II, Tel: 6440054. **Sachdeva**, 49 Golf Links, Tel: 611418. **Shervani Fort View**, 11 Sunder Nagar, Tel: 611771. **Sodhi Lodge**, E-2 East of Kailash, Tel: 6442381. **YMCA International Guest House**, Sansad Marg, Tel: 311569. **Youth Hostel**, 5 Nyaya Marg, Chanakyapuri, Tel: 3011969.

CAMPING SITES: **Jawaharlal Nehru Marg**, Tel: 3278929. **Qudsia Gardens**, Qudsia Road, Near I.S.B.T.

Bookstores and Libraries
E.D. Galgotia & Sons, 17B Connaught Place. **Teksons Bookshop**, N.D.S.E. Part I. **Bahri & Sons**, Khan Market. **Bookworm**, 29B Connaught Place. **The Book Shop**, Khan Market. **Picadilly Bookstore**, 64 Shankar Market.

LIBRARIES: **Sahitya Akademi**, Rabindra Bhawan, Ferozeshah Road, Tel: 388667/8/9. **American Information Center**, 24 Kasturba Gandhi Marg, Tel: 3316841. **Max Mueller Bhavan**, 3 Kasturba Gandhi Marg, Tel: 3323269. **National Museum Library**, Janpath.

Hospitals
All India Institute of Medical Sciences, Ansari Nagar, Sri Aurobindo Marg, Tel: 661123. **Aaslok Hospital**, 25 A Safdarjang Enclave, Tel: 608407. **Batra Hospita**l, 1 Tughlakbad, Institutional Area, Tel: 6433509. **East West Medical Centre**, 38 Golf Links, Tel: 699229. **Escorts Heart Institute and Research Centre**, Okhla Road, Tel: 6844820. **Holy Family Hospital**, Okhla Road, Jamia Nagar, Tel: 6845900. **Safdarjang General Hospital**, Ring Road, Tel: 665060. **Dr. Sharma's Clinic**, 19A Kailash Colony, Tel: 6431896. **Summit Clinic**, 9 Palam Marg, Vasant Vihar, Tel: 673432.

Museums
Archaeological Museum, Red Fort, Tel: 3267961, 10 am-5 pm, closed Fri. **Crafts Museum**, Pragati Maidan, Tel: 3317641, 10 am-6 pm. **Gandhi Museum**, Opp. Raj Ghat, Tel: 3311495, 9.30 am-5.30 pm. **Musical Instruments Gallery**, Rabindra Bhavan, Feroz Shah Rd., Tel: 387246, 10 am-6 pm. **National Gallery of Modern Art**, Jaipur House, India Gate, Tel: 382835, 10 am-5 pm. **National Museum**, Janpath, Tel: 3019538, 10 am-5 pm, guided tours available. **Rail Transport Museum**, Chanakyapuri, Tel: 601816, 9.30 am-5.30 pm. **Tibet House Museum**, 1, Institutional Area, Tel: 611515, 10 am-5 pm, closed Sun. (Unless otherwise stated, the museums above are closed on Mondays.)

An inexpensive monthly publication, *The City Guide*, gives the lowdown on film, theater, exhibitions and cultural events for the current month.

Post / Telegraph / Telephone
Head Post Office, Sansad Marg, Tel: 385605, open 10 am-8 pm, Sun 10 am-5 pm. **Eastern Court Post & Telegraph Office**, Janpath, Tel: 3324214 (Telegraph: 311599), 10 am-8 pm, Sun 10 am-5 pm. **G.P.O. Ashoka Place**, Tel: 322012, 8 am-7 pm, closed Sun (Poste Restante facility available). **Overseas Communication Service**, Bangla Sahib Road. Open 24 hours. International calls and overseas telegrams.

Restaurants
CHINESE: **Bali Hi**, Welcomgroup Maurya Sheraton, Sardar Patel Marg, Tel: 3010101. **Chinese Room**, Nirula's, L-Block, Connaught Place, Tel: 3322419. **House of Ming**, Taj Mahal, 1 Mansingh Road, Tel: 3016162. **Pearls**, Hyatt Regency Delhi, Bhikaji Cama Place, Tel: 609911. **Tea House of The August Moon**, Taj Palace Intercontinental, Sardar Patel Marg, Tel: 3010404. **Taipan**, The Oberoi, Dr. Zakir Hussain Marg, Tel: 4363030.

CONTINENTAL: **Burgundy**, Ashok, 50 B Chankyapuri, Tel: 600121. **Captain's Cabin**, Taj Mahal, Tel: 3016162. **Club de France**, Maurya Sheraton, Tel: 3010101. **Curzon Room**, Oberoi Maidens, Tel: 2525464. **Orient Express**, Taj Palace Intercontinental, 2 Sardar Patel Marg, Tel: 3010404.

INDIAN / TANDOORI / MUGHLAI: **Bukhara** and **Dum Pukht**, Welcomgroup Maurya Sheraton, Tel: 3010101. **Chor Bizarre**, Broadway Hotel, Tel: 3273821 (Kashmiri). **Darbar**, Ashok, Tel: 600121. **Dhaba**, Claridges, 12 Aurangzeb Road, Tel: 3010211. **Frontier**, Ashok, 50 B Chanakyapuri, Tel: 600121. **Kandahar**, The Oberoi, Tel: 4363030. **Tandoor**, Hotel President, Asaf Ali Road, Tel: 3277836.

Shopping

Connaught Place is Delhi's main business and shopping area. Shops on **Janpath** sell a variety of goods - ready to wear, costume jewelry, books, furnishings etc. Antiques are available near **Jama Masjid** in Old Delhi, in **Sunder Nagar**, the **Qutab Complex**, shops in Connaught Place and in the shopping arcades of hotels. Boutiques worth a visit include **Anokhi** (Santushti Shopping Arcade, near Ashok Hotel) **Khazana** (at the Taj Mahal Hotel) and **The Collection** at the Taj Palace. A visit to **'Once upon a Time'**, Bina Ramani's exclusive boutique in **Hauz Khas**, behind the Qutab is a must. State emporia selling handicrafts and fabulous textiles from each state are located on **Baba Kharak Singh Marg**, a stone's throw from Connaught Place, closed on Sundays and national holidays. **The Central Cottage Industries Emporium**, Janpath, **Handloom House** and **Khadi Gram Udyog**, Connaught Place, are also worth a visit.

Excursions

Day trips can be undertaken to tourist spots in the neighboring states. **Haryana**: Badhkal Lake (32 km); angling and boating facilities. Ballabgarh (36 km); ideal for anglers. Karna Lake (132 km); facilities for boating and fishing. Maur Bund (32 km); a snake charmers' village. Sohna (56 km); hot springs. Surajkund (18 km). For Haryana, you have the option of hiring a taxi or taking a bus. **Uttar Pradesh:** Agra (203 km). The city of the Taj Mahal, and also of handicrafts (marble and soft stone inlay work, carpets, leather goods, brocade). **Rajasthan**: Jaipur (256 km). Once again a city of architectural marvels and exquisite handicrafts (textiles, mirror-work, jewelry, enameled brass-ware, blue pottery, *pichwai* paintings, ivory carving). There are daily conducted tours run by ITDC and other agencies (by deluxe coaches) to Agra and Jaipur.

Tourist Information

Government of India Tourist Office, 88 Janpath, Tel: 320005-8. Counters at the International Arrivals hall at the airport, (Tel: 391315 Extn. 2377/2440). **Delhi Tourism Development Corporation**, N Block, Connaught Place. Tel: 3313637. Also a 24-hour counter at the Indira Gandhi International Airport, Tel: 391213; Delhi Emporium, Tel: 343287. These tourist offices organize city tours as well. The following tourist information offices are located on Bara Kharak Singh Marg: Andhra Pradesh, Tel: 343894; Assam, Tel: 3321967; Bihar, Tel: 311087; Gujarat, Tel: 3322107; Karnataka, Tel: 343862; Kerala, Tel: 310151; Maharashtra, Tel: 343281; Orissa, Tel: 344580; Tamil Nadu, Tel: 343913; West Bengal, Tel: 3323840. The tourist offices for Haryana, Tel: 344911, Rajasthan, Tel: 3322332 and Uttar Pradesh, Tel: 3322251, are located in Chandralok Building on Janpath. A five-minute walk away is the Kanishka Shopping Plaza with the tourist information offices of Himachal, Jammu & Kashmir, Tel: 345373; and Madhya Pradesh, Tel: 3321187, 344764. For information on Sikkim, Tel: 3324589, walk down to Hotel Janpath (on Janpath); and for Andaman & Nicobar Islands, Tel: 387015, and Lakshadweep, Tel: 386807, Curzon Road Hostel.

Access / Transport

The **Indira Gandhi International Airport** is situated at the city's limit (17 km from Connaught Place). Terminal I handles domestic flights (there is a separate terminal for airbus departures) whereas Terminal II, some kilometers further out, handles only foreign flights.

For airport-city transfers there are metered taxis, auto-rickshaws and a prepaid taxi service. Coaches to the city stopping at selected points take about 45 minutes to 1 hour. There are transfer coaches from the international to the domestic airport. There are three major railway stations - Delhi Main (also referred to as Old Delhi), New Delhi and Hazrat Nizamuddin.

An extensive network of roads links the capital to neighboring states. Inter-state buses leave regularly from the Inter-State Bus Terminus near Kashmere Gate (in Old Delhi). The chief mode of local transport is the blue-yellow bus, run by Delhi Transport Corporation. Local taxis (black bodied and yellow topped) are metered while tourist taxis, generally white, charge anywhere between Rs. 2 to Rs. 5 per km.

Auto-rickshaws are metered. Rates are often revised. The fare conversion chart will indicate the revised fare. Between 11 pm and 6 am there is a 30 percent surcharge.

HARYANA AND PUNJAB

New Delhi is surrounded to the north, west and south by the state of Haryana, which was once part of the huge state of Punjab. Today, Punjab lies northwest of Delhi beyond Haryana: the northernmost part of the old state is now Himachal Pradesh, the westernmost part is across the border in Pakistan.

This area was the traditional route for invaders from the northwest. It has seen some of India's fiercest battles, and the cards of history have been dealt at places like **Panipat** and **Karnal** in Haryana. Here, many mausoleums and cenotaphs scattered across the countryside are testimony to the forces of history and change, of human triumph and disaster. Further north is **Kurukshetra**, the scene of the

epic battle narrated in the *Mahabharata* and the occasion for Lord Krishna's *Bhagavad Gita*. Here devout Hindus flock to temples and sacred tanks.

The people of Haryana and Punjab are basically pastoral: strong and hardy and fiercely attached to the soil. They have colorful folk dances (the most famous being the vigorous *Bhangra* of Punjab) and festivals celebrating the seasons and harvest.

Haryana

Minor historical monuments are scattered throughout Haryana: Mughal ruins and fortresses which have seen many desperate battles, and the beautiful ornamental gardens of **Pinjore** near **Chandigarh**. **Surajkund** (20 km or 13 mi from Delhi), an 8th-century Hindu **Sun temple**, and also **Sohna's hot springs** have been developed recently into pleasant tourist excursion spots. Surajkund also has a small golf course. Every year, in February, it becomes the venue for a

Above: Bullock carts remain an indispensable mode of transportation in India. Right: The Bhangra dance reflects the robust character of the people of Punjab.

Crafts Mela (fair) at which craftsmen from all over the country display their skills and wares. The imperial route from Delhi to Agra once passed through Haryana and even today the Mughal *Kos Minar* (milestones) can be seen along the highway. The bird sanctuary at **Sultanpur**, 40 km (25 mi) from Delhi, is particularly interesting in winter. Haryana has almost purely pastoral plains, subject to a merciless, scorching sun in summer and extreme cold in winter, with the monsoon giving life from June to September.

In winter the fertile fields of Haryana are often a carpet of yellow: the mustard crop has ripened. The rhythmic tonk tonk of small oil and flour mills can soon be heard from villages. It is not uncommon, also, to find many peacocks and the occasional nilgai (blue bull: a type of antelope) in the fields of Haryana. Neither is ever harmed by villagers. The absence of mammoth urban development in these two states leaves room for unspoiled nature: the sound of doves and partridges

calling amid the mustard, wheat and sugar-cane fields is complemented by the murmur of irrigation pumps and the flow of water.

Most of the peasantry are Jats, a religious, pastoral race known for their robustness and typical country bluntness. Many members of the Sikh peasantry in Punjab are also Jats. There is a language difference: Punjabi is a distinct language with its own script, while Haryanvi, spoken by the Jats, is a dialect of Hindi.

Though few tourists do so, traveling through Haryana by road is pleasant as the state has created tourist and leisure spots along major highways to make up for the lack of more important attractions. These include artificial lakes and comfortable facilities for overnight stay.

Chandigarh

Chandigarh, the capital of both Haryana and Punjab, is famous for its design and layout. This city was planned by the French architect Le Corbusier, and today

remains one of India's most pleasant state capitals, with the hills of Himachal Pradesh beginning just on the outskirts. Chandigarh is also famous for its tree-lined avenues, giving it a unique atmosphere and charm, especially during the flowering season.

Morni, near Chandigarh, provides the opportunity to see a protected forest in picturesque hilly terrain. **Sukna Lake**, in Chandigarh itself, gives the city its green space and provides the people with recreation and the opportunity to watch migratory waterfowl stopping over in winter. The city has a fine rose garden, and a park where statues have been made from scrap material.

Punjab

The main city of this state is **Amritsar**. The incredible jewel of Punjab, the **Golden Temple**, is here, making it the holiest

Above: The Golden Temple at Amritsar is the most sacred shrine of the Sikhs.

of holy places for Sikhs all over the world. The city is over 400 years old, the temple only a little younger. It is built in the middle of a pool of holy water. The great Sikh ruler Maharaja Ranjit Singh used 400 kg of gold leaf to rebuild and cover the domes of the temple in 1803, hence the name.

The temple complex is huge, and is thronged with many pilgrims on special days. The gleaming golden dome and the holy waters of the Harmandir Sahib make it one of the most beautiful religious structures in the whole country.

A spectacular festival is enacted at another Sikh holy shrine, **Anandpur**, at the base of the Himalaya, one day after Holi, the nationwide festival of spring and color. Besides the Sikh shrines, Punjab also has a Muslim center of pilgrimage, **Sirhind**.

Nowadays, despite its serene green landscape, Punjab is a strictly controlled area because of political disturbances, and foreigners are advised to conform to current rules regarding entry.

CHANDIGARH
Accommodation

LUXURY: **Piccadily**, Himalaya Marg, Sector 22B, Tel: 322223-7. **Sunbeam**, Udyog Path, Sector 22B, Tel: 32057, 41335, 41260. *MODERATE:* **Chandigarh Mountview**, Sector 10, Tel: 41773, 45882. **President**, Madhya Marg, Sector 26, Tel: 40840, 33233. **Rikhys International**, SCO 301-302, Sector 35B, Tel: 26764, 40033. *BUDGET:* **Kapi**l, SCO 303-304, Sector 35B, Tel: 33366. **Maya Palace**, SCO 325, Sector 35 B, Tel: 32118, 33277. **Shivalikview**, Sector 17, Tel: 67131/36. **Pankaj**, Sector 22, Tel: 41906, 25083. **YMCA** (men only) Sector 11, Tel: 26532. **YWCA** (women only), Sector 11, Tel: 43224.

Hospitals

Post Graduate Institute of Medical Sciences and Research & Nehru Hospital, Sector 12, Tel: 32351-58. **Health Center & Poly Clinic**, Sector 22, Tel: 26164. **General Hospital**, Sector 16, Tel: 26165.

Local Festivals

Lohri (mid-January) is celebrated with bonfires and sharing sweets made from jaggery and sesame seeds. An annual event of international repute is the *Rose Festival* (February - March) held at the sprawling Rose Garden. *Baisakhi* (April 13) coincides with the beginning of the harvest season. In the last quarter of the year, when the tourist season starts, the *Regatta* on Sukhna Lake and the festivals of *Dussehra* and *Diwali* (October-November) take place.

Museums

Government Museum and Art Gallery, Sector 10 C, Tel: 25568, 10 am-4 pm, closed Mon and public holidays. **Museum of Fine Arts**, Arts Block, Punjab University, Tel: 22779, 2-5 pm (summer); 10 am-1 pm (winter), closed Mon.

Post / Telegraph / Telephone

General Post Office, Sector 17, Tel: 21070, open 10 am-5 pm). **Central Telegraph Office** (24 hrs). Sector 17, Tel: 23033.

Restaurants

CHINESE: **Dragon**, Sector 15. **Ginza**, Sector 14. *FAST FOOD*: **Hot Shoppe** &**Hot Millions**, S. 17. *CONTINENTAL*: **Four in One**, Sector 17, Tel: 26516. **Kwality**, SCO 20, Sector 17, Tel: 33183. *INDIAN* : **Mehfil**, Sector 17, Tel: 29439. **Bawarchi**, Sector 9, Tel: 21361. **Indian Coffee House**, Sector 22, Tel: 25504.

Shopping

Chandigarh is a show window for a variety of handicrafts. *Bagh* and *phulkari* embroideries adorn bedspreads, handbags, table linen and ready-made dresses. *Panja* durries are made in attractive geometric motifs. The main shopping areas are Sector 17 and 22.

Tourist Information

Chandigarh Tourism, Sector 17, Tel: 22548. **Punjab Tourism**, Sector 8, Tel: 40859. **Haryana Tourism**, Sector 17, Tel: 21955.

Access / Local Transport

Flights to Delhi, Leh, Jammu, Kulu, and, within Punjab, for Ludhiana and Amritsar. Bhatinda and Patiala have air connections with Delhi, too. The railway station, 8 km from the city, services trains from Delhi, Calcutta and Bhiwani (Haryana). Buses and taxis are available in all towns and cities. The main bus stand, Sector 17, has buses operating to Delhi, Jammu-Srinagar, Shimla and towns in Punjab. Auto-rickshaws and cycle-rickshaws supplement the city bus service. Deluxe coaches offer local sightseeing.

Miscellaneous

Parts of Punjab are closed to foreigners. Seek advance information from your local GITO.

AMRITSAR
Accommodation

LUXURY: **Mohan International**, Albert Road, Tel: 34146, 52864-5; *MODERATE*: **Airlines**, Coper Road, Tel: 44545. *BUDGET:* **Grand**, Queen's Rd., opp. Railway St., Tel: 62787.

HARYANA

The state lies en route to Uttar Pradesh, Himachal Pradesh, Rajasthan and Punjab. Its towns are well-equipped with facilities for overnight stay or for use as transit points. (Distances from Delhi unless otherwise specified.)

Delhi-Chandigarh

Sonepat (43 km), Tel: 2282; Samalkha (70 km), Tel: 10; Panipat (92 km), Tel: 3579; Karnal (124 km), Tel: 4279, 4249; Pipli and Kurukshetra (152-155 km), Tel: 250; Ambala (200 km; 55 km from Chandigarh), Tel: 58352; Panchkula (270 km); Morni Hills (45 km from Chandigarh); Yadavindra Gardens, Pinjore (270 km; 22 km from Chandigarh), Tel: 455, 959, Kalka Exch.

Delhi-Rajasthan

Dharuhera (70 km), Tel: 25; Sohna (64km) - the nearby Damdama Lake offers angling and boating facilities; Gurgaon (32 km), Tel: 20683; Rewari (80 km), Tel: 2084.

Delhi-Punjab

Rohtak (72 km), Tel: 4594; Jind (127 km), Tel: 293; Hissar (160 km), Tel: 2602; Sirsa (259 km), Tel: 21996; Abub Shehr (335 km). Surajkund (20 km), Tel: 825357, 6830766; Badkhal Lake (32 km), Tel: 26901; and Sultanpur Bird Sanctuary (46 km), Tel: 42 Farakhnagar Exch.

THE PLAINS OF UTTAR PRADESH

The alluvial plains of Uttar Pradesh (popularly known as U.P.) lie at the foothills of the Himalaya and are nourished by the Ganga and its tributaries. This fertile land nurtured the process of Indian civilization during which Hinduism found sophisticated expression, Buddhism and Jainism emerged, and small states and principalities grew into great kingdoms and empires.

Mathura, Jaunpur, Agra and Fatehpur Sikri were each, at different moments in history, great centers of learning, culture and political power, created by those who came in conquest from across the formidable natural barriers of the northwest. They brought Islam and cultural strains that were not only absorbed but creatively synthesized into a new tradition

Above: Memorial to a beloved wife. The Taj Mahal is the supreme example of a garden tomb.

with a distinct identity. Uttar Pradesh, in particular, is a stronghold of this tradition, most evident in architecture but also present in the schools of music, in dance forms such as *Kathak* and in the Urdu language and poetry.

Today the state is among the most densely populated in the country, and a hotbed of politics. Large areas of it remain backward, but for the traveler it holds some breathtaking attractions, particularly at Agra and Varanasi.

Agra

For several centuries a place of secondary importance, **Agra**, located on the banks of the Yamuna, gained prominence in 1504 as Sikander Lodi's capital when it evolved into a center of power. As such, it was obvious that Babur, the founder of the Mughal Empire, would settle here.

As a city of the Mughals, Agra's monuments express both the individual taste of successive emperors and the evolution of an architectural tradition, finding unique perfection in the Taj Mahal.

For two centuries and more, travelers and poets have lavished praise on the **Taj Mahal**. In more recent years its portrayal through visual media has made it synonymous with India. Yet the visitor is never prepared for the overwhelming impact, which transcends the merely visual.

The Taj Mahal

The death of his beloved queen, Mumtaz Mahal, in 1631, moved the Mughal Emperor Shah Jahan, a builder *par excellence*, to enshrine her memory in a mausoleum of matchless beauty. It took 22 years to build, with the help of the most outstanding talent available, and some 20,000 laborers. The architect remains unknown, though records seem to indicate that 37 people were involved in this. Stainless white marble was excavated from the quarries of Makrana, sandstone was brought from Fatehpur Sikri, precious and semi-precious stones were chosen from within and without the boundaries of the empire, while the legendary imperial coffers flowed without any restraint.

Conceived as a garden tomb on the lines of those of Khan Khanan and Humayun in Delhi, the Taj Mahal (which is a colloquialism of the queen's name) eclipses its predecessors. Here, the mausoleum rises at the far end, instead of the center, of the garden in a setting that highlights the perfect symmetry of the entire plan. It also reveals the complementary nature of the immense gateway, the spacious garden and the auxiliary buildings – the mosque and the mirror-image Mehman Khana or guest house. Each is planned in proportion to the central structure; together they define the space from which the Taj rises "like a beautiful princess, surrounded by four ladies-in-waiting."

Descriptive detail can reduce the merit of a creation such as the Taj to mere technicalities. But it is worth mentioning its almost sculpturesque quality whereby form is balanced – the fullness of the dome with the rising, recessed arches of the doorways, and these, in turn, with the arched alcoves set in the chamfered angles of the tomb; or, again, the luminous masses of white marble with the lyrical but restrained use of color. Beneath the dome, in the central hall are the cenotaphs of Mumtaz Mahal and Shah Jahan, who was later buried there by his son, Aurangzeb. (The actual graves are in a chamber below.) Here, in particular, the *pietra dura*, or inlay work, is exquisitely intricate; often as many as 48 tiny pieces of semi-precious stones were shaped and embedded to give the desired tonal variation to a single flower. (Craftsmen, who live near the Taj, and draw constant inspiration from it, still excel in marble inlay work.) Soaring to a height of almost 75 m (246 ft), the Taj Mahal, luminous and chaste, retains a jewel-like quality. The play of light on the marble makes it a monument of many moods. Some feel that the Taj is best seen under a full moon; others that it is most ethereal at dawn and most sensuous at sunset; while yet others insist that on a moonless night it has a haunting luminosity.

For sheer presence, the imposing **Agra Fort**, on the banks of the Yamuna, has no rival. It was built by Akbar on the established Mughal lines. However, most of the palaces and buildings built by Akbar within the fort were destroyed, to be replaced by the more lyrical marble creations of his grandson, Shah Jahan. Apart from the solid sandstone ramparts which stretch for 2.5 km (1.5 mi) and the towering gateways, the **Jehangir Mahal,** with its fretwork and carving, is the only surviving structure of Akbar's time. It is the largest private residence within the fort and the architecture has strong Hindu overtones.

85

The **Diwani-i-Khas**, the exclusive hall of private audience, was built by Shah Jahan. Its spaces are defined by the elegant pillars and its foliated arches which were to become a hallmark of his style. The world-famous peacock throne was kept here before it was taken to Delhi. Adjacent to the Diwan-i-Khas are those "paradise-like apartments" which Shah Jahan built for Mumtaz Mahal (the Chosen One of the Palace). They include the **Khas Mahal**, the **Jasmine Tower**, the **Octagonal Tower**, the **Shish Mahal** or Palace of Mirrors, and the **Hamam** or Turkish baths. Ironically, Shah Jahan was to spend his last years confined to these apartments by his ambitious son Aurangzeb. There are also two mosques within the fort – the **Pearl Mosque** and the **Nagina Masjid**. These two palaces are supreme examples of an architectural style born of the fusion of Islamic and Hindu traditions, and culminating in Shah Jahan's "reign of marble." Within the fort is the superbly proportioned **Diwan-i-Am** or hall of public audience, with its inlaid marble throne. There are contemporary accounts which describe the Emperor receiving petitions amid elaborate protocol that enhanced his magnificence. Much of the gold, silver and precious stones used in these buildings – as in the other monuments in Agra – was pillaged by the Jats in the 18th century.

Across the river, 3 km (1.5 mi) downstream, is the mausoleum of Mirza Ghiyas Beg, the father-in-law of Jehangir. After proving his worth at the Mughal court, he was granted the title of Itmad-ud-Daula (Pillar of the State). His mausoleum was completed under the patronage of his daughter Nur Jahan in 1628. This "jeweled casket" is a gem of Mughal architecture. In its use of marble and inlay work (aptly described as stone embroidery) it is a forerunner of the Taj Mahal.

Close to Itmad-ud-Daula is the **Chini-ka-Rawza**, built by Afzal Khan, a promi-

nent official at the court of Jehangir. This structure is dominated by a single dome, and the remains of enamel tiles reveal a strong Persian influence.

Further north is **Ram Bagh**, the first Mughal garden, laid out by Babur as relief from the "hot and dusty plains of Hindustan." It is presently in a state of neglect. The Dyal Bagh complex is only 10 km (6 mi) from Agra. Here, a **Radha Swami Temple** has been under construction for the last 80 years. Skilled craftsmen are working on this marble edifice, but the style of their work is far removed from the elegance of the 17th century creations in Agra.

More interesting are the **Kinari** and **Jauhari bazaars** within the city of Agra,

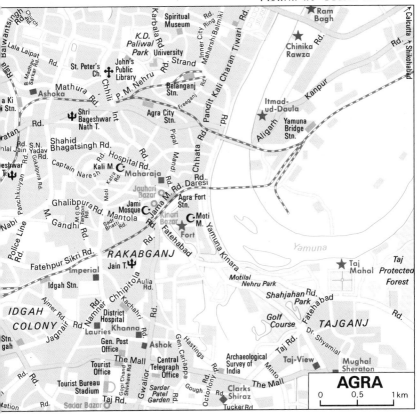

and the bustling streets that converge at the **Jami Masjid**, a mosque built by Shah Jahan. Agra is the largest shoe manufacturing center in the world. It is also famous for its variety of inlaid marble goods, *zardozi* or goldembroidered items, carpets, and *petha* (crystallized gourd) and *dalmoth* (savory lentils).

Akbar's mausoleum is located near Sikandra, only 10 km (6 mi) from Agra. The excessively ornamented gateway leads to an immense sandstone tomb which is topped by marble pavilions. Started by Akbar himself, but completed by his son Jehangir the structure is a self-conscious combination of Hindu and Islamic styles and has appropriately been described as an "amorphous curiosity."

Fatehpur Sikri

Fatehpur Sikri, 37 km (23 mi) west of Agra, is a magnificent deserted city, partly in ruins. However, the red sandstone imperial residence is so well preserved that it seems as though Akbar left but yesterday. There is a story behind its creation. On the barren ridge above the village of Sikri there lived a Sufi saint, Sheikh Salim Chishti. It is said that Akbar sought his blessings for a male heir. In course of time three sons were born to his queens. At the birth of the first (Jehangir) in 1569, Akbar built the grand **Jami Masjid** near the saint's dwelling. When a second son was born in 1571, the grateful emperor decided to create an imperial city. The best architects and builders were already constructing Agra Fort. Enthused by Akbar's personal interest, they created a magnificent city at Sikri, "bigger and better than London." In 1573, to commemorate his triumph over Gujarat, Akbar renamed it Fatehpur, the City of Victory.

Ralph Fitch, an Englishman who visited Fatehpur Sikri in 1585, records that the route from Agra was a crowded bazaar which extended up to the palace walls, and where the treasures of the East were sold. The city, surrounded by a 10-km-long (6 mi) wall, was built along the ridge with the palace complex to the east where the ground sloped away from the highest point occupied by the Jami Masjid. Below the palaces were the houses of the nobles, bazaars and caravanserais, workshops, schools, baths and stables (with as many as 5,000 elephants, more than 1,000 cheetahs and 30,000 horses).

The Abode of Fortune

The **Agra Gate** is still the point of entry and the road leads through ruins where recent excavations have revealed arms and pottery. After these ruins, the **Diwan-i-Am** comes as a surprise. The immense courtyard, the collonaded arches and the carved sandstone appear untouched by time. Here, Akbar made himself accessible to the public. Judgments were passed and in the midst of hearings there were performances by jugglers and jesters and acrobats, in whom the Emperor is known to have delighted.

A doorway (nobles had to kiss the threshold) leads to the **Daulat Khana** or the Abode of Fortune, as the imperial residence was called. At the southern end of this immense space are the **Anup Talao** (Peerless Pool), Akbar's private

Right: Krishna steals the Milkmaids' Clothes. (Bhagavata Purana series, 18th century).

chambers and the one-roomed, exquisitely carved **Turkish Sultana's Palace**. A large quadrangle known as the Pachisi courtyard is where Akbar played a game of chess using dancing girls instead of pawns. **Raja Birbal's palace**, the **Treasury** and the **Astrologer's Seat** are to its north. Nearby is one of the architectural wonders of Fatehpur Sikri, the use of which is still uncertain. It is variously known as the **Diwan-i-Khas**, the **Ibadat Khana** (the House of Worship) and the **Jewel House**. What is certain is that the Emperor's throne was at the top of the ornately carved pillar that is linked by narrow bridges to the corners of the building. But we do not know whether he conferred with his nobles here, listened to learned divines or inspected his jewels. Towering above the Daulat Khana is the **Panch Mahal**, where Akbar enjoyed the cool air of a summer evening with the ladies of his vast harem.

It would be well, in the midst of these deserted palaces, to try to visualize the scene 400 years ago. This was the nerve center of a legendary empire ruled by an emperor who was a contemporary of Elizabeth I of England, Henry IV of France and Shah Abbas of Persia; a remarkable statesman driven by the conviction that God had chosen him "for the unfolding of some great design;" an extraordinary general who had a passionate interest in many diverse aspects of life, and who even attempted to start a new religion, Din-i-Illahi. Within the circle of the court there were outstanding generals and financiers, poets and biographers, theologians of various religious disciplines and the renowned musician, Tansen. A library of 24,000 manuscripts was created at Fatehpur Sikri with the help of the best artists and calligraphers. Mughal miniature painting was born in its workshops, while Sanskrit classics and Turki chronicles were translated into Persian in the Makhtab Khana. The court in those days was a lively and creative center.

To the west of the Daulat Khana is the **Harim Sara**, the splendid abode of the royal ladies. **Jodha Bai's palace** (she was Akbar's favorite queen) and the **Sunahra Makan**, with its painted ceiling, are especially beautiful. At the western extremity of the ridge is the **Jami Masjid**. Sheikh Salim Chishti is buried in the courtyard, in an exquisite tomb of white marble, which was raised by Jehangir. It is revered as a wish-fulfilling tomb, especially by those who want children. The Jami Masjid is one of the finest built by Akbar. In 1573, he commissioned the immense Buland Darwaza, which rises to a height of 40 m (131 ft). A huge rain water cistern below the quadrangle still provides water for the mosque.

Akbar lived in Fatehpur Sikri for only 14 years. Some believe that he left because of an acute water shortage; others, that the problems in the northwest necessitated his presence in Lahore. By 1610, the city was already deserted, with only the imperial residence preserved for later emperors who came to pay homage to the saint. Real destruction was caused by the Jats in the 18th century, but there was little they could do to the sandstone.

Mathura

Mathura, on the banks of the Yamuna, is revered as the birthplace of Lord Krishna. Mentioned in the accounts of Ptolemy and Fa Hsien, this predominantly Hindu town is still an important place of pilgrimage, one of India's holiest and oldest cities. The **Mathura Museum** has a vast collection of antiquities from the Maurya, Sunga and Gupta periods. Its collection of Kushan art is said to be the finest in India. Today, Mathura's most visited places are the **Dwarkadesh Temple**, the **Geeta Mandir** and the **Keshav Deo temple** (see also the Seven Sacred Cities). Nearby, **Vrindavan** is equally enriched by its association with Krishna. The most famous temple here is the **Govind Deo**. The **Jugal Kishore**, **Radha Ballabh** and **Madan Mohan** are other temples worth visiting.

Eastward to Lucknow

The site of an ancient Hindu fort and the scene of hectic military activity in ancient times **Aligarh** is today best known for the Aligarh Muslim University which specializes in Islamic studies. **Rampur** was ruled by nawabs who were connoisseurs of art and also gourmets as well. The bazaars (daggers are a specialty) and the **Jami Masjid** are worth a visit. Of much more interest is the **Hamid Manzil** which houses the **Raza Library**. Its collection of old miniature paintings and rare manuscripts attracts scholars and art lovers from all over the world. **Kanpur**, on the banks of the Ganga, has little of tourist interest, being an industrial city famous for its leather and textile industries. Historically, Kanpur's importance is linked with the revolt

Above: Lucknow railway station captures the mood of this one-time city of nawabs. Right: The Bara Imambara where Shia Muslims gather for ritual mourning on Mohar-

of 1857, and the Memorial Church contains tablets commemorating the British who died at that time.

Lucknow

On the banks of the Gomti river stands **Lucknow**, the capital city of Uttar Pradesh. Despite modernization it bears the legacy of its former rulers, the Nawab Wazirs of Awadh whose lifestyle encouraged cultural growth but proved too decadent to sustain political power. The city of Lucknow rose in importance under the Nawabs of Awadh. The creator of Lucknow as it is today was Asaf-ud-Daula. The city gradually acquired fame as a center of Urdu poetry and courtly diction and reached its acme during the reign of the last Nawab, Wajid Ali Shah, a renowned connoisseur of music and poetry. However, as a ruler he was a disaster for his country and was deposed and deported by the British in 1856.

Parts of Lucknow bear testimony to this bygone era. Close to the **Chowk** with

its narrow, crowded bazaars, selling traditional silver, *zari* and *chikan* embroidered items (both crafts dating to the time of the Nawabs), and authentic Muslim cuisine, is the **Bara Imambara** built by Asaf-ud-Daula in 1784. The most distinctive feature of this huge pillared hall built for ritual mourning during Moharram is the absence of beams and supporting pillars. Within are numerous *tazia* (replicas of the tombs at Karbala), some in stained glass, and the *bhul bhulaiya*, a maze with a series of endless corridors where a guide is essential. Right beside the Imambara stands the **Rumi Darwaza**, an ornamental gateway of brick and colored stucco, also referred to as the Turkish Gate because it resembles one in Constantinople. The Bara Imambara was built to give employment at the time of a famine. Food was served free and in order to ensure a steady supply the new method of slow steam cooking, called *dum pukht*, was devised. The Nawab sampled this and fancied the subtle flavors retained by this method. As a result,

dum pukht was introduced in the royal kitchens where it evolved into a culinary art.

Of less impressive dimensions is the **Chota Imambara** (sometimes called the **Husainabad Imambara**) built by Mohammed Ali Shah in 1837 as his own mausoleum. A central tank lies before this heavily ornamented structure with its gilded domes. Facing the tank stands the **Baradari,** or summer house, and the clock tower.

To the west is the **Jami Masjid**, the mosque built by Ali Shah and one of the few closed to non-Muslims. In another part of the city is the **Shah Najaf Imambara**, a simple white structure deriving its name from the town of Najaf about 200 km (124 mi) south of Baghdad where the saint Hazrat Ali is buried. This Imambara, which is actually the tomb of Ghazi-ud-din Haider Khan, contains a large number of exquisite chandeliers made of Venetian and Czechoslovakian glass and somber portraits of former rulers.

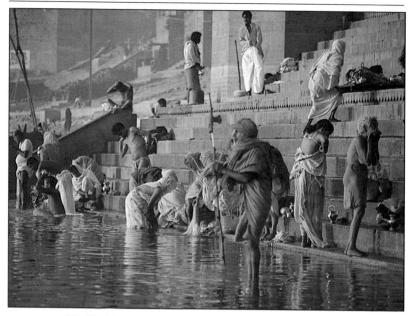

The Residency

The **Residency** epitomizes the British legacy. Within the green lawns are a few ruined buildings. Built for the British Resident in the 18th century, it was the scene of dramatic events during the revolt. Today, the broken and scarred walls tell the story of the British community who were besieged and finally overcome by the Indian mutineers. The now ruined church close by contains the graves of the 200 men, women and children who lost their lives during the revolt.

The model room within the complex is interesting, as it shows the buildings as they were and the sequence of events that took place. Another distinct structure is the **La Martinere** school built by Claude Martin, a soldier of fortune and an opportunist who amassed enormous riches. His palatial house, a strange mixture of Indian and western architectural styles, was

Above: A timeless image - pilgrims bathing at the ghats of the Ganga in Varanasi.

later converted into a school where the famous writer Rudyard Kipling studied for some years. The **Kaisar Bagh**, a beautiful garden with several buildings, **Lakshman Tila**, the original site of the town (today the site of a mosque) and the **Zoo** are among Lucknow's other attractions. The city's charm, however, lies in a distinctive culture that is evident, for instance, in the poetic turn of phrase of even the common people.

Ayodhya and Allahabad

Close to **Faizabad**, once the capital of Awadh, is the small town of **Ayodhya** on the banks of the Ghagara. It is believed to be the birthplace of Rama, the hero of the epic *Ramayana*. One of the seven sacred cities of Hinduism, it has numerous temples and *ghats*. The **Babri Masjid mosque**, claimed by militant Hindus to have been built on the site of an ancient Ram temple which was destroyed by Babur the moghul king, was demolished by a mob of nearly 20,000 militant Hindus on December 6, 1992. A heated controversy between the miliant Hindus and Muslims followed, each group wanting to build their own place of whorship on this site, the Muslims want the Mosque rebuilt and the Hindus insist on building a new Ram temple. The Government of Prime Minister P.V. Narasimha Rao has promised to build both the mosque and the temple. Whatever the final outcome, the Ayodhya question is likely to remain a burning topic in Indian politics and likely to erupt into a frenzy of communal violence again.

The city of **Allahabad** stands at the confluence of two of india's holiest rivers, the Yamuna and the Ganga. It is the *sangam* (the confluence) which is Allahabad's nucleus, and many feel that a visit to the city begins and ends there. Passing the **Hanuman Mandir**, interesting because the idol is supine, a short walk leads to the river's edge. Behind is the fort built by the Mughal Emperor Akbar, ahead the river and in the distance the place where the "white and dark streams" meet. Revered for centuries, the Sangam is visited by hundreds of pilgrims who swell to thousands during the annual *Magh Mela* and the more sacred *Kumbh Mela* which is held every twelve years. The last Kumbh Mela took place in January 1989.

The Source of the Mythical River

The massive **Fort** built by Akbar is a protected area and visits require prior permission. Much of its original beauty is now lost although the magnificent outer wall still stands intact. Of what has remained within, visitors are only allowed to see the **Asokan pillar** and **Saraswati Kup**, a well said to be the source of the mythical subterranean Saraswati river. In keeping with his benevolent attitude, Akbar did not touch the **Patalpuri Temple** that lies below.

In another part of the city, **Anand Bhavan**, ancestral home of the Nehrus, was donated to the nation by the late Indira Gandhi. Surrounded by well-maintained gardens it was once intimately connected with the national struggle in India and the scene of many historic events which are brought to life through photographs and the memorial museum. Close to Anand Bhavan is the **University**. It was one of the foremost universities in the first half of this century.

Varanasi

Varanasi (also known as Benares), the oldest continuously inhabited city in the world, situated on the banks of the Ganga, is also India's holiest. Through the centuries pilgrims have come here in search of salvation and spiritual solace. This ancient city draws all into its vortex for beneath the squalor it is alive and vital. It confronts the visitor with all life in almost panoramic detail. This, perhaps, is its greatest fascination.

Nowhere is this more apparent than at the *ghats* (stepped embankments) where, from dawn to dusk, a steady flow of people, swelling to thousands on auspicious days, approach the river. Unmindful of observers and undisturbed by the mundane activities that go on alongside, pilgrims perform rituals firm in the faith that the sins of a lifetime will be washed away. Beneath shady umbrellas sit the *ghatias*, ready to help with the rituals. Some people are disturbed by the first sight of the *ghats* – the noise, the chaos, the cremation grounds. Religion and its message seem far away. There is too much sordid detail, too much of life itself. But gradually, the dissonance recedes and a pattern, a harmony almost, can be perceived in the whole scenery.

The spectacular 4 km (2.5 mi) sweep of the *ghats* is a unique sight, best viewed at dawn, in that "soft first light" when the river and *ghats* have a "timeless, ethereal appeal." It is best to hire a boat and go

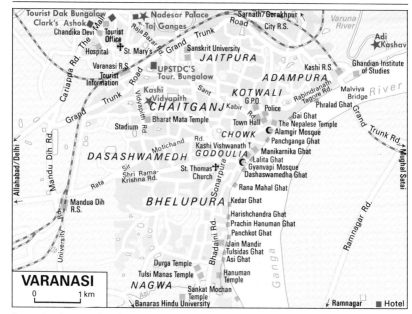

Map labels: Tourist Dak Bungalow, Clark's Ashok, Chandika Devi, Tourist Office, The Mall, Chandni Rd., Hospital, St. Mary's, Varanasi R.S., Tourist Information, Cariappa Rd., Mandu Dih Rd., Allahabad/Delhi, Grand Trunk, Vidyapith Rd., Kashi Vidyapith, Stadium, DASASHWAMEDH, Motichand, Sir Shri Rama-Krishna Rd., Rata, Mandua Dih R.S., University, BHELUPURA, Bhadaini Rd., Durga Temple, Tulsi Manas Temple, NAGWA, Asi, VARANASI, 0 1 km, Nadesar Palace, Taj Ganges, Raja Bazar Rd., Grand Trunk Road, Sanskrit University, JAITPURA, UPSTDC'S Tour. Bungalow, Sant, CHAITGANJ, Bharat Mata Temple, Bhuta Mata Temple, Rd., St. Thomas Church, Sonarpura, Sarnath/Gorakhpur, City R.S., Kashi R.S., KOTWALI, G.P.O., Kabir, Police, Town Hall, KOTWALI, CHOWK, Kashi Vishwanath T., GODOULIA, Lalita Ghat, Dashaswamedha Ghat, Rana Mahal Ghat, Kedar Ghat, Harishchandra Ghat, Prachin Hanuman Ghat, Panchkot Ghat, Jain Mandir, Tulsidas Ghat, Asi Ghat, Hanuman Temple, Sankat Mochan Temple, Banaras Hindu University, Varuna River, Adi Kashav, Ghandian Institute of Studies, Malviya Bridge, River, Rabindranath Tagore Rd., Phralal Ghat, Gai Ghat, The Nepalese Temple, Alamgir Mosque, Panchganga Ghat, Manikarnika Ghat, Gyanvapi Mosque, Grand Trunk Rd., Mughal Sarai, Ramnagar Rd., Ganga, Ramnagar, Hotel

down the river to absorb the scene slowly, as the oars lap the water and the panorama unfolds. The *ghats* begin at the point where the Varuna river enters the Ganga, and end at the Asi Ghat where the Asi River enters the Ganga; hence the name Varanasi.

Over 100 *ghats* line the river, but only a few can be approached by a motorable road. The **Dashaswamedha Ghat** is one of these. To its right is the small **Shitala Temple**, dedicated to the goddess who guards against smallpox, but which also houses a *linga* that commemorates the origin of the *ghat* as the site of the ten horse sacrifices, the merit of which is said to attend all those who bathe in the *ghat*. A submerged **Shiva Temple** looks misplaced as does the garish palace of the Dom Raja, who is said to have amassed a fortune by virtue of his profession. (*Doms* are hereditary managers and concessionaires of the burning *ghats*.) While being cremated at Varanasi adds to the merit of a lifetime (and many bodies are brought to the city for that purpose),

dying here ensures liberation from the cycle of rebirth. A lot of people nearing the end of their lives come here, waiting to die. The *doms'* purview are the **Harishchandra** and **Manikarnika** *ghats*. Boatmen are quick to point out both to tourists with morbid pleasure. For Hindus, death is a part of living, and there is no attempt to shroud what is an inevitable fact of life. Cremation is acceptable to Hindus who still believe that the body, which merely houses the soul, should be destroyed to allow its release. It is the indestructible soul that is of concern and a series of elaborate rituals ensure its passage to the other world.

Close to the Dashaswamedha Ghat is **Vishwanath Gali**, a narrow lane lined with shops selling traditional Benares brocade, wall hangings, carpets, brassware and other items. Shopkeepers, with infallible instinct, call out to Indians in the language of their state; some even have an elementary knowledge of English, French and German. The street terminates at the **Vishwanath Mandir**, the main temple of the city, dedicated to its presiding deity, Lord Shiva. Varanasi is said to be the point at which the first *jyotirlinga*, the fiery pillar of light by which Shiva manifested his supremacy over other gods, broke through the earth's crust and flared towards the heavens. Hence Varanasi's second name, **Kashi**, meaning the City of Light. Today, more than the bathing *ghats*, even more than the Ganga, the Shiva *linga* remains the devotional focus of Varanasi.

Also referred to as the Golden Temple, the **Vishwanath Mandir** was rebuilt on the original site by the Holkar queen Ahilya Bai in 1776, the gold plating being provided by the Maharaja Ranjit Singh of Lahore. Within the *sanctum*, the gleaming black lingam rests on an altar of gold. The precincts are dark and cramped; there is noise, crowds and the numerous chanting priests are caught up in their own business; but this is the devotional heart of the city where at the five daily offerings men and God unite in ritual.

An elaborate ritual identifies each predetermined path of pilgrimage. These include visits to various temples most of which are not open to non-Hindus, but are worth seeing because the approach roads are full of character. Among the prescribed temples are the **Durga Kund**, the **Sankat Mochan**, the **Tulsi Manas** and the **Kal Bhairav**. The last houses a primitive deity workshipped by followers of the Tantric tradition. The **Alamgir Mosque** built by Aurangzeb is a reminder of Muslim rule.

Of more interest is the **Chowk** area where numerous shops sell traditional foods and handicrafts – in particular Benares brocade. The tradition of brocade weaving dates to Mughal times. Benares brocade is not just an exquisite but also a very worthwhile buy, whether from shops or the more interesting wholesale market called *Satti*. These Benares brocades are available as scarves, stoles, saris and yard lengths.

SARNATH

Since ancient times Varanasi has been a city of learning, and a center for great Sanskrit scholars. The **Banaras Hindu University** was founded at the beginning of the century as a center for the study of Indian art and culture, and Sanskrit. For the tourist, a visit to the **Bharat Kala Bhavan Museum** is an absolute must, for it contains a prized selection of miniature paintings, medieval sculptures, manuscripts and textiles.

Across the river at the town of **Ramnagar**, is the imposing palace of the erstwhile Maharaja of Benares, where a **museum** houses some interesting artifacts including a profusely carved ivory carriage which he used for traveling around. For one month each year before the festival of *Dussehra*, Ramnagar comes to life; scenes from the *Ramayana* are enacted every evening, with the Maharaja himself presiding over the celebrations.

A visit to Varanasi must by all means include **Sarnath** (14 km or 9 mi) – where the Buddha preached his first sermon more than 2500 years ago.

AGRA
Accommodation
LUXURY: **Welcomgroup Mughal Sheraton**, Taj Ganj, Fatehabad Road, Tel: 361701. **Clarks Shiraz**, 54 Taj Road, Tel: 72421-26. **Taj View Hotel**, Taj Ganj, Fatehabad Rd., Tel: 64171. *MODERATE:* **Agra Ashok**, 6B Mall Road, Tel: 76223/7. **Amar**, Tourist Complex Area, Fatehabad Road, Tel: 360695-99. **Mumtaz**, Fatehabad Rd., Tel: 64771. **Grand Hotel**, 137 Station Rd., Tel: 74014, 76311. **Jaiwal**, 3 Raj Road, Sadar Bazar, Tel: 64141-2. *BUDGET:* **Agra**, 165 Cariappa Rd., Tel: 72330. **Imperial**, M.G. Road, Tel: 72500. **Lauries Hotel** (camping facility), M.G. Road, Tel: 72536. **Mayur Tourist Complex**, Fatehabad Road, Tel: 67302. **Rajit**, 263 Station Rd., Tel: 64446.

Hospitals
Lady Lyall Hospital, Noori Gate Rd., Tel: 74184. **S.N. Hospital**, Hospital Rd., Tel: 72222. **Verma Nursing Home**, Delhi Gate, Tel: 73787.

Museums
Archaeological Museum, Taj Mahal, 10 am-5 pm, closed Fridays and national holidays. Paintings, mosaic work, manuscripts.
At **Mathura** (53 km en route to Delhi) is the **Mathura Museum** (Dampier Nagar, Tel: 92), finest collection of Kushan art, daily except Mon 10.30 am-6.30 pm (July 1 to April 15); 7.30 am-12.30 pm (16th April to 30th June).

Post / Telegraph / Telephone
Head Post Office, The Mall, Tel: 74000. **Central Telegraph Office** (24 hrs), The Mall, Tel: 76914.

Restaurants
The best restaurants are in the luxury and moderate hotels. Others are listed below:
CHINESE: **Chungwah**, Taj Road, Sadar. **Kwality**, Taj Road, Sadar, Tel: 72525.
INTERNATIONAL: **Capri**, Hari Parbat, Tel: 72077. **Taj Restaurant**, Western Gate, Taj Mahal, Tel: 76644. *VEGETARIAN:* **Lakshmi Vilas**, Taj Road, Sadar, Tel: 63873.

Shopping
The city specializes in artifacts made of marble and soapstone. Brocades and embroidered clothes, leather footwear, fashion garments, durries, carpets, jewelry and enameled brassware are also available. The main shopping areas of Agra are Hari Parbat, Sadar Bazaar, Kinari Bazaar, Munro Road, the Taj Mahal Complex; also shopping arcades in good hotels.

Tourist Information
Government of India Tourist Office, 191 The Mall, Tel: 727377. Information counter at Kheria airport (10 km). **UP Government Tourist Bureau**, 64 Taj Road, Tel: 75852. Also a counter at Agra Cantt. Railway station, Tel: 61273.

Access / Local Transport
Air links exist with Delhi, Khajuraho, Varanasi, Bombay, Jaipur and Kanpur. Major express trains connect Agra with the rest of the country. Bus services operate to Delhi, Lucknow, Jaipur, Gwalior and other places of tourist importance. Two trains, the Taj Express and Shatabdi Express, link Agra to Delhi, making a one-day trip to Agra possible. Auto-rickshaws, unmetered taxis, tourist taxis with fixed rates, cycle rickshaws and *tongas* are modes of local transport.

VARANASI
Accommodation
LUXURY: **Clarks Varanasi**, The Mall, Tel: 42401-6. **Taj Ganges**, Nadesar Palace Grounds, Cantt., Tel: 42481, 42491.
MODERATE: **Varanasi Ashok**, The Mall, Tel: 446020-30. **Pallavi International**, Hathwa Market, Chetganj, Tel: 56939-43.
BUDGET: **Barahdari**, Maidagin, Tel: 52206. **Diamond**, Bhelupur, Tel: 310696-700. **Gautam**, Ramkatora, Tel: 44015-17. **De Paris Hotel**, 15 The Mall, Tel: 46601-08. **Hindustan International**, C 21/3 Maldhaiya, Tel: 57075.

Restaurants
The best restaurants are in the luxury and moderate hotels. Others include the following:
CHINESE: **Winfa**, Lahurabir.
INTERNATIONAL: **The Aces**, Gadolia, **Blue Fox**. *INDIAN:* **Konamey**, Deepak Cinema.

Hospitals / Chemists
Benares Hindu University Hospital, B.H.U. Campus, Tel: 66833. **Ishwari Memorial Hospital**, 180 beds. *CHEMISTS:* **Arun Medical Store**, K65/67 Kabir Rd., Tel: 63618. **Kaladhar Prasad & Sons**, Bichibagh, Tel: 52652.

Local Festivals
Some of the festivals listed here are either exclusive to this holy city, or their manner of celebration is distinct: *Mahashivaratri* (March), dedicated to Varanasi's patron-god, Shiva; *Panch Kroshi* (April), month of austerity and penance when a stream of pilgrims visits Varanasi; *Buddha Purnima* (May full moon), a fair is held at Sarnath and relics of the Buddha are displayed; *Rathyatra* (August); *Ramlila* (October), at Ramnagar, recounting episodes from the *Ramayana*. *Bharat Milap* (October-November), the return from exile of Lord Rama, hero of the *Ramayana*; *Nagnathaiya* (November), episodes from Lord Krishna's life; *Chetganj Nakkatiya* (November), harking back to an amusing anecdote in the *Ramayana;* and *Ganga Dussehra*, commemora-

ting the eventful day when the waters of the holy Ganga reached Haridwar.

Museums

Archaeological Museum, Sarnath, Tel: 63708, 10 am-5 pm, closed Fri. **Fort Museum**, Ramnagar, Tel: 64002, 8.30 am-12 noon (summer); 9 am-12.30 pm, 2-6 pm (winter). Collection: Royal paraphernalia. **Bharat Kala Bhawan**, Benares Hindu University, 11 am-4.30 pm, closed Sun and University holidays. Sculpture, terracottas, excellent miniature paintings and textiles.

Post / Telegraph / Telephone

Head Post & Telegraph Office, Biseshwarganj, Tel: 67150. **Head Post Office**, Cantt. Tel: 42783. **Central Telephone Office**, Cantt. Tel: 42014.

Shopping

Varanasi has a long tradition of handicrafts – by far the most important is silk weaving. Most of the raw material comes from South Indian states, local weavers hav set up looms at their residences. Brassware, ivory, jewellery and silk products are available in the main shopping areas of the City Chowk, Godoulia, Vishwanath Lane and Thatheri Bazaar.

Tourist Information

U.P. Government Tourist Office, Parade Kothi, (opp. Railway Station), Cantt, Tel: 43486, 43413. Also a counter at Varanasi Cantt. Railway Station (Tel: 43544), and Babatpur Airport.

Access / Local Transport

Air connections to Delhi, Bombay, Agra, Khajuraho, Lucknow, Allahabad, Hyderabad, Patna, Kanpur, Calcutta and Kathmandu (in Nepal). The airport at Babatpur, 22 km from Cantt. Varanasi, is connected by rail to major centers in India by two networks, Northern and North-Eastern railways. Locally, autos and cycle rickshaws, horse-drawn tongas and buses are available. For viewing life along the Ganga, boats are for hire.

LUCKNOW

Accommodation

LUXURY: **Hotel Clarks Avadh**, 8 Mahatma Gandhi Marg, Tel: 240131-3, 236501-10. *MODERATE:* **Carlton Hotel**, Shahnajaf Road, Tel: 44021-24. *BUDGET:* **Hotel Kohinoor**, 6 Station Road, Tel: 35421-5. **Capoor's Hotel & Restaurant**, 52 Hazrat Ganj, Tel: 243958. **Avadh Lodge Tourist Hotel**, Tel: 43821. **UPSTDC's Hotel Gomti**, 6 Sapru Marg, Tel: 34282, 84. **Mohan**, Char Bagh, Tel: 52251. **Tourist Bungalow**, Sapru Marg, Tel: 32257.

Hospitals / Chemists

Balrampur Hospital, Gola Ganj, Tel: 244040. **Dufferin Hospital**, Gola Ganj, Tel: 244050. **Arya Medical Stores**, Raja Bazaar, Tel: 4463.

Museums

State Museum, Banarsi Bagh, Tel: 43107, 10.30 am-4.30 pm, closed Mon and important holidays. **Children's Museum**, Motilal Nehru Marg, Tel: 52313, 10.30 am-5.30 pm, closed Mondays.

Post / Telegraph / Telephone

General Post Office, GPO Square, Vidhan Sabha Marg, Tel: 242887. **Head Post Office**, Mahanagar, Tel: 247771.

Restaurants

CHINESE: **Ninja** and **Manchao Hut** on Mahatma Gandhi Road. *TANDOORI / MUGHLAI:* **Sayeed Hotel**, Lalbagh. **Kabab Corner**, Hotel Gomti, Sapru Marg. **Kwality**, Hazratganj, Tel: 43331. **Ranjana**, Hazratganj, Tel: 45946.

Shopping

A specialty is *chikan* embroidery on garments, kurtas, saris, scarves and table linen. Also *zari* (gold thread embroidery) and sequin work. The town is famous for *ittar* (perfume), incense sticks and Indian sweets. The main shopping areas are Ameenabad in the Old Town with idyllic lanes, and the modern shopping centers on Hazratganj, Lalbag, Janpath.

Tourist Information

U.P. Govt. Tourist Reception Centre, Railway Station, Charbagh, Tel: 52533. **U.P. State Tourism Development Corporation**, 3 Naval Kishore Road, Tel: 248349.

Access / Local Transport

Air connections to Delhi, Calcutta, Agra, Varanasi, Patna, Kanpur and Bombay. The Amausi airport is 14 km from downtown. Lucknow is linked by road and rail to major towns in north India. Local transport is by metered taxis, autorickshaws, *tongas* and cycle-rickshaws.

ALLAHABAD

Accommodation

BUDGET: **Presidency**, 19D Sarojini Naidu Marg, Tel: 604460. **Allahabad Regency**, Tashkent Road, Tel: 56043. **Samrath**, 49A Mahatma Gandhi Marg, Civil Lines, Tel: 604854-888. **Yatrik**, 33 S.P. Marg, Civil Lines, Tel: 601713-14. **UPSTDC's Tourist Bungalow**, 35 M.G. Road, Tel: 53640.

Hospitals / Chemists

Dufferin Hospital, Chowk, Tel: 55088. **Swaroop Rani Nehru Hospital**, Tel: 52452. **Agarwal Medical Stores**, 95 Zero Rd., Tel: 52126. **Balsons Chemists**, near Kamla Nehru Hospital, Tel: 52683. **B.N. Ram & Co. Chemists**, 24 M.G. Marg, Civil Lines, Tel: 2308.

Tourist Information

Regional Tourist Office, 35 Mahatma Gandhi Road, Civil Lines, Tel: 53883.

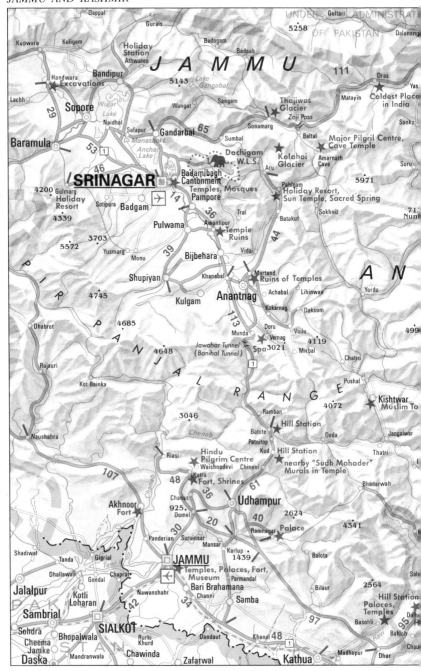

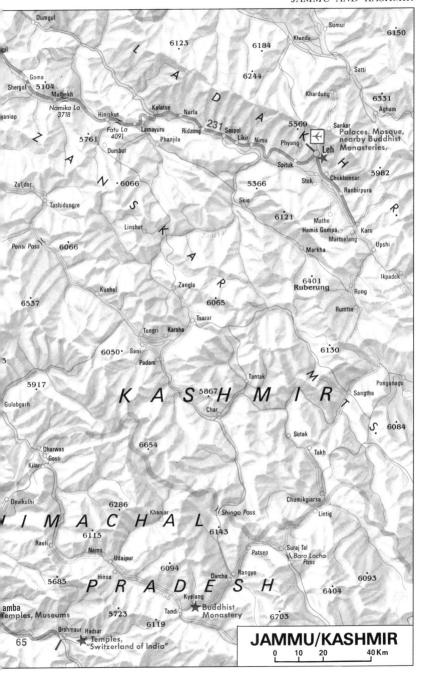

Dumgul

Sumur

6150

Klunda

6123

6184

6244

Satti

Goma

5104 Mulbekh

Khardung

6331

Shergol

Namika La
3718

Agham

aniap

Hiniskut

Kalatse

Nurla

Sankar

5569

Palaces, Mosque,
nearby Buddhist
Monasteries,

Fatu La
4091

Lamayuru

Ridzong

231

Saspol

5761

Phanjila

Likir

Nimu

Leh

Dumbur

Phyang

Spituk

5982

6066

Stok

Choklamsar

Ranbirpura

Zuljdor

5366

Tashidongze

Skio

6121

Matho

Pensi Pass

Linshot

Zanskar

Hemis Gompa

Karu

6066

Martselang

Upshi

Markha

Kushol

Zangla

6401
Ruberung

Rong

Ikpadok

6537

6065

Rumtse

Tsazar

Tongri

Karsha

6130

6050 Sani

Padam

Tantak

Pongunagu

5917

5867

Sangtha

Gulabgarh

Char

6084

KASHMIR

Dharwas

6654

Sutak

Gosti

Takh

Kilar

Devikolhi

6286

Chumikgiarsa

Khanjar

Shingo Pass

Lintig

6115

6143

Raoli

Namu

Patseo

Suraj Tal
Bara Lacha
Pass

Udaipur

6094

5685

Hinsa

Darcha

Rangyo

6093

PRADESH

Kyelang

6404

amba
Temples, Museums

5723

Tandi

Buddhist
Monastery

6703

65

Brahmaur Hadsar

6119

Temples,
"Switzerland of India"

JAMMU/KASHMIR

0   10   20   40 Km

IN THE LAND OF AWESOME MOUNTAINS

JAMMU AND KASHMIR

LADAKH

HIMACHAL PRADESH

HILLS OF UTTAR PRADESH

JAMMU AND KASHMIR

India's northernmost state, referred to often as J&K, is a good example of the country's genius in combining contrasting cultures in vastly different terrain under a single administration. **Jammu** is characteristically the lower hills of the Lesser Himalayas inhabited by the Dogras; they are largely Hindu hillmen well known beyond their borders for their prowess with both pen and sword.

Ladakh, on the other side of the Himalayan range, presents the character of the Tibetan Plateau where the colorful ritual of Mahayana Buddhism, which was recently wiped out in Lhasa, continues to enliven the high altitude desert watered by the Indus, known locally as the "Lion River."

Between these two extremes lie the fabulous lakes of the Vale of **Kashmir**, as lush in its promise of a relaxed lifestyle as in the fulfilment of its craftsmens' extraordinary skills. Since the late 14th century Islam has been the presiding religion. Some centuries later, in the 19th century, the Dogras took over the valley and through their energetic general, Zora-war Singh, gained possession of

Preceding pages: A view of the picturesque Dal Lake in Srinagar, Kashmir.

Ladakh. During the turbulent partition of 1947 the Hindu ruler of Kashmir merged his state with the Indian Union.

Jammu

The town of **Jammu** is the railhead from Delhi (591 km or 367 mi) for traffic to Kashmir and Ladakh. Despite the low profile of the Shivaliks (the outermost range of the Himalayas), the town has an attractive setting with the old, impressive **Bahu Fort** overlooking the Tawi River. With its plethora of temple spires, reached by some narrow spiraling roads, Jammu has considerable character.

The array of gilded temples that constitute the **Raghunath** complex reflects the princely lifestyle of this old capital of the Dogras. The **Dogra Museum** in **Gandhi Bhavan** has an extensive collection of Pahari miniature painting, especially of the Basohli school. The **Amar Palace** also houses a good museum of local arts and is built in a charming style called "royal French exotic."

Places of scenic beauty outside the town include the lakes at **Suroinsar** (45 km or 28 mi) and **Mansar** (80 km or 50 mi). Near Mansar are the mysterious ruins of **Manor Ghar**. The temples at **Babor** (72 km or 45 mi), **Billawar** and **Sukrali** all lie southeast of Jammu, as does **Purmandal** (39 km or 24 mi), a lavish uncompleted place of pilgrimage built by the Sikh ruler Maharaja Ranjit Singh. Both **Akhnoor** (32 km or 20 mi) and **Riasi** (80 km or 50 mi) overlook the Chenab River, Riasi being the ancestral seat of Zorawar Singh. The road to Riasi passes **Katra** (48 km or 30 mi from Jammu), the terminus for traffic to the temple of **Vaishno Devi**, the richest and most popular temple in north India. To reach the small Hindu cave-shrine which honors three forms of the Mother Goddess, the pilgrims have to climb a paved 12-km (7.5 mi) path. Helicopter services are now available.

Towards Srinagar

The main road from Jammu to **Srinagar** continues to **Udhampur** from where an unsurfaced road leads southeast to the interior town of **Basohli**. East of Udhampur is the **Palace of Colors** (**Rang Mahal**) with wall paintings in the Pahari style. Ten km (6 mi) from Udhampur is a cluster of old temples at **Krimchi**. As the road climbs to cooler ranges there are several places to stop overnight. **Kud**, **Patnitop** and **Batote** offer bungalows set amidst conifer forests. From Batote, a rough motor road runs to **Kishtwar** (216 km or 134 mi from Jammu) a remarkably unspoilt town on the Chenab surrounded by magnificent waterfalls. This is the base for treks east to **Lahaul** and north over the Great Himalayas; also to the blue sapphire mines at **Paddar** (114 km or 71 mi), with a policeman on duty at 4,000 m (13,123 ft)!

The **Banihal Tunnel** (200 km or 124 mi from Jammu) marks the fascinating transition from the Hindu sphere to the Muslim. Vehicles traveling to Kashmir need windscreen wipers and lights to pass through the 2.5 km (1.5 mi) tunnel.

To emerge from the bland scenery of the Jammu Hills into the tingling landscape of Kashmir is an exhilarating experience. The two-hour drive across the valley passes along corridors of willows and through aisles of stately poplar. In summer, the valley is emerald with rice paddies, and in autumn ablaze with red and yellow leaves. At **Pampore**, (16 km or 10 mi from Srinagar) the fields turn purple under the saffron crop. East of the **Jawahar Tunnel** from Banihal is the spring at **Verinag**, one of the sources of the River Jhelum. Winding its way through the Vale of Kashmir into the Old City of **Srinagar** it continues northwest to the large lake of **Wular**. The Mughal Emperor Jehangir enclosed the spring in 1612 and eight years later his famous son Shah Jahan laid out a formal garden.

At **Anantnag**, (56 km or 35 mi from Srinagar) there are hot springs. The narrow road to **Pahalgam** turns off here. Along this road (8 km or 5 mi) is Kashmir's most impressive Hindu temple built by Lalitaditya Mukhtapada, around A.D. 730. Though badly ruined, the site is magnificent and the remains show that this was a ruler of extraordinary refinement. Several other formal gardens can be found along the road to Srinagar, including the towns of **Acharbal** and **Kokarnag** southeast of Anantnag. The Hindu temples at **Avantipur** (29 km or 18 mi from Srinagar) date back to the 9th century, and here again the ruins show the vigorous culture of their builder, King Avantivarman. Five km (3 mi) before Srinagar the small temple of **Pandrethan** is a classic in the Kashmiri style of architecture, dating from A.D. 900.

Srinagar

A great part of the magic of **Srinagar** (1,768 meters or 5,800 ft), the capital of Kashmir, is its flavor of Central Asia although it lies on the same latitude as southern Spain. After Buddhist and Hindu dynasties, Islam continued the tradition of communal harmony through its mystic school of Sufis which offset the bigotry shown by a handful of rulers. The polarization of religion is a recent phenomenon.

Staying on one of the houseboats is an experience that should not be missed in Kashmir. The Maharaja would not allow foreigners to own land in his kingdom and so the houseboat, which first appeared in 1888, was a compromise. The European fascination for the lakes dates back to 1664 when Bernier declared, "There is nothing like it in the world for so small a kingdom." If **Dal Lake** is brimming with life and the stream of smaller boats (*shikara*) – selling everything from a sticking plaster to a postage stamp – too distracting, **Nagin Lake**, west of Dal Lake, is more secluded and has deeper water for swimming and water sports. **Anchal Lake** (13 km or 8 mi) caters for bird watchers and puts on a dazzling display of lotuses in summer. Life on a houseboat here has a special magic that Venice can only hint at. Kashmiri food and the memorable tea served in between makes lazing on the lake the consummate way to relax. If you wish to enter into the Kashmiri way of life, take haggling seriously. If you start dividing local prices by two, people will respond warmly to those who know the rules! To see the town you can sail by *shikara* along the Jhelum or hire a bike. The good-natured chaos of the bazaars cannot conceal the skill that makes almost every object a tempting buy.

A City Tour

Proceeding in a clockwise direction around the outskirts of Dal Lake you pass from **Dal Gate** into **Azad Road** along which stand some famous clubs and hotels, including **Nedou's**. Running parallel with the river is the **Bund**, a popular walk that starts from **Zero Bridge**.

The nine old bridges of the city go by their numbers, each covering a *kadal* or city ward. Between **Zero Bridge** and

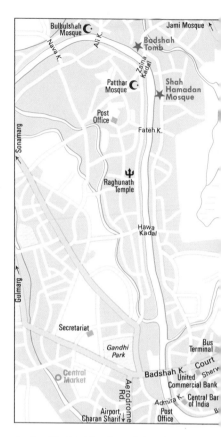

Amira Kadal (the first of the nine) you pass near the **Tourist Reception Centre**, the **Government Handicrafts Emporium** (in the old British Residency) and the **Museum**. **Hawa Kadal** is the heart of the town and the golden spire (twin to the Raghunath temple in Jammu) marks the largest Hindu temple. **Fateh Kadal**, the third bridge in the center of Kashmir's crafts industry is as interesting a place to shop as "Suffering Moses" on the bund.

The soaring elegance of the **Shah-I-Hamdan Mosque** catches the eye, and the most remarkable feature of this tiered structure is that it is made of wood. First built in 1395, it has been rebuilt twice after damage by fire. Opposite is the **Pathar** (or stone) **Mosque** built by the

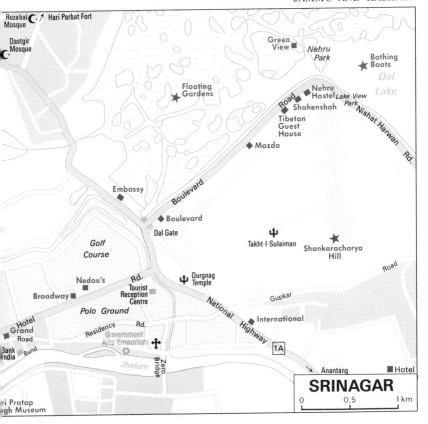

Mughal Empress Nur Jahan in 1623. Between the **Zaina Kadal** and **Ali Kadal** is the tomb of the popular ruler called Badshah, son of the king who erected Kashmir's biggest mosque, the **Jama Masjid**. Nearby stands the **Mosque of Bulbul Shah**, a renowned mystic and poet of the valley. (Bulbul means nightingale.) By the seventh wooden bridge at **Safa Kadal** is the site of the old **Yarkand Market** where traders prepared for the punishing corpse-strewn trail across the Karakoram Pass to join the Silk Route to China.

Now you must leave the river and turn back towards the lake to admire the bulk of the **Jama Masjid.** Raised by Sultan Sikander in 1385, this building has been ravaged by fire no less than three times in its history. The architecture, however, is still outstanding and impressive for the 300 full-grown cedar trunks which support the roof.

Also situated in the Old City is **Rozabal Mosque** where, a local tradition avers, Jesus lies buried. (Hemis monastery in Ladakh once possessed a *Life of Jesus* detailing how he came to India. **Yusmarg** meaning "the meadow of Jesus," is another reference to this legend.) You leave the bazaar now and pass to the western shore of Dal Lake.

The massive walls that guard **Hari Parbat Fort** (unforunately not open to the public), were begun in the reign of Emperor Akbar (1586). He also planted the 1,200 trees at **Nasim Bagh**, the Garden of the Morning Breeze, the oldest of the Moghul gardens, situated at the northwest corner of the lake.

The road passes **Nagin Lake** on the west, and a causeway to the east runs across Dal Lake to make a shortcut back to the other side. But first you should visit the undisputed pride of the valley, the lustrous marble dome of **Hazratbal Mosque** which rises from the lakeside. This impressive modern building enshrines a hair of the Prophet Muhammad which was brought to India in 1634 and reached the valley in 1700. The holy relic is displayed on only ten days during the year. After having admired the gleaming white marble mosque, one can return to Dal Gate by boat or cycle across Dal Lake over the causeway.

This will bring you out at the northeast end near the best known of the formal gardens, **Shalimar Bagh**, 15 km (9 mi) from Srinagar. The gardens were laid out in 1616 by the Emperor Jehangir for his wife Nur Jahan. A *son et lumière* performance records their romance and many of the *shikaras* on the lake carry honeymooning couples, testifying to the power of romantic legends!

Returning to your starting point along the eastern edge of Dal Lake you pass **Nishat Bagh** (11 km or 7 mi from the city), the largest of the gardens with ten terraces, built by the brother of Nur Jahan in 1633. Apparently, the Emperor was so jealous that he had the water supply cut off. This was restored by the gardener who risked the death penalty for disobeying Jehangir's decrees. Since both ruler and subjects loved the flowers, the gardener's life was spared. Further along this road, on the hillside, is the ruined **Pari Mahal** (Fairy Palace), once a renowned college of religious harmony built by Dara Shikoh. His title of Great Mughal was later usurped by the fanati-

Right: Up the Fatu La Pass, the topmost point on the winding road to Leh.

cal Aurangzeb. Nearby is the small, well-maintained garden of **Chashmi Shahi** (the Royal Spring.) Nearing **Nehru Park** and the **Boulevard** you can see two small islands in the lake and also the famous **Floating Gardens**.

The vegetable market is best seen in the early morning when haggling reaches a crescendo. The **Kotar Khana** (Pigeon Loft) in the lake is a royal summer house used by the ex-Maharaja of Kashmir. His palace, now converted into the **Oberoi Palace Hotel**, lies inland. From the Boulevard with its jewelers' shops you can climb the steps to the ancient **Temple of Shankaracharya**.

Kashmir's Hill Stations

Three main excursions from Srinagar offer a cross section of the stirring natural beauty that awaits you at Kashmir's hill stations.The village of **Pahalgam** (2,130 m or 6,988 ft), though eastward from Srinagar, is reached by a winding route (95 km or 59 mi). Watered by the sparkling Lidder River, famous for its trout fishing, the small bazaar gives way to attractive alpine scenery. Walks include a three-day trek to the **Kolahoi Glacier**, or a more serious trip across the Himalayan range to the **Suru Valley** (eight days and a 4,500-m or 14,764 ft pass). Pahalgam also gives you a chance to see the Gujjar shepherds at home in their underground log chambers. It is the friendly presence of these shepherds on the trail that remains in the memory, along with the mind-blowing photographs.

Gulmarg is the classic hill station of Kashmir with majestic conifers and riotous carpets of flowers on the meadows. At 2,730 m (8,957 ft) (52 km or 32 mi west of Srinagar), Gulmarg is always cool and warm clothes are needed throughout the year. The golf course in summer (famous for its altitude record) and the ski slopes in winter (famous for the quality of the snow) make this a

fashionable resort. The trails around Gulmarg give dramatic views of **Nanga Parbat** (8,126 m or 26,660 ft), the westernmost peak of the Great Himalayan Range, which was first climbed by Hermann Buhl in 1953.

Lakes in the Mountains

The long trail to **Yusmarg** (2,700 m or 8,858 ft) leads you through the best flowerspangled meadows in Kashmir. Traveling north from Srinagar to the third hill station of **Sonamarg** you pass **Dachigam**, the wildlife reserve (21 km or 13 mi from Srinagar) which has a unique species of local deer (*hangul*). At **Gandarbal**, where the tumbling white waters of the River Sind finally reach the valley, the roads for Sonamarg and **Wular Lake** divide.

Wular Lake lies 50 km (31 mi) to the west and is the biggest freshwater lake in India. It offers a houseboat holiday quieter than any on Dal Lake. Not to be missed is the green and placid beauty of

Manasbal Lake (28 km or 17 mi) which has another of Nur Jahan's gardens on its shore. The lotuses in summer and birds in winter make this one of the highlights of the Kashmir Valley. **Sonamarg** (2,748 m or 9,016 ft) means the Golden Meadows and, as the last township before the bleak areas of the Trans-Himalaya, it does not disappoint in the bracing beauty of its setting. Travelers on their way to the Zoji La often use Sonamarg as their final stop before ascending the pass.

A popular short trek, giving access to the splendors around each valley corner is the 4-km (2.5 mi) walk to **Thajiwas Glacier**. More demanding is the trail westwards to the remote **Gangabal Lake** (3,572 m or 11,719 ft), involving one week of camping out.

Ahead of Sonamarg, at the start of the climb to the **Zoji La,** is the encampment at **Baltal,** the base for the short but very dangerous climb to **Amarnath Cave**. Look your last on the lush meadows of Kashmir. Ahead lies a barren but magical wilderness across the Himalayas.

LADAKH

The road to **Ladakh** over the **Zoji La Pass** (3,529 m or 11,578 ft) is one of the most thrilling in the world. The drive to Leh is the most outstanding cultural trip in the whole Himalayas. Flights to Leh from Srinagar (and Chandigarh) tend to get delayed owing to bad weather, and so the two-day journey by road sometimes proves to be quicker than the booked half-hour flight.

The 434-km (270 mi) road from Srinagar to **Leh** is usually covered in two stages with a night's halt at **Kargil** (2,650 m or 8,694 ft), 204 km (127 mi) from Srinagar. The first 80 km (50 mi) are along the Sind Valley northeast of the capital. Owing to the one-way traffic system you may have to wait a whole day or more before being allowed to join the convoy over the pass. The bleak scenery immediately hits you at the crest and from the

Above: A colorful gathering of Ladakhis at the Matho winter festival.

lush greenery of the valley you run down to a stark plateau looking almost lunar in places.

Drass, the first town, claims to be the coldest place outside Siberia in winter. Then the villagers stay indoors, engulfed by 20 m (66 ft) of snow, weaving woolen goods including carpets. The road then follows the turbulent Drass river to **Kargil**, an oasis of poplar and willow trees which is lined with small transit hotels and the only filling station between Srinagar and Leh.

This old trading town preserves its Shia religious culture and the entire **Suru Valley** looked to Ayatolla Khomeni for its spiritual leadership until his death in 1989. Archery is about the only sport not frowned upon. From Kargi,l a road runs through Suru Valley and over the **Pensi La**, which separates the Muslim culture from that of Buddhist Zanskar. Up to **Parkachik** (near the base of Nun-Kun), the road is surfaced but on to **Padum**, capital of **Zanskar** (240 km or 149 mi from Kargil), it is in a terrible condition.

On the main road to Leh the first signs of Buddhism occur at **Shergol** (33 km or 21 mi) where a small cave monastery can be seen. Eight km (5 mi) further, at **Mulbekh**, stands the massive, rock-carved **Maitreya Buddha**, 7 m (23 ft) in height and dating back more than 2,000 years. The road winds through inspiring desert scenery to cross two high passes, the **Namika La** (3,718 m or 12,198 ft) and the **Fatu La** (4,094 m or 13,432 ft), the topmost point on the road to Leh.

The vast blueness of the sky experienced on these passes gives the feeling of being on the roof of the world. Now comes the climax to this dramatic road, the outlines of the **Lamayuru Monastery**, which spills down the mountainside near to a weird geological display of undulating yellow clay. Visitors to monasteries are welcome (unlike the mosques in Kashmir) but a token entrance fee is usually charged (except in Zanskar).

From there the road descends in an incredible series of spirals, called the **Hangroo Loops,** to meet the Indus at **Khaltse** (97 km or 60 mi from Leh). You now follow the north bank of the Lion River. This stretch past bare rocks has side roads leading off to interesting monasteries such as **Ridzong** and **Likir**, both set in fine gorge scenery. The latter is the monastery of the brother of the Dalai Lama.

Alchi is the most impressive of all the *gompas* (monasteries) in this region, and sits across the river from **Saspol** (62 km or 39 mi from Leh). The drive from **Nyemo**, where the Zanskar River joins the Indus, involves more desert terrain for 35 km (22 mi) until the monastery at **Spitok** above the Leh airfield announces your arrival at the capital of Ladakh.

Leh

Though now ruined and austere, **Leh Palace** still creates an unforgettable backdrop to the mud city with its flat roofs bristling with brushwood used for winter fuel. At a height of 3,505 m (11,500 ft) the climate is hot and very dry. Along the main street the Buddhist women in their tall hats chatter freely as they sell vegetables, in complete contrast to the Muslim areas of J&K. When making a deal, the Ladakhi will stick to it. Used to a barter economy, the local people have not yet been seduced by the lure of cash. Despite their hard life the people are cheerful and friendly and their religion is colorful and omnipresent.

Lamas are held in high regard and the Dalai Lama is their specific God Incarnate. Everywhere will be found *chortens* (relictuaries) and *mani* walls carrying the carved refrain *Om mani padme hum*, a mystical formula that means "The jewel in the heart of the lotus."

The true flavor of the old religion of Tibet can now be found only in Ladakh. Lamaism contains features of the pre-Buddhist Bon religion which continue to influence its art. The Indian sage Padmasambhava is credited with having introduced Buddhism into Tibet more than 1000 years ago.

Historically as well as culturally, Leh has looked to Lhasa for inspiration. A Ladakhi king took control of Kashmir in 1324 and changed his religion to become the first Muslim ruler of the valley. Two hundred years later, the Namgyal dynasty furthered Ladakh's influence. With the rise of the Dogras under Maharaja Gulab Singh (1834), both Kashmir and Ladakh fell to his energetic general, Zorawar Singh. The holes in Leh Palace are souvenirs of his visit!

Today, the unpleasant line of actual control from Jammu to Leh runs very near to the motor road, and visitors are not allowed to move or film west of it.

It is often the custom in Ladakh for one family of brothers to share a wife, to save the land from subdivision. Ladakhi architecture is simple and elegant. The kitchen enjoys pride of place in the home and the polished stove will always be surrounded by gleaming copper and brass vessels combining beauty with utility.

Up until 1986, Leh did not have a jail. The polo ground under the palace sees regular matches played vigorously on local Zanskar ponies. The **Ladakh Ecological Development Group** devises appropriate technology for the villages and also runs a restaurant where visitors can learn about local cuisine and culture.

Thirty-five km (22 mi) above Leh (but closed to visitors) is the **Khardung La Pass**, the highest motor road in India (above 5,500 m or 18,045 ft). Of the many *gompas* in the vicinity of the town the **Leh Monastery,** perched above the palace, gives a splendid view. Nine km (5.5 mi) from Leh, on the road to **Hemis**, is **Choglamsar** where Buddhist novice monks are trained. Another 6 km (4 mi) on is the old **Shey Gompa,** on top of a huge rock and part of a former palace. Shey is famous for its oracle who goes into a trance and predicts events. The monastery has the largest **Golden Buddha** in Ladakh. Next door (5 km or 3 mi), in the fort-like *gompa* of **Tikse** you can see a resplendent large modern Buddha statue, proving that the Lamas have not lost their touch.

Hemis, probably the best known of all the Indus Valley *gompas*, lies only 25 km (16 mi) from Tikse, but on the southern bank of the river. The large rambling building is located partly concealed in a gorge. Its **Annual Religious Festival** is famous for the mask dances when the monks go through an elaborate ritual to depict Tantric teaching. Returning to Leh along the south bank of the Indus River, the road passes the *gompa* at **Matho,** with another sought-after oracle. The **Stakna Gompa** stands out, being sited on a rock. **Stok**, opposite Leh (across the Indus) has a fine palace still used by the former royal family. The **Palace Museum** is excellent and worth a visit. The road from here back to Leh (16 km or 10 mi) crosses a bridge at Choglamsar.

Trekking around Leh is rewarding because the snow line is very high. (For mountaineering, permission has to be sought from New Delhi.) Always carry a length of rope to help with river crossings. Once outside Leh, Kargil and Padum, nothing in the way of supplies can be bought. The villagers exist on a diet of *tsampa* (roast barley flour) and butter tea (containing more barley flour!). The weather north of the Great Himalaya is never really wet though it can rain enough to make a tent welcome. The nights are as cold as the days are hot. Sun hat, sun glasses and face cream are basic equipment. (The trade mark of a trekker in Ladakh is his tomato-red nose.) The **Zanskar Gompas** are well worth a visit. Karsha, near Padum, is magnificently sited, while downstream of the Zanskar River (15 km or 9 mi) is **Zangla**, the seat of the former king. Csoma de Koros stayed here for a year in 1826, when collecting material for his dictionary of the Tibetan language, the first to be published in English.

The passes from Zanskar into Himachal and Kishtwar need to be treated with respect and horses are recommended as an aid in river crossings. It is an advantage to hire local Zanskar pony men instead of outsiders, for then you share the lifestyle of the villages you pass through. The villagers, though grindingly poor, possess the strength of character that comes from self-sufficiency. As Buddhists, they do not take life but enjoy eating meat when offered. The greeting throughout Ladakh is *Julley*, except in Muslim villages where Salaam alaikum is used. Trekking in the wilderness requires stamina and resourcefulness, but you will be rewarded with sublime mountain scenery and some very rare glimpses of wild species like the ibex, the wolf and the legendary snow leopard. The fragile nature of Ladakh's high altitude heritage makes it vital that all visitors should tread softly.

SRINAGAR
Accommodation
LUXURY: **Centaur Lake View Hotel**, Chashmishahi, Tel: 75631-33. **The Oberoi Palace**, Gupkar Road, Tel: 71241/2.
MODERATE: **Welcomgroup Nedous**, Maulana Azad Road, Tel: 74006. **Hotel Zabarvan**, The Boulevard, Tel: 71441/2. *BUDGET:* **Boulevard Hotel**, Tel: 77089. **Nehrus Hotel**, The Boulevard, Dal Lake, Tel: 73641. **Asia Brown Palace**, Tel: 73856. **Broadway Hotel**, Maulana Azad Road, Tel: 75621-23. **Gulmarg**, The Boulevaard, Tel: 71331-35. **Tramboo Continental**, The Boulevard, Dal Lake, Tel: 73914.

Museums
Sri Pratap Singh Museum, Lal Mandi, Tel: 72078, 10 am-5 pm, closed on Wednesdays and government holidays.

Post / Telegraph Office
General Post Office, Tel: 76494. **Central Telegraph Office** (24 hrs), Maulana Azad Rd.

Restaurants
CHINESE: **Lhasa** (and Tibetan cuisine), Boulevard. **Alka Salka**. **Daitchi**, Boulevard. **Capri**, Polo View. *FAST FOOD:* **Tao Cafe** (also Continental food), Shervani Road. *CONTINENTAL:* **Hollywood**, **Grand** and **Solace** on Shervani road. Also **Broad View**, New Secretariat Road. **Kwality**, Hari Singh Street. *INDIAN:* (Kashmiri & Mughlai): **Ahdoo's**, **Mughlai Darbar**, Shervani Road. Also **Kashmir Darbar** and **Gulal** on the Boulevard.

Shopping
Shopping areas: Residency Road, Boulevard, Dal Gate, Polo View, Budshah Chowk, Lal Chowk, Maulana Azad Road and Hari Singh Street. **Kashmir Government Arts Emporium** on Shervani Road (Tel: 73011/12) and the Boulevard (Tel: 77466).

Access / Local Transport
Flights from Srinagar, Jammu and Leh to Delhi (among other places). The railhead for the state is Jammu. From here, an all weather road leads to Srinagar. State buses ply this route taking under 12 hrs to cover a 293-km distance. Leh is best approached by road, since this allows one to get acclimatized to the change in altitude, and to enjoy the landscape. The journey takes two days with a night halt at Kargil.

Miscellaneous
All foreigners visiting the state are required to register their arrival and departure with Foreigner's Regional Registration Offices at the airport (New Srinagar Airport, Tel: 31521-29) and in the city (office of the Senior Superintendent of Police, Shervani Road, Tel: 77298).

Festivals
Festivals with a distinct Kashmiri style are *Baisakhi* (April), *Id-ul- Milad* (October-November), Prophet Mohammad's birthday, *Shab-e-Miraz* (March-April; relics of the Prophet are displayed). *Navreh* (March-April, the new year's day of Kashmir Pandits) and *Amar Nath Yatra* (July-August; a pilgrimage concluding on *Shravan Purnima* at the Amarnath Cave - a Shaivite shrine). Annual festivals: *Thiksey* (September), *Phayang* (July), *Lamayuru* (April), *Stok* (February) and *Leh* (January-February). Ladakhis celebrate *Losar* in the manner that Buddhists all over the world do.

LEH
Accommodation / Restaurants
BUDGET: **Indus**, Tel: 166. **Kangri**, Tel: 51. **Ladakh Sarai**, Tel: 181. **Lungse Jung**, Tel: 193. **Yak Tail**, Tel: 118. **Dragon**, Tel: 139. **Dreamland**, Tel: 89. **Hill View**, Tel: 58. **New Artdope**, Tel: 86. **Kangla**, Tel: 162, and economy class lodges. *Restaurants:* **Burman Chopsticks**; **Hill Top**; **Kargia Chein**; **Nepali**; **Potala**; **Snow Lion** and **Yak Boy** - these serve Ladakhi, continental, Tibetan, Indian and Chinese cuisine.

Museums
Stok Palace Museum (17 km from Leh), Tel: 131, open 7 am-6 pm.

Post / Telegraph / Telephone
Head Post & Telegraph Office.

Shopping
Fine paintings of the Buddha and of dragons on paper or cloth can be purchased from the **Handicrafts Centre** in Leh.

Tourist Information / Miscellanous
J & K Tourist Office, Tel: 97. The Road between Srinagar and Leh is closed from October to May.

Accommodation
JAMMU
LUXURY: **Asia Jammu-Tawi**, Nehru Market, Tel: 49430/32. 3930/32. *MODERATE:* **Hotel Jammu Ashok**, opp. Amar Mahal, Tel: 43127. *BUDGET:* **Cosmopolitan**, Vir Marg, Tel: 47561. **Mansar**, Denis Gate, Tel: 46161.

PAHALGAM
MODERATE: **Pahalgam Hotel**, Tel: 26, 52, 78. *BUDGET:* **Mount View**, Tel: 21. **Nataraj**, Tel: 25. **Ornate Hill Park**, Tel: 79. **Senator Pine-N-Peak**, Tel: 11. **Woodstock**, Tel: 27.

GULMARG
MODERATE: **Highlands Park**, Tel: 207, 230. *BUDGET:* **Hotel Ornate Woodlands**, Tel: 68.

SONAMARG
Tourist Huts, **Tourist Bungalow** and **Rest House**.

HIMACHAL PRADESH

Himachal Pradesh means "the land of the snowy mountains." As a modern Himalayan state it provides excellent facilities for visitors to enjoy its superb mix of scenery. The green, rolling **Kangra Valley** unfolds before the running white ridge of the **Dhaula Dhar**, one of several parallel snow-girt ridges that rise between the forested valleys with their lively local culture. Himachal is the best example of Hindu hill lifestyle; and its temples are among the most picuresque in India. Across the **Rohtang Pass,** in the arid but bracing **Lahaul** and **Spiti** region, a Buddhist civilization survives like a rare flower clinging to a rock. Both entry points from the south (**Kalka**) and west (**Pathankot**) provide a rail service to the interior, rather slow but very scenic, as the Kangra Valley line is among the most spectacular light railways in the world.

Towards Shimla

The road from Kalka to **Shimla** (88 km or 55 mi) follows the great Indian watershed that divides the west-flowing Indus from the waters of the Ganga, draining east. It continues beyond Shimla and becomes the **Hindustan-Tibet Road** running up to the **Shipki La Pass** where the Sutlej, the most important river of Himachal, rushes out of Tibet to carve a passage through the Himalayas. The road to Shimla is marked by several small hill stations. East of the Shimla road lies the old princely state of **Sirmur** with its elegant little capital of **Nahan** (932 m or 3058 ft) nestling amid luxuriant forests. At **Kala Amb** (14 km or 9 mi) is a fascinating **Fossil Park** and **Museum**. Further east is the Sikh shrine of **Paonta Sahib** on the banks of the Yamuna (45 km or 28 mi). From Paonta, an unsurfaced road returns to the main road to Shimla via **Renuka**, a former fishing retreat of the Sirmur rulers and now a lake surrounded by

a lush **Safari Park**, with lions on the loose. The road runs from **Dadahu** to **Haripurdhar** near **Churdhar** (the highest peak in the Lesser Himalaya) and is part of the Himalayan Car Rally route. You join the Shimla road at **Solan** (1,350 m or 4,429 ft) famous for its brand of whisky "Solan No.1." Ahead of Solan at **Kandaghat** is a road to **Chail Palace**. Now a hotel, this was once the summer residence of the Maharaja of Patiala, a well-known sportsman. An alternative route to Shimla passes **Kufri**, with ski slopes for beginners.

Shimla

Shimla (2,130 m or 6,988 ft) is the capital, and has retained something of British tradition. Founded around 1822, the town became an official seat of power in 1870, when a **Viceregal Lodge** was built. It was during the "superior Curzon's" viceroyalty that the town earned its reputation for fast living, gossip, intrigue and impressive imperial display, with liveried rickshaw jampanies being the only native Indians allowed on **The Mall**.

The buildings and walks here remain largely unchanged although temples are in more demand than churches, which stand as forlorn monuments to a proud era. Shimla's houses still stand on top of one another as they did in Kipling's day. **Scandal Point** retains its function if not its name and **The Gaiety Theatre** has been preserved as a monument to a golden age. Lord Curzon named his daughter after the beauty spot **Naldhera**, 23 km (14 mi) north of the town. On the way you pass **Mashobra** and **Craignano**, well-known picnic spots. Driving northeast to **Narkanda** you pass **Wildflower Hall** (13 km or 8 mi), the stately residence of Earl Kitchener who, as Commander-in-Chief, plotted to have Curzon dismissed. The main road to the **Kangra** and **Kulu Valleys** runs west but

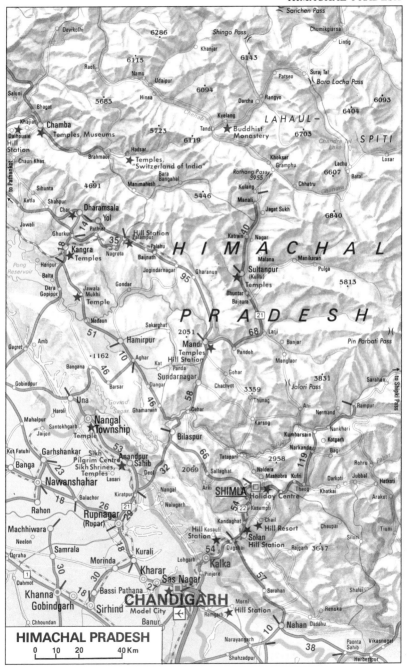

HIMACHAL PRADESH

0   10   20   40 Km

113

there is a jeepable road north over the **Jalori Pass. Narkanda** is 64 km (40 mi) from Shimla and overlooks the snow peaks of Kinner Kailash and its outriders (6,743 m or 22,123 ft). There are excellent walks in the jungles around the hill of **Hathu** which has popular ski slopes in winter. The road north drops steeply to the Sutlej. One branch runs to **Kotgarh**, the center of Himachal's apple industry. This was founded by the American missionary Rev. Stokes, and, having married locally, his family still maintain orchards. The other road runs to **Rampur**, the capital of the famous old hill state of **Rampur-Bushehr** (76 km or 47 mi from Narkanda). The magnificent temple of **Bhimkali** at **Sarahan** is a fitting climax to a visit to these border areas.

On the way back to Shimla, a road leads east at **Theog** and runs to **Tiuni** in Uttar Pradesh. It passes **Jubbal**, another small former capital and **Hathkoti** (104

Above: A charming beauty from the mountains. Right: A terraced farm in Himachal.

km or 65 mi from Shimla) on the Pabbar River, renowned for its delicious trout. Nearby is **Rohru**, a fisherman's retreat. Hathkoti is famous for a large bronze image of the Mother Goddess. Going west from Shimla, you drive down to **Arki**, an old capital with a small fortress, and join the main road to **Mandi** and **Kulu** at **Bilaspur** (90 km or 56 mi). This modern town lies upstream of the **Bhakra Dam**, one of India's most prestigious hydroelectric projects. (Himachal depends on these schemes for much of its revenue.) The lake level fluctuates throughout the year and sometimes old, flooded temples reemerge.

Kangra Valley

The low-lying town of Mandi marks both the end of the **Kangra Valley** and the start of the Kulu. Kangra is unique in the entire Himalayan region in possessing a gentle aspect, and it was here, under Raja Sansar Chand, that the most famous school of miniature painting arose in the Pahari (hill) style. The ancient town of **Kangra** (19 km or 12 mi from Dharmsala) was much damaged during a terrible earthquake in 1905, but the **Fort** ruins still remind one of its impressive role in Indian history. The riches of the Kangra temples were legendary. 27 km (17 mi) southeast of the town is the important temple of **Jwalamukhi**, "the tongue of the Goddess." This name refers to the eternal gas flame that flickers forth out of the rocky hillside. Not far is the woody retreat of **Nadaun** on the River Beas, one of Sansar Chand's capitals. This great patron of the arts (1775-1823) moved his court from place to place according to his esthetic mood.

After entering the Kangra Valley from Pathankot, you come first to **Nurpur**, named after the Mughal Empress Nur Jahan in 1622. A seasonal road runs north to **Dalhousie** (80 km or 50 mi) but it is much safer to go via **Chakki**, near Pa-

thankot. A quiet hill station, characterized by winding lanes and sleepy old bungalows, Dalhousie makes a noticeable contrast to **Chamba**, another 56 km (35 mi) towards the interior. One was a cool British retreat, while the other was the capital of a vigorous hill Raja with a distinctive culture and some remarkable temples.

The local herdsmen, known as Gaddis, hail from **Brahmaur** (65 km or 40 mi), an area full of challenging trekking routes. By foot, crossing the Dhaula Dhar to Dharamsala takes a week, whereas by road it is only one (very long) day.

The sacred lake of **Manimahesh** (3,950 m or 12,959 ft) lies 35 km (22 mi) from Brahmaur. Returning to the Kangra Valley, the town of **Dharamsala,** nestling at the foot of the Dhaula Dhar range, became famous when the exiled Dalai Lama settled here. The Tibetan enclave is situated at **McLeodganj,** 750 m (2,460 ft) up the hill (13 km or 8 mi by motor road). On the road is **Forsythganj,** a small bazaar which marks the beginning

of thick forests. Before entering McLeodganj, you pass the cemetery and **Church of St. John in the Wilderness**, whose spire fell during the 1905 earthquake. In the cemetery can be seen the grave of Lord Elgin who died here in 1863. From a quiet British hill station McLeodganj has been transformed into a bustling center of Tibetan culture. Continuing your journey along the Kangra Valley, **Palampur** (35 km or 22 mi) is renowned for its tea gardens. Another 16 km (10 mi) brings you to **Baijnath** where an extremely old **temple of Shiva** (built in A.D. 804) is the goal of many pilgrims. **Jogindernagar** marks the end of the railway and from here a trolley ascends to view a hydroelectric scheme.

Mandi (150 km or 93 mi from Pathankot), though warm, presides over the union of two rivers and possesses some very fine temple images. The **Palace** in the town square proves that this was once a state of some consequence. Twenty-four km (15 mi) above the town is a sacred lake at **Rewabar**.

Kulu Valley

The scenic Kulu Valley starts as a narrow gorge, then opens out at **Bhuntar** where the airfield is situated, 10 km (6 mi) south of **Kulu** town. Forty-five km (28 mi) to the east are the **Hot Springs** at **Manikaran**, a place of Sikh pilgrimage. Beyond, the trail leads to the **Pin Parbati Pass** (4,802 m or 15,755 ft). The village of **Malana** is remarkable for the religious rites that surround the local god Jamlu. Kulu is pleasantly sited in unusual flat, open land (at 1,200 m or 3,931 ft). At the autumn festival of *Dussehra* all the gods of the valley are carried in their palanquins to pay their respects to Raghunathji (except, of course, Jamlu, who watches from the other side of the river). For cooler parts of the valley head north to **Manali** (40 km or 25 mi). Across the river from **Katrain**, a road winds up to **Naggar Castle,** now converted into a tourist bungalow with a commanding view of the entire valley (1,768 m or 5,800 ft). The alternative road to **Manali** (18 km or 11 mi) passes **Jagat Sukh**, with an old wood-carved temple. Manali is the base for treks and has a renowned **Institute of Mountaineering**. The motor road follows the River Beas to its source and climbs steeply for 51 km (32 mi) to reach the **Rohtang Pass** (3,915 m or 12,844 ft).

Lahaul and Spiti

Now you are leaving the green magic of Kulu for the gray mystique of **Lahaul** and **Spiti**.After the bright woolen shawls worn by the Kulu women you will now see the long black tunics (with silver piping) and the brightly colored silk waistcoat of the ladies of Lahaul. In this sparsely populated area villagers worship both Hindu and Buddhist symbols. From **Khoksar** a road runs east to Spiti, the last wild area of India. The Buddhists of **Kibar** (4,205 m or 13,796 ft) are be-

lieved to inhabit the world's highest village. To the west a tortuous road has been carved out of the unstable walls of the Chenab gorge leading to **Udaipur**. From there a trail leads to the almost forgotten **Pangi Valley** and eventually on to **Kishtwar**. The Chenab, which flows to Jammu, rises in Lahaul as two separate rivers, the Chardra and Bhaga, flowing from different ends of the **Bara Lacha La Pass**. A motor road crosses the western end of the pass but is only open to military traffic at present. While the rest of Himachal welcomes thousands of tourists throughout the year, Lahaul is cut off for seven months after the Rohtang Pass gets the first heavy snow in October. It will reopen the following June. Despite its bleak landscape, the area is fascinating. The scenery is a dramatic mixture of river and mountain, and the people embody sterling virtues such as kindness and independence.

Trekking

One of the best treks in the whole Himalaya is to **Chandra Tal**, a beautiful high-altitude lake at 4,320 m (14,173 ft), requiring 11 days on the trail. The small, peaceful town of **Keylong** is a day's bus ride from Manali. Situated above the Bhaga River it makes an ideal base for walking or studying the several **Buddhist monasteries** in the area. **Darcha**, between Keylong and the Bara Lacha La, is the take-off point for treks into **Zanskar** which will take you at least a week.

The shortest route over the crest of the Himalayas is via the **Shingo La Pass**. Alternatives, involving a detour via the Bara Lacha Pass, are the **Sarichen La** and **Phirtse La** (the highest). All supplies have to be brought in from Manali and horses will be needed to ferry your luggage over the tough terrain. Though poor, the local people are hospitable and share their butter tea, sitting round the kitchen stove.

SHIMLA
Accommodation
MODERATE: **Asia The Dawn**, Tel: 5858, 6464. **Himland Hotel East**, Circular Rd., Tel: 3595-96. **Oberoi Clarkes**, The Mall, Tel: 6091-95. *BUDGET*: **Dalziel Hotel**, Dalziel Estate, Tel: 2691. **Gulmarg**, The Mall, Tel: 3168-69. **Harsha Hotel**, The Mall, Tel: 3016-17. **Kufri Holiday Resort**, Kufri, Tel: 8300, 8341/2.

Museums
Himachal State Museum, near Chaura Maidan. Tel: 2357, open 10 am-5 pm, closed on Mondays and public holidays.

Restaurants
Fascination, Tel: 2202. **Seven-Eleven**, Tel: 3214. **Embassy**, Tel: 2271. **Alfa**, Tel: 5142.

Shopping
The main shopping areas are The Mall, Lower Bazaar and Lakkar Bazaar.

Tourist Information
Himachal Pradesh Tourism Development Corporation offices at Shimla: Ritz Annexe, Tel: 4472; The Mall, Tel: 3311; Panchayat Bhawan, Cart Road, Tel: 4589.

Access / Local Transport
Shimla and Kulu are connected by air. The convenient railheads for Kulu-Manali are Chandigarh, Jogindernagar (narrow gauge with a change at Pathankot) and Shimla, from where road transport is available. Taxis and private cars available.

Festivals
The *Kulu Dussehra* held on the Dhalpur Maidan is the main festival. Palampur is the site of a colorful fair at the local temple on *Holi* (March/April). The Tibetan Institute of Performing Arts organizes an annual 10-day folk open in April, 1 km from McLeodganj. In the same month, floral offerings are made exclusively by women and children on *Suhi Mela* in Chamba. The district is also famous for the *Minjar* (July/August) fair. The Cedar forest of Deongri (1.5 km from Manali) provides the grand setting for the 3-day fair held in honor of Goddess Hadimba in May. A winter carnival is also organized in February (10-14). Unique in its style of celebration is the 7-day *Shivaratri Mela* at Mandi (March).

KULU
Accommodation
LUXURY: **Span Resorts**, Kulu-Manali Highway, Tel: 38-40 (Katrain Exch).
MODERATE: **Ramneek Hotel**, Dhalpur, Tel: 2558; **Hotel Sarvani** (HPTDC), Tel: 2349; **Hotel Silver Moon** (HPTDC), **Hotel Shangrila International**, **Naveen Guest House** (Tel: 2228) and **Empire Hotel** (Tel: 2559).

Shopping
The main shopping area is Akhaara Bazaar. There is a Weavers' Colony at Bhutli (6 km).

Restaurants
Café Monal and restaurants in the **Hotel Daulat** (Tel: 2358), **Hotel Rohtang** (Tel: 2303).

Tourist Information
Tourist Information, Tel: 2349.

MANALI
Accommodation
MODERATE: **Hotel Piccadily**, The Mall, Tel: 113. **Hotel Preet**, Kulu-Manali Highway, Tel: 129. **HPTDC's Log Huts**, Tel: 39. **Tourist Cottages**, **Tourist Lodge**, **Hotel Beas** and **Youth Hostel**.

Museum / Art Gallery
Roerich Art Gallery, Naggar (78km from Kulu).

Restaurants
Restaurants in the **Hotel Greenfields**, Panchratan Resort, Tel: 163/73; **Hotel Preet**, Tel: 129; **Hotel Piccadily**, Tel: 113.

Shopping
Main Market, Tibetan Bazaar, Tibetan Carpet Centre.

Tourist Information
Tourist Information, Tel: 25, 116. Himalayan Mountaineering Institute, Tel: 42.

DHARAMSALA
Accommodation
HPTDC's Hotel Dhauladhar, Tel: 2256. **Hotel Sun-n-Snow**, Tel: 2423 (Shimla Tel: 2650). **Rose Hotel**, Tel: 2417. **Hill View Hotel** (all in Kotwali Bazaar).

Shopping
Kotwali Bazaar and McLeodganj.

Tourist Information
HPTDC's Tourist Information Office, Kotwali Bazaar, Tel: 2363.

Further Accommodation
CHAMBA: HPTDC's Hotel Iravati and **Hotel Champak**. Reservations: Tel: 36. There are several lodges too.

DALHOUSIE: HPTDC's Hotel Geetanjali, Tel: 36. **Youth Hostel**, near the bus stand, Tel: 89. **Mehar's Youth Hostel**, The Mall, Tel: 79. **Hotel Devdar** (HPTDC), Khajjiar (also a youth hostel 27 km away, 14 km from Chamba). Several hotels are located on The Mall and near the bus stand.

CHAIL: Chail Palace Hotel, Tel: 37, 43. **Wood Rose Cottages**; **Himneel Hotel**.

KANGRA: Palace Motel Taragarh, Tel: 34.

LAHAUL-SPITI: Tourist Bungalow Keylong.

THE HILLS
OF UTTAR PRADESH

Situated between Western Nepal and Himachal Pradesh, the two hill regions of **Kumaon** and **Garhwal** in Uttar Pradesh (known collectively as **Uttarakhand**) are considered to possess the most beautiful mountain scenery in High Asia. Lacking the temperate climate that gives Kashmir and Himachal their conifer forests, Uttarakhand makes up for it with a sumptuous array of snow peaks visible from any point in the region.

Garhwal

Starting in the west, one of the most splendid views is from the British-built hill station of **Chakrata**. This **Jaunsar-Bhabar** district bordering Himachal has not yet been developed and therefore odd customs, such as polyandry, linger from the past. At **Lakhamandal** (65 km or 40 mi west of **Mussoorie**) are some sculptures in the temple compound that date back to the 4th century A.D. Further south at **Kalsi**, in the same Yamuna Valley, is an **Asokan Edict** (250 B.C.) carved on a polished white boulder, announcing the Emperor's desire to encourage non-violence in his kingdom.

Between the Yamuna and Ganga rivers lies the fertile **Doon Valley** with its fragrant variety of rice. Above **Dehra Dun** sits the hill station of **Mussoorie** (2,005 m or 6,578 ft) which, despite its unplanned development, retains much charm in the wooded walks along the 15-km (9 mi) length of its spread. The cantonment, higher in **Landaur**, has an even more bracing climate and is only six hours from Delhi.

The Yamuna is part of the Tons river system which rises in the wonderful trekking area of **Har-ki-Doon**, the unspoiled northwest corner of Garhwal where, according to Hindu mythology, the heroes of the epics ascended to heaven. The

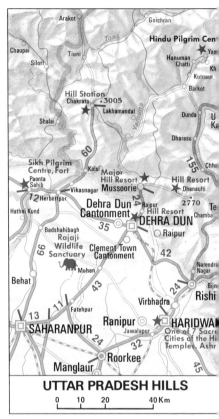

UTTAR PRADESH HILLS

0   10   20   40 Km

source of the Yamuna introduces you to the first of the *Char Dham*, the four sacred shrines of Uttarkhand that every Hindu aspires to visit. Following custom, you should travel from west to east. Most pilgrimages start at **Rishikesh**, though there is a direct road to **Yamnotri** from Delhi. This goes as far as **Hanuman Chatti**, leaving a fairly easy 14-km (9 mi) climb to the source (3,185 m or 10,449 ft). The path passes through jungle and along a splendid gorge. The scalding hot springs here are traditionally used to cook one's rice and potatoes.

Returning to the road after your picnic you can cross the river to **Kharsali** to view its pagoda-style temples framed against the peak of Bander Punch (6,315

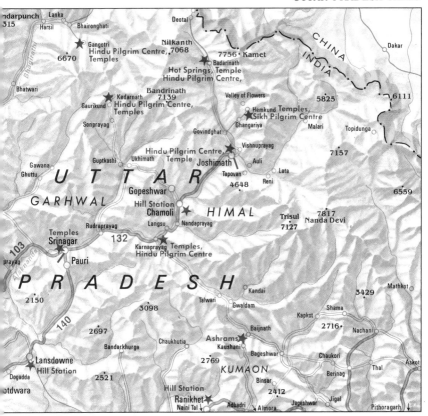

m or 20,719 ft). In winter, the River Goddess resides in Kharsali.

Shrines and Confluences

The next shrine is **Gangotri** (see To the Source of the Ganga). Traveling from **Barkot** via **Uttarkashi**, you can reach the Gangotri temple in one long and tiring day (228 km or 142 mi). Gangotri is situated amid tall cedars, and the gorge hewn out by the river is almost like a Henry Moore sculpture. From Gangotri, the road returns to Uttarkashi (100 km or 62 mi) and **Tehri** (another 65 km or 40 mi). From Tehri, there are two roads to **Kedarnath**, both about the same distance (243 km or 151 mi). The narrow road via **Chirbatia** is more scenic while the other, via **Srinagar,** is more reliable. Another road runs from Tehri to **Ghuttu** which is the base for treks to the series of lakes culminating in **Sahastra Tal**.

Another breathtaking trail follows the **Khatling Glacier** and takes a high altitude route to **Kedarnath** via **Masar Tal**. The winding road to Kedarnath goes as far as **Gauri Kund** (where there are **hot springs**) leaving a fairly easy but crowded climb to the third temple (14 km or 9 mi). This is the most magnificent setting of the four shrines, against a stunning backdrop of the Himalayas (3,584 m or 11,791 ft). Even holier, however, is the temple at **Badrinath** which lies about 243 km (151 mi) east of Kedarnath. A

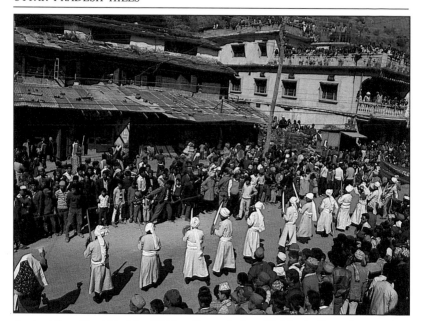

short cut from **Gupt Kashi** to **Ukhimath** (where the Lord of Kedarnath spends the winter) takes you over one of the most scenic roads in Uttarakhand to **Gopeshwar**, the site of another famous old temple. Note the tall iron trident in the courtyard.

From the top of this road (**Chopta**) the highest shrine in Garhwal is only 3 km (1.5 mi). This is the **temple of Tunganath** at 3,680 m (12,074 ft), with a view of the Nanda Devi peak. **Chamoli**, near Gopeshwar, brings you to the main Rishikesh-Badrinath pilgrim road crowded with buses when the temple is open from May to November.

You are now following the other great tributary of the Ganga, the Alaknanda. Along the course of this river are five *prayag*, auspicious places where rivers meet. The first is **Deoprayag**, 70 km (44

Above: A rare picture of Bhotia dancers in the remote village of Dharchula, Kumaon. Right: Queen of the jungle. A tigress at Corbett National Park, Kumaon.

mi) from Rishikesh. Here, the river first takes the name of Ganga. Another 35 km (22 mi) brings you to the old capital of Garhwal at **Srinagar**, but this town has suffered severely from floods and is a shadow of its former self. Standing above the broad valley is the British town of **Pauri** (30 km or 19 mi), and continuing towards the plains, the town of **Lansdowne**, home of the Garhwal Rifles.

Thirty-four km (21 mi) from Srinagar is **Rudraprayag**, where the road splits for Kedarnath. Four km (2.5 mi) before the junction look out for the notice that marks the spot where the great hunter-writer Jim Corbett once shot a man-eating leopard that had killed 300 people.

The green Mandakini river joins the glacial gray of the Alaknanda at Rudraprayag, the first flowing from Kedarnath, the second from above Badrinath. The next prayag is **Karnaprayag** (31 km or 28 mi) where the River Pindar from Kumaon joins the main stream. Next comes **Nanda Prayag** (22 km or 14 mi) and the roaring torrent Nandakini, pouring off

the slopes of Nanda Ghunti and Trisul. To reach the base camp of these peaks is a 10-day trek along the Nandakini Valley. Crossing the trail is another exhilarating 10-day walk from **Gwaldam** to **Tapovan**, a favorite journey of the much-traveled Viceroy and known as "The Curzon Trail."

Traveling along the Alaknanda Valley you next pass the Birehi Ganga, the scene of several landslide disasters that formed lakes which then overflowed to cause devastation downstream. **Joshimath** (40 km or 25 mi) at 1,890 m (6,200 ft) is not a prepossessing town but it has historical associations with the saint Shankaracharya and makes an excellent base for treks to the surrounding alps known as *buggial*, among the most scintillating of all Himalayan views. In winter, the Lord of Badrinath comes to Joshimath.

At **Auli Buggial** above the town are the best ski slopes in the Himalayas, with a stunning close-up of Nanda Devi. Nowhere else can you be on the crest of the Great Himalayas and so near to the comforts of civilization. Twenty-five km (16 mi) east of Joshimath are the hot springs at **Tapovan** and another 10 km (6 mi) bring you to **Renni** on the Rishi Ganga. In this village, the Chipko (tree-hugging) Movement to protect the environment began. Three km (1.5 mi) away is the village of **Lata** with an old temple of Nanda Devi guarding the entrance to her sanctuary, at present closed to visitors. Coming from Joshimath, the main road to Badrinath (50 km or 31 mi) crosses the Alaknanda River near **Vishnuprayag** and pierces a rocky gorge to **Govindghat** (18 km or 11 mi). From here, a trail climbs alongside the Lakshman Ganga for 14 km (9 mi) to **Gangharia**, a clearing within a cypress forest (3,048 m or 10,000 ft).

A steep ascent of 5 km (3 mi) brings you to the lake of **Lokpal** (4,329 m or 14,202 ft) with a modern Sikh shrine, **Hemkund Sahib**. Another 4-km (2.5 mi) trail from Gangharia leads to the **Valley of Flowers** (3,658 m or 12,000 ft) which is in bloom only during July and August.

Badrinath is situated in the open valley of Mana across the Great Himalaya. The small temple is always crowded. To the Hindu, this is the ultimate pilgrimage. Hot springs and a fascinating small bazaar selling religious items are set breathtakingly against the backdrop of **Nilkanth peak** (6,596 m or 21,640 ft).

Garhwal is called *Dev Bhumi*, the land of the gods, because all the tributaries of the Ganga (except one) rise in the region. The exception is the Pindar river which rises in Kumaon. To reach that province you have to follow the Pindar up its course from Karnaprayag. Gwaldam, at an altitude of 1,829 m (6,000 ft), is the last village in Garhwal and gives a superb close-up view of Trisul.

Kumaon

Compared to Garhwal, the scenery of the **Kumaon Hills** is much less harsh and the fertile valleys give good harvests. The road winds down through pine forests (tapped for resin) to **Baijnath,** an ancient capital with elegant temples containing some of the finest Indian art. From here, the broad valley leads east to **Bageshwar**, once famous for its winter-solstice fair, attended by traders from Tibet. Beyond Bageshwar the road climbs to **Chaukori** (46 km or 29 mi), formerly a profitable tea-garden and now a tourist bungalow that offers splendid snow views at the right time of the year.

Towards the Sacred Mountain

From here, the road continues for 58 km (36 mi) to **Pithoragarh**, a little visited corner of Kumaon which also has memorable views of the snow range. The trek to **Kailash-Manasarovar** in Tibet (at present restricted to Indian citizens) starts here. Seventy-two km (45 mi) south of Pithoragarh you come to the old capital of **Champavat** with some outstanding stone-carved ruins.

Almora

The modern capital of **Almora** is situated 132 km (82 mi) northeast of Champavat. Thirty km (19 mi) short of the town is an exquisite cluster of temples in a cedar forest at **Jageshwar**. To reach Almora from Garhwal there are two roads. One runs to **Ranikhet** past **Adbadri** (30 km or 19 mi from Karnaprayag), another old capital site with finely carved temples. The second runs via Baijnath to **Kausani,** a small resort offering fabulous snow views and made famous by a visit by Mahatma Gandhi.

A road also leads to Almora from Bageshwar passing **Binsar**, perhaps the ultimate snow view, giving a panorama of almost 500 km (311 mi). These roads are open in winter, and the ideal time to see Kumaon is in March when the rhododendron trees are in full bloom. **Almora** (1,646 m or 5,400 ft) is a pleasant town with some attractive domestic architecture in the upper paved bazaar. Forty km (25 mi) east is the sylvan resort of **Ranikhet** with an interesting mix of hill and military culture.

South lies the bigger hill station of **Naini Tal** (60 km or 37 mi) spread around its busy lake. North of the lake there are excellent walks in the thick jungle around **Cheena Peak** (2,611 m or 8,566 ft). East of Naini Tal are the lakes **Bhim Tal**, **Sat Tal** and **Naukuchia Tal** at lower altitudes. The snow view from **Mukteshwar** (2,438 m or 8,000 ft) is one of the best though furthest from the main range. Another superb view is from the road that runs from Ranikhet west to the gates of **Corbett National Park** (70 km or 43 mi). In this unbroken panorama you can see the most beautiful and elusive Himalayan peak, Changabang (6,864 m or 22,520 ft). This road takes you from the pine forests to forests of teak where most of Corbett's man-eaters were shot. Near Corbett Park is **Kaladhungi**, where the great *shikari* had his home.

MUSSOORIE
Accommodation
MODERATE: **Savoy**, The Mall, Library, Tel: 2510, 2620. **Solitaire Plaza**, Picture Palace, Kincraig Rd., Tel: 2937, 2998. *BUDGET:* **Hakman's Grand Hotel**, The Mall, Tel: 2559. **Roanoke**, Kulri, Tel: 2215. **Filigree**, Camels Back Rd., Kulri, Tel: 2380. **Shiva Continental**, The Mall, Tel: 2980. **Hotel Shilton**, Library Bazaar, Tel: 2842.

Local Festivals
Nag Panchmi at the Nag Mandir (July/August); *Janmashtami* Fair (August/Sept.); and the Autumn festival which coincides with the annual *Dussehra* (September/October) celebrations.

Post / Telegraph / Telephone
Post & Telegraph Office, Kulri Bazaar, Tel: 2802.

Shopping
Woolens and wickerware. Areas: Library, Kulri and Landour Bazaars.

Tourist Information
U.P. Tourist Bureau, The Mall. Tel: 2863. **Garhwal Mandal Vikas Nigam** (GMVN), Library Bus Stand, Tel : 2258. **U.P. Tourism's Regional Tourist Office**, 45 Gandhi Road, Dehradun, Tel: 23217/26894. **Mountaineering & Trekking Division**, Yatra Office, **GMVN Ltd.**, Muni-ki-Reti, Rishikesh, Tel: 372, 357. **General Manager (Tourism), GMVN Ltd.**, 74/1 Rajpur Road, Dehradun, Tel: 26817.

Access / Local Transport
Dehradun's Jolly Grant Airport (60 km from Mussoorie) receives flights from Delhi. The nearest rail-head is Dehradun (35 km).

Miscellaneous
Trekking is risky during the monsoon. Foreigners require special permits and advance booking with the **Indian Mountaineering Foundation**, Benito Juarez Road, New Delhi (Tel: 671211), and **Garhwal Mandal Vikas Nigam**, 74/1 Rajpur Road, Dehradun, (Tel: 26817). **Note:** Foreigners cannot visit Mana (beyond Badrinath) or Chakrata.

Further Accommodation
HARIDWAR: **UPSTDC's Tourist Bungalow**, Belawala, Tel: 379. **Hotel Gurudev**, Station Road, Tel: 101; **Hotel Kailash**. Tel: 789.

RISHIKESH: **Hotel Basera**, 1 Ghat Road, Tel: 767, 720; **Inderlok Hotel**, Railway Station Road, Tel: 555; **GMVN's Tourist Bungalow**, Muni-ki-Reti, Tel: 372.

There are **GMVN Tourist Bungalows/Youth Hostels** at Kedarnath, Badrinath, Chamoli, Devaprayag, Rudraprayag, Karnaprayag, Nandprayag and Auli.

NAINI TAL
Accommodation
MODERATE: **Shervani Hilltop Inn**, Shervani Lodge, Mallital, Tel: 2504, 2498. **Grand Hotel**, Nainital, The Mall, Tel: 2406. **Swiss Hotel**, Nainital, Tel: 2603. *BUDGET:* **Arif Castles**, Nainital, Tel: 2801-3. **Vikram Vintage Inn**, Mallital, Tel: 2877/79, (reservation: New Delhi 643-6451). **The Naini Retreat**, Ayanpatta Slopes, Nainital, Tel: 2108/05.

Local Festivals
The *Uttaraini* Festival is celebrated in mid-January. Before harvesting, the local people celebrate *Hariyala* (July/August). Of major importance is the *Nanda Devi fair* in memory of the goddesses Nanda and Sunanda (August/Sept).

Post / Telegraph / Telephone
Main Post Telegraph Office, Mallital, Tel: 2599. Also at Tallital (Tel: 2704).

Restaurants
VEGETARIAN: **Ahar Vihar**, The Mall, Tel: 2446. *NON-VEGETARIAN:* **Capri Restaurant**, The Mall, Tel: 2690; **Embassy Restaurant**, The Mall, Tel: 2597; **Kwality**, The Mall, Tel: 2506; **Flatties Restaurants**, The Mall, Tel: 2567.

Tourist Information
U.P. Government's Tourist Bureau, The Mall. Tel: 2337. **Parvat Tours & Tourist Information Centre**, Tallital, Tel: 2656. The main **KMVN office** is housed in the Old Secretariat Building (Tel: 2509, 2543). The **KMVN Tourist Reception Centre**, Tallital, Tel: 2570.

Access / Local Transport
The nearest airport is Pantnagar (72 km). A coach service links the airport with the town (journey time: 2 1/2 hrs). For travel in and around Nainital coaches, taxis, cycle and handdrawn rickshaws are available. (No vehicular traffic is allowed on the Mall after 5 pm in the tourist season.)

Further Accommodation
ALMORA: **KMVN's Holiday Home**, Tel: 2250. **RANIKHET**: **West View Hotel**, Mahatma Gandhi Road, Tel: 61, 196. **Moon Hotel**, Sadar Bazaar, Tel: 58. **Nortons Hotel**, Upper Mall, Tel: 177. **KMVN's Tourist Cottages**, The Mall, Tel: 97.

BINSAR: **KMVN's Tourist Bungalow**. Estates of Travel Corporation of India and private individuals where foreign tourists are taken as paying guests. There are **KMVN Tourist Bungalows** at Pithoragarh, Chaukori and Bageshwar.

Miscellaneous
Entry to areas beyond Janljubi (Tehsil Dharchula) is prohibited as Pithoragarh is a border district and permits are required. Photography is banned in these restricted areas.

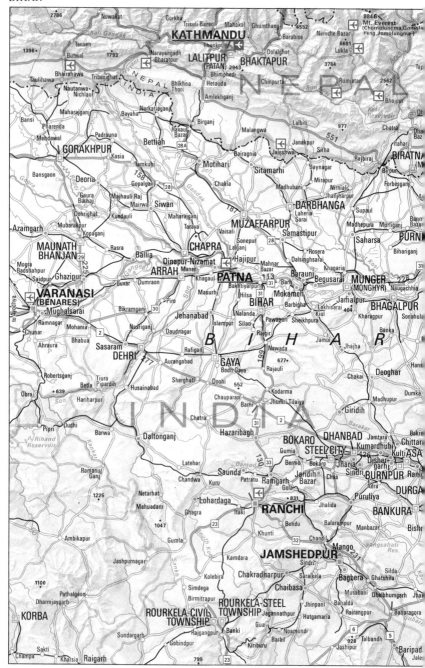

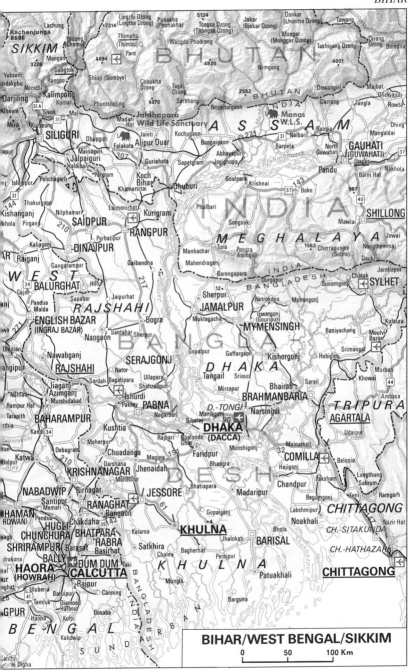

BIHAR/WEST BENGAL/SIKKIM

0   50   100 Km

1	Arunchal Pradesh	7	Assam
2	West Bengal	8	Nagaland
3	Himachal Pradesh	9	Meghalaya
4	Punjab	10	Manipur
5	Haryana	11	Tripura
6	Sikkim	12	Mizoram

LAND OF SAGES
AND POETS

BIHAR

CALCUTTA

WEST BENGAL

BIHAR

Bihar offers a wide variety of sights but few amenities because its small urban middle class has not yet severed its ties with the ancestral villages where holidays are spent in preference to resorts. However, all the places mentioned below are accessible from Patna, Ranchi and Jamshedpur, where some hotels provide reasonable facilities.

Distances mentioned are from Patna, except for the jungle trails, which are from Ranchi, except those specifically stated as from Jamshedpur.

The lack of facilities is all the more acutely felt when considering that the places worth a visit include the earliest known habitation in the entire Ganga basin. The world's most ancient highway, the nuclei of the first empire and second civilization on the Indian subcontinent, the earliest of the cave temples, Himalayan vistas, the world's largest fair, and water holes where tigers quench their thirst are some of the exceptional highlights which Bihar offers the tourist.

Chirand's mound, near Chapra (112 km or 70 mi) has excavated levels that have yielded radiocarbon-materials dat-

Preceding pages: Elephants for sale at the Sonepur cattle fair, near Patna.

ing to around 3200 B.C. As yet, no other sites in the Ganga basin are known to be as old.

The Grand Trunk Road

Around 1000 B.C. people using copper tools settled in Bihar. They carted the metal to the centers of consumption from mines in **Singhbhum** (the abandoned mines have been located) along a 500-km (311 mi) road which deserves to be reckoned as the world's oldest highway. In the 4th century B.C., Emperor Chandragupta Maurya extended it to Taxila and its length to 3,200 km (1,988 mi) – comparable in extent and antiquity to the Great Wall of China – and elevated its status to that of an imperial highway. Renovated in the 16th century by Sher Shah Suri and again in the 19th century, the Grand Trunk Road continues to be used more than the Wall, though, being less spectacular, it is not visited so often. Sites along the Grand Trunk Road do attract pilgrims. Jains visit the temple on Parasnath Hill (249 km or 155 mi) dedicated to Parasnath who died there in the 9th century B.C. Buddhists visit the site of **Bodh Gaya** (181 km or 113 mi) where the Buddha attained Enlightenment.

The Hindu temples of **Kalyaneshwari** (325 km or 202 mi) and **Mundeshwari**

(196 km or 122 mi) at the eastern and western ends of the road in Bihar are fine specimens of 11th-century architecture. An **Asokan edict** can be seen in a nearby cave.

Rajgir

Rajgir (101 km or 63 mi), the nucleus of the Magadhan state, was situated so that it could dominate both the Copper Age road and the Ganga waterway. History began at Rajgir in the 6th century B.C. after a 50-km (31 mi) long wall was built along the crests of the surrounding hills. **Ajatsatru's fort** has crumbled away, but ruts bitten into the shale of the valley floor by racing chariots can still be seen. Rajgir is sacred to the Jains, for their Lord Mahavira taught here. Rajgir, **Nalanda**, **Vaishali** and **Bodh Gaya** have many associations with the Buddha. **Pawapuri** (97 km or 60 mi) has two splendid **Jain temples** as memorials to Mahavira, the founder of Jainism who died there in the 5th century B.C.

Patna

With the introduction of iron and iron tools about 800 B.C. the importance of copper declined as did the road along which it was brought. On the other hand, the importance of the river route began to increase. In the closing years of the 6th century B.C. the Magadhans built a fort on the banks of the Ganga, and subsequently made it their capital. This city has borne various names: Kusumpura, Pataliputra, Asimabad and **Patna**.

By 323 B.C., when Alexander appeared on the northwest of the subcontinent, the Nandas of Magadha were ruling over the greater part of north India. The Macedonians did not fight the Nandas but started on the homeward journey. While here, they had been friendly to Chandragupta Maurya who later overthrew the Nandas, and further extended Magadhan territory to a common frontier with Seleucus Nikator. The Magadhan capital grew into a big city. Megasthenes, who resided here, left an account which has been corroborated by excavations revealing a hall with sandstone pillars behind a wooden palisade. The excavated site can be seen at **Kumhrar**, 5 km (3 mi) east of Patna Junction railway station.

For a place in continuous occupation for 3,000 years, Patna is poor in monuments. That some must lie buried under the alluvium is probably true but in actual fact few Indian cities have many monuments dating to the period before A.D. 1200. Patna ceased to be an imperial capital around A.D. 600, and was not even a provincial capital for three centuries after 1196. The *viharas* (Buddhist monasteries), from which the state later derived its name, and the universities at **Nalanda** and **Vikramshila** (242 km or 150 mi to the east) were destroyed by Bakhtiar Khilji in the 13th century. No monuments dating to the period between **Kumhrar** (4th century B.C.) and **Sher Shah's Qila** (1545) exist today. Patna's loss of importance after the Khilji incursion is evident from the fact that whatever was built was outside this city, and, in the custom of the time (12th to 16th centuries), they were all domed tombs: **Ibrahim Baya's** on the ridge at **Bihar Sharif** (77 km or 48 mi), those of **Yaha** and **Shah Daulat** at **Manes** (30 km or 19 mi) and of **Sher Shah**, his father and a son at **Sasaram**. Patna regained its importance with the start of trade with Europe. Sher Shah built his **fort** and **mosque** about the same time as the Portuguese established a new trading port at **Hugli**.

The second mosque was built in 1621, soon after the Dutch and the British came to buy saltpeter, indigo, textiles and opium. The Dutch left a handsome building which is now **Patna College**. The British opium trade was later associated with commissioning artists of the Patna school of painting to produce miniature portraits on ivory which came to be known as (East India) Company art. With the arrival of photography the demand for miniature portraits dwindled, and the last painter of Patna had to move to Calcutta to teach traditional technique to the Bengal School, active in the earlier part of the present century.

The administrative functions were assumed by the British in 1771, and they moved west of the city (unwalled but with two localities called East and West Gate), and built for themselves **Bankipur**, nostalgically trying to recapture the typical atmosphere of an English village – a church overlooking a green. That green is now the **Gandhi Maidan**. An odd building was the **Golghar**, a hemispherical granary rising to 27 m (89 ft) and erected in 1786 for meeting shortages during the frequent famines. It affords a panoramic view of the city.

The city did not lose its importance immediately. A handsome church, **Padre Ki Haveli**, was built in 1775 in order to receive the Capuchin (Austrian) missionaries who were beeing expelled from Tibet. **Harmandir**, a *gurudwara*, was built as late as the 19th century around the room in which the tenth and last Sikh guru, Gobind Singh, had been born 200 years earlier. It is among the holiest shrines of the Sikhs.

Forster's India

Bankipur is the place where the first part of E.M. Forster's *A Passage to India* is located. Forster changed the name to Chandrapore, as he did that of Barabar to Marabar. The **church**, the **maidan** and the **club** are easily identified, even the mosque to which Mrs. Moore slipped out is there at the head of **Asoka Rajpath** which runs through **Muradpur** and past **Fielding's College** to the city. The Eng-

Right: Rowing across the huge expanse of the Ganga at Patna after sunset.

lish writer had a friend named Khuda Baksh, whose collection of rare oriental manuscripts and miniature paintings is housed in the **Khuda Baksh Oriental Library**. Some of the manuscripts had been saved from the violent evacuation of Cordoba in Spain four years before Columbus set sail on his famous voyage. One other collector needs a mention: R.K. Jalan, whose collection of jade, Chinese porcelain and other curiosities at **Qila House** draws many visitors.

The new city of Patna, capital of Bihar, was built around 1920, west of Bankipur. Five major buildings – **Government House**, **High Court**, **Legislative Chambers**, the **Secretariat** and the **General Post Office** – attempt to lessen the summer heat and glare through thick walls, high ceilings and deep verandahs. At the Secretariat gate is a memorial to those killed there during the 1942 Quit India agitation against the British.

Only two buildings have tried to achieve a revivalist Indian façade - the **Museum**, built in the late 1920s and the **Patna Women's College** built after World War II. The latter is run by American Catholics. The **Museum** has an excellent collection of Mauryan and Gupta statuary, terracotta and bronzes. The prize exhibits are the **Didarganj Yakshini** and the **Lohanipur tirthankaras**, the terracotta laughing boy, and a pair of Pink Headed Ducks, now an extinct species.

The Ganga River at Patna is wide, with stretches of silver sand. There is a long promenade for pedestrians on the embankment in the university area. The **Bankipur Club** has a turfed terrace overlooking the river. There is also a floating restaurant. A wildlife park and a golf course are sited near the airport.

In the **Barabar Hills** (52 km or 32 mi) are cave temples which were excavated long before Kanheri or Ajanta or any other. Two of them bear inscriptions stating that the caves were gifts from Asoka

(264-225 B.C.) and a relative of his. The interiors still gleam with the polish imparted to them 2,300 years ago. Granite crockery is still produced and sold in the village below the cave.

Each *Kartik* (November) full moon, a fair is held at **Sonepur** (25 km or 15.5 mi) on the north bank of the Ganga, where the Gandak mingles with the waters of the sacred river. Primarily a cattle fair there is a wide range of livestock for sale, from elephants and camels to rabbits and white mice. Situated in a very thickly populated area, more than a million people assemble at the fair each year, transact their sales and purchases, and amuse themselves.

Himalayan Vista

There is a spectacular view of the Himalayan snow from the barrages on the Kosi (380 km or 236 mi) and the Gandak (177 km or 110 mi). The mountains rise from the plains, barely 100 m (328 ft) above sea level, to heights of 8,000 m (26,250 ft) or more. The grander view is from the Kosi barrage for though Mt. Everest is hidden behind a lesser but nearer giant, its five neighbors, all above 8,000 m high, are visible, in addition to many other summits. From the Gandak barrage only two 8,000-m peaks, Annapurna and Dhaulagiri, can be seen.

The Gandak barrage is named **Valmikinagar** because the national epic *Ramayana* was composed in the neighborhood. **Ayodhya** whose prince Rama was, lies to the west. Rama's consort, Sita, was the princess of **Janakpur** which lies 218 km (135 mi) to the east. She was born at **Sitamarhi**. **Mithila**, as the area is called, is scenically attractive – with lotus ponds after every 5 km (3 mi) or so of shady mango orchards and rows of slender betel nut palms.

There are several temples at Sitamarhi and Janakpur. The latter lies in the Terai within the lowland strip of Nepal just across the border. **Madhubani** (154 km or 96 mi), is a center of vibrant folk painting and is freely accessible.

131

Ranchi and Jamshedpur

Ranchi (326 km or 203 mi), once a summer retreat for the British, is in the uplands 700 m (230 ft) above sea level. Today it has lost its cool climate due to large-scale deforestation. At the base of Ranchi Hill is an artificial lake which is flanked by fine temples.

In **Jagannathpur**, 10 km (6 mi) southwest, is a Jagannath temple, a copy of the one in Puri. Two circular **jungle trails** start from this holiday resort, around which are four waterfalls. The farthest fall, **Hirni**, is 74 km (46 mi) away, whereas the tallest, **Hundru**, (86 m or 828 ft), **Jonha** and **Dussomghagh** are within a range of 45 km (28 mi). The wilder trail leads past **Hirni** and **Chaibasa** to **Hatgamaria** and thence via **Tensa**, **Kiriburu**, **Kumri** and **Tholkobad** to the steel town of **Rourkela**, and then northeast to Ranchi. The round trip is 600

Above: An artist from Madhubani, Bihar, working on a traditional folk painting.

km (373 mi), mostly over tarmac with all rivers bridged. The forests are too dense to permit a sight of wild animals. The other route leads through drier and more open country in which wild animals can be seen. This route is via **Netarhat** (155 km or 96 mi and 1,250 m or 4,100 ft) and the **Mahuadanr Valley** to **Betla** and back via **Latehar**. The round trip will be 500 km (310 mi), but the sight of bisons at Netarhat and of bisons, spotted deer and tiger at Betla is assured. On the border of Madhya Pradesh, 150 km (93 mi) from Ranchi, is the village of Neterahat, known for its scenic location.

Jamshedpur (455 km or 283 mi from Patna and 129 km or 80 mi from Ranchi) is a new industrial town. **Dimna Lake**, **Rivers Meet** and **Dalma Hill** are ideal places for recreation. The **Tata Youth Centre** has laid several rock climbs in the hills around. **Seraikela** (40 km or 25 mi) is known for *chhau* (masked) dances. Different objects made of soapstone are available at **Chaibasa** (80 km or 50 mi) and **Dhalbhumgarh** (64 km or 40 mi).

PATNA
Accommodation
LUXURY: **Welcomgroup Maurya Patna**, South Gandhi Maidan, Tel: 22061. *MODERATE:* **Chanakya**, Birchand Patel Marg, Tel: 23141/42. **Pataliputra Ashok**, Beer Chand Patel Path, Tel: 26270/79. **Republic**, Lawly's Buildg., Exhibition Rd., Tel: 55021-24. *BUDGET:* **Avantee**, Fraser Rd., opp. Dak Bungalow, Tel: 220540-42. **Jaysarmin**, Kankar Bagh Rd., Tel: 55573. **Samrat International**, Fraser Road, Tel: 220560-67.

Hospitals
Dinapur Civil Hospital, Tel: 7315. **Kurji Holy Family**, Tel: 62516. **Patna City Hospital**, Tel: 41817.

Museums / Libraries
Radha Kishan Jalan Museum, Oila House, Tel: 41121, visits by appointment, closed weekends. **Patna Museum**. Buddha Marg, Tel: 23332, 10.30 am-4.30 pm, closed Mon and public holidays. **Khuda Baksh Oriental Library**.

Restaurants
Vaishali, Hotel Maurya, South Gandhi Maidan. **Palli**, Hotel Pataliputra Ashok, Beer Chand Patel Path. **Amber**, Fraser Road. **Ta Sindong**, Biscomaun Bhawan, West Gandhi Maidan.

Shopping
A number of quality handicrafts are for sale, the specialty being gold and silver embroidery (Patna); silver jewelry; brocade and tussar silk (Bhagalpur); lacquered toys (Ranchi); papier maché, bamboo products, decorative articles in *sikki grass*, handlooms (Chotanagpur); vases and bowls in stone (Bodhgaya); folk paintings (Mithila region); beaten white metal statues and leather goods. The shopping areas in Patna are Patna Market, Ashok Rajpath, Bari Road, New Market, **Bihar Emporium** on New Dak Bungalow Road and near East Gandhi Maidan; **Bodhgaya**: Khadi Bhandar and Prashad Buddhistic corner. **Rajgir**: stalls at the foot of the aerial ropeway including an India Tourist Handicrafts Emporium. **Nalanda**: stalls at the entrance to the ruins displaying locally made costume jewelry and stoneware. **Vaishali**: village workshops around Vaishali.

Tourist Information
Government of India Tourist Office, Tourist Bhawan, Beer Chand Patel Path, Tel: 26721. **Tourist Information Centre**, Government of Bihar, Mazharul Haq Path, Fraser Road Tel: 25295.

Access / Local Transport
Air, rail and road links exist between Patna and the major towns of India. From Patna, Sonepur and Vaishali are accessible by road. Rajgir and Nalanda are linked by rail and road to Patna and Varanasi. Gaya is a major railhead from where buses and shared auto-rickshaws run to Bodhgaya. Ranchi and Jamshedpur are linked by air, road and rail. The national parks of Palamau and Hazaribagh have road links with Patna and Ranchi. Ranchi, though not the nearest, is a more convenient railhead for the two. *Local transport:* Tourist taxis and unmetered local taxis are available in Patna, Jamshedpur and Ranchi; buses, auto-rickshaws, cycle-rickshaws and tongas in Patna, Jamshedpur, Ranchi, Gaya and Rajgir.

Festivals
Since a lot of Hindu, Sikh, Buddhist, Jain and Muslim shrines dot the state, there is almost a festival a day. As they represent socio-cultural aspects of Bihar, the tourist department has selected seven for official patronage. Patna is the site of the month-long *Pataliputra festival. Dussehra/Durga Puja* are celebrated in October-November. The sun is worshipped at the banks of the Ganga on *Chhath Puja*, six days later. The two-week long Sonepur fair is held a fortnight after *Diwali*, with a sale of livestock and grain, folk performances and magic shows. Buddhists from India and abroad congregate at Bodhgaya and Rajgir on *Buddha Jayanti* (April-May) to offer prayers. The six-week long annual (December) retirement of the Holy Dalai Lama in Bodhgaya draws thousands of Buddhist pilgrims to attend morning prayer meetings. The two major Jain festivals are *Mahavir Jayanti* (April) and *Deo Deevali* (10 days after *Diwali*), the former at Parasnath Hill. A unique festival of the region is the *Samath Sabha* (June), held at Madhubani for a fortnight. This is a large marriage mart where parents bring horoscopes of their children and negotiate marriages. The marriage season coincides with the spring festival of *Holi*, when Kama, the god of Love, is the presiding deity.

Further Accomodation
NALANDA
PWD Rest House. Bookings through SDO PWD Rajgir.

RAJGIR
Centaur Hokke Hotel (closed in summer), Tel: 92. **Tourist Bungalows I & II** (Bihar Tourism), Tel: 39. **PWD Rest House**. Bookings through SDO, Rajgir.

BODH GAYA
Hotel Bodh Gaya Ashok. Tel: 22708-9. **Tourist Bunglows I & II**. (Bihar Tourism). **PWDIB**, bookings through Executive Engineer, Gaya. Lodges attached to monasteries (contact the monk in charge).

CALCUTTA

The teeming metropolis of **Calcutta** (population 11 million) is one of India's overpowering experiences. The city evokes strong reactions, both favorable and unfavorable; few persons can remain indifferent to its vitality.

Its character has been shaped by the Raj; by commerce; by the fact that it was a center of social reform and continues to generate vigorous cultural, political and intellectual activities; and not least by the mass of humanity it has drawn into its vortex. Calcutta has been called "the city of dreadful night," a city which has been "much discussed, much misunderstood and fiercely defended, claimed alike by poet, revolutionary and industrialist." It should figure prominently on any itinerary that seeks to find the varied facets of Indian reality.

The British Era

Among the youngest European settlements in Asia, Calcutta reckons its rapid growth into a city from 24 August 1690. That was the day Job Charnock chose a site in the village of Kalikata to build a warehouse for the East India Company. Real growth started in 1774, after Robert Clive had defeated the armies of the Nawabs of Bengal and Oudh and extracted the right to collect revenue from the provinces of Bengal, Bihar and Orissa. As a result, Calcutta became the capital of British possessions in India. It remained so until 1911, when the capital was moved to Delhi.

Fort William, named after William I, was built in 1773, but the Maratha ditch dug in 1740 as an impediment to raiders, had not been filled. Britons living in the city were called Ditchers, a nickname they retained long after the ditch was

Right: An angel of mercy. A nun at Mother Teresa's home for the destitute.

converted into the Circular Road. The fort was built to guard against an attack by land, because by 1759 the French at Chandernagar and the Dutch at Chinsura had ceased to be rivals. During World War II, fighter aircraft used the Red Road outside the fort as a runway. At present, the fort serves as the Eastern Command headquarters.

As the seat of the Governor-General, Calcutta resembled a minor court. Warren Hastings was married in the newly constructed **St. John's Church** (1773). A monument in the garden commemorates the victims of the infamous "Black Hole" tragedy of June 1756, when 113 Britons, imprisoned by the Nawab of Bengal in a single room, died of suffocation. This room once stood where the G.P.O. is now located. The church is near the tomb of Charnock, and the former residence of Hastings is in a street which, until recently, bore his name. Now this street is called Kiran Shankar Roy Road, and the building is used as a shop for selling government publications. (So many locality and street names have been changed that it is advisable to acquire a directory listing the old names and their new substitutes. The old names, however, still remain popular.)

Several European painters flocked to the new "court" at Calcutta: Tilly Kettle (1770), Thomas Hickey (1775), William Hodges (1780), Johann Zoffany (1783) and the famous Daniels, both uncle and nephew, in 1786. The **Victoria Memorial** has a collection of their work which gives a vivid description of how the city and its residents looked at that time. Also on display are the works of Dutch and German engravers. The growing city drew European architects as well, and Bishop Heber wrote in 1826 that Calcutta's style was as much Palladian as that of Petrograd. Government House, built in 1802 and now called **Raj Bhavan**, is a good example of that style which continued through the 19th century to the

early years of the 20th. The **Town Hall** and the former **War Office**, on roads leading west and east of Raj Bhavan, are built in the same style as **Metcalfe Hall** in Hare Street, and, with various modifications, **Writers Building** (which once housed writers of the East India Company, and is now the seat of the West Bengal Government), the **Old Mint** and the **New Mint**, **Hastings House** and **Belvedere**. The last two are in Alipore.

Horse-drawn coaches arrived in Calcutta in 1740 but took time to become popular with the Ditchers who were accustomed to riding or using palanquins. Boats were used along the waterfront to visit Chandernagar and Chinsura. A large part of the city is riven with narrow lanes, and around the **Maidan** (Calcutta's green space) and **BBD Bagh** (previously **Dalhousie Square**) the roads intersect so frequently that traffic jams are the order of the day.

The closing years of the 18th century saw the arrival of men with American associations. Sir William Jones came to Calcutta in 1783 as a Supreme Court judge, and founded the **Asiatic Society** (Park Street). Lord Cornwallis, who had lost the war against the colonists in America, arrived three years later as Governor-General. David Ochterlony was a general in 1818 when he won the war against Nepal. He had an Indian wife for which he suffered ostracism. The monument to him (at the northern end of the Maidan), now called **Shahid Minar**, has an Egyptian base, Syrian tower and Turkish cupola. Portraits of the three Americans are displayed in the Victoria Memorial. Trade with the U.S.A. developed quite early, and one of the treasures brought by American ships and much valued in the city's long and exhausting summer was ice.

During the 19th century there were fewer commissions for portraits, for in 1839, **Bourne & Sheppard** opened a photographic studio which is the oldest

among those still in business throughout the world. Italian architects came to the city, once steam navigation had reduced the duration of the voyage from Europe. Then the style of architecture changed, and Gothic Revival came into vogue. **St. Paul's Cathedral** (1847) and the **High Court** (1852) are the only buildings in this style. The cathedral has a large piece of stained glass by Burne-Jones and a painting by Zoffany. Italian and Swiss confectioners also flourished in the latter part of the 19th century.

Claude Martin, a French soldier of fortune living at Lucknow, amassed a fortune which he bequeathed to establish schools in Lucknow, Lyons and Calcutta. **La Martiniere** in Calcutta, founded in 1836, is a memorial to him. Some French officers even took employment with the British and lived in this city. Catherine Grand, the wife of one of them, was a beauty who later became notorious when Philip Francis, the arch rival of Warren Hastings, was found clambering through a window into her bedroom. The Grand house in Alipore can no longer be identified, but her town residence on Chowringhee has been incorporated in the **Grand Hotel**. Next to the Grand Hotel is a building whose broad mosaic horizontal bands are in the style of Frank Lloyd Wright. It replaces an older colonial building where the American writer Mark Twain stayed during his visit over 80 years ago.

Some institutions which have endured to the present day were established by the English in the 19th century. The oldest golf club outside the British Isles was founded in Calcutta in 1829; but horse racing is older by ten years. The **Race Course** is on the **Maidan**, and events here have been attended by visiting royalty and dignitaries. Polo has been played in its central oval since 1861. Some of the jockeys later went to Britain and Australia and distinguished themselves. The season is October to March, but the principal fixtures are in the latter part of De-

cember and early January. The **Calcutta Cricket Club** came into being around 1860, and the Indian Football Association shield has been enthusiastically competed for since 1884.

The Chinese came to Calcutta around 1830 to manufacture sugar, as carpenters and leather workers, and to start the first tea plantations in Assam and Darjeeling. The Chinese New Year, which falls in January, is celebrated at **Ah Chi Ghat**, near **Budge Budge**, where the first sugar factory was located. Chinatown is no longer as impressive as it was before wide roads cut through it, but meanwhile a new settlement has grown up at **Tangra** in the eastern part of the city where local families provide Cantonese meals.

The Bengal Renaissance

Calcutta became the nerve center of the Bengal Renaissance which dates to

Above: Images of Calcutta - a friendly beggar; and a rickshaw-puller waiting for work.

1783, when William Jones founded the **Asiatic Society**, the first learned society in the world to study all matters pertaining to the Orient. Two institutions owe their genesis directly to the Asiatic Society – the **Botanical Garden**, with its herbarium across the river at **Sibpur,** and the **Indian Museum** on Chowringhee. The banyan tree in the Botanical Garden has been a memorable sight since the gardens were laid out in 1787. Aerial roots have spread over 382 m (1,253 ft) in circumference. The main tree at the center used to be 28 m (92 ft) high but was attacked by a fungus and removed in 1925 to prevent the spread of the infection.

Many German, French and American researchers corresponded with the Asiatic Society or studied manuscripts in its possession. Max Mueller, the most distinguished among them, never actually came to India although he published many biographical sketches of the leading personalities of the Bengal Renaissance. Rammohun Roy and Dwarkanath Tagore, grandfather of the poet Rabindranath, became ardent advocates of progress. English education was started at the Hindoo College (now **Presidency College**) in 1817 and one of the teachers was Henry Derozio, Calcutta's first poet in the English language. An art school was established in 1856.

From the middle of the 19th century onwards, the Bengal Renaissance was mainly a literary movement, though three major achievements in social reforms are to its credit – the statutory prohibition of *sati*, or the burning of widows, legalization of the remarriage of Hindu widows, and a gradual raising of the marriageable age of girls.

Though religious controversies raged, the attempt all through was to evolve a universal religion which found expression in Ramakrishna Paramhansa's experiments. By turn he lived as a Muslim and a Christian although he was the priest of a Hindu temple. At the conclusion of these experiments he declared: "All religions lead to the same God." His disciple Vivekananda attended the World Congress of Religions in 1894 at Chicago and built the **Belur Math** with donations from two Americans. The building incorporates distinctive features of the houses of worship of different faiths.

Rabindranath Tagore was the culmination of the Bengal Renaissance. He was a poet, playwright, storyteller and novelist. He composed the melodies for his songs and thereby created a new branch of Indian music now called *Rabindra sangeet*. During the last 20 years of his life he turned his hand to painting and found a very modern style.

The **Rabindra Sadan** on Cathedral Road is a memorial to Tagore, where various dramatic performances and concerts are staged. **Jorasanko**, on Sir Hariram Goenka Street, had been the home of six generations of Tagores. The house in which Rabindranath lived is now the **Rabindra Bharati University**, where his original works are displayed.

The English language theater in Calcutta never recovered from the death, in 1842, of the actress Esther Leach after her clothes caught fire from the footlights. Since then only amateur productions have been staged. The site where Leach had been acting that evening is now occupied by **St. Xavier's College**. However, in 1895, Gerasim Lebedeff, a Russian, produced a startling play in Bengali and started a theatrical tradition that has since flourished and produced such famous personalities as Girish Ghosh, Binodini, Sisir Bhaduri, and Tripti and Shambhu Mitra.

Successive novelists and playwrights have also enabled the city to be the home of famous film directors: Pramathes Barua, Bimal Roy and Ritwick Ghatak in the past, and Satyajit Ray and Mrinal Sen in the present.

Offshoots of the Bengal Renaissance also emerged in the fields of science and politics, for example the **Indian Association for Science** was founded in 1876. By the 1920s several eminent scientists in the **Calcutta School of Physics** and the **School of Tropical Medicine** on Chittaranjan Avenue were engaged in research which earned international recognition.

The Indian Political Association was founded in 1878 and was the forerunner of the Indian National Congress. Outstanding political leaders from the city have been Surendranath Banerjea, C. R. Das, M. N. Roy and Subhas Chandra Bose. The last two had excellent international links: Roy was prominent in the Communist International between 1920 and 1929, and Bose raised an army to fight alongside the Japanese during the Second World War.

Between 1910 and 1935, as many as 399 young men from Calcutta and its environs were transported for life to isolated jails in the Andamans on charges of conspiracy to overthrow the British Indian Government.

Calcutta Today

The future decline of Calcutta has been prophesied often enough over the last 118 years, but both its population and its area continue to grow, making it the largest city in India and among the largest in the world. The occasions for these prophecies of doom were the cutting of the Suez Canal in 1869 which put this port on the wrong side of the peninsula for trade with Europe; the moving of India's capital to Delhi in 1911; Partition, which brought the international frontier within 90 km (56 mi) of the city, and a flood of refugees; the Bangladesh war, which brought more refugees; and, finally, the election of Marxists to power in 1977. But Calcutta has survived, and while Calcuttans complain about pressures of population they would rather not go elsewhere. They will admit to signs of decay, but are quick to show the contrary. In the

Above: Cinema hoardings crowd the façades of Calcutta's busy Esplanade.

last few decades, they say, two enormous stadiums have been built, at **Eden Gardens** and at Salt Lake, for cricket and soccer fans. Silt dredged from the river bed has been used to fill salty marshes to house 300,000 people. The **Girish Mancha Auditorium** and a library devoted to the theater in memory of a 19th-century playwright and actor, have been established. Of course, the city recalls with nostalgia several earlier periods of glory. For instance, between 1920 and 1940 when Tagore was writing, Sisir Bhaduri was acting, Uday Shankar was dancing, Jamini Roy was painting, while Pramathes Barua was making films. But each of them, except Tagore, has a present-day successor. Mother Teresa has taken the place of Ramakrishna Paramhansa as the living saint of the city, loved and admired by people irrespective of the religion they follow. Born an Albanian, she came in 1931 to teach at a convent here. She founded her **Missionaries of Charity** (the mother house of the order is in Lower Circular Road) in 1948. Now, her order has 350 houses in 71 countries, as many as 146 being in India.

Other markers, less expressive of the live of a city but considered more trustworthy, also point to growth: Land prices continue to soar, communications have improved, and Calcutta is the only city in India with a metro.

One completed project is a metropolitan bypass running to the east of the city, which provides access to all localities from **Dum Dum Airport**. Though they still frequent Kalighat Temple, Tipu's mosque, New Market, Chowringhee and the Esplanade, beggars are less often seen in the streets now than 20 years ago, because rural prosperity follows better prices for agricultural produce. Pavement dwellers come mainly from Bihar and Andhra Pradesh where large populations of the landless are unable to find an adequate living in the villages.

Museums

Few Indian cities have as much to offer in the study of painting and sculpture; Calcutta can boast some fine museums. The **Victoria Memorial** (along with **Howrah Bridge**, today known as **Rabindra Setu**) is still one of Calcutta's landmarks. This imperial monument was the brainchild of Lord Curzon during whose viceroyship Queen Victoria died. Funds were raised by subscription, and work began in 1906. The memorial was opened to visitors in 1921. The Victorian Age roughly coincided with the Bengal Renaissance, and here a considerable collection is representative of both.

However, there are also artifacts belonging to earlier times. Of great interest to those who love arms are the rockets used by the troops of Tipu Sultan and the cruel Mughal Emperor Aurangzeb. Statues of the heroes of the Raj, which once lined Red Road, are now scattered through the grounds of the Victoria Memorial.

The **Indian Museum** has been the repository of many collections of numerous scientific surveys for 200 years. The present building dates from 1878 and has 36 galleries. The natural history, ethnographic and archaeological sections are particularly rich. Artifacts of the Indus Valley civilization, Mughal paintings, including the works of two masters, Mansur and Ghulam, and the stone railing of the Barhut stupa are among the many prize exhibits.

The **Asutosh Museum** in Calcutta University focuses on folk art. Tagore originals can be admired at **Rabindra Bharati**, while the **Academy of Fine Arts** has a collection of paintings of the Bengal School (early 20th century) as well as contemporary art. The **Birla Art Academy**, on Southern Avenue, apart from sculptures in stone and bronze dating to the first century B.C. also houses modern art. The **College of Arts and Crafts**, and the house of the late Jamini Roy, one of Bengal's finest painters, are also worth visiting.

The quaint **Marble Palace** of Raja Mullick on Muktaram Babu Street, built in 1835 and still occupied by his descendants, has a collection of art that includes sculptures by Michelangelo and Houdon and paintings by Rubens, Reynolds and Gainsborough. Calcutta also has the prestigious **National Library** (once the Viceregal Lodge) which receives a copy of each book published in India. In addition, it has been buying books published elsewhere for more than 150 years and has received several large private collections. It has an excellent collection of manuscripts in languages prevalent in the country at various periods. The **Birla Planetarium** was the first to be built in India. Near it is the **Nehru Children's Museum**. Calcutta also has a large **Zoo** (1816) famous for its "tigons" and "litagons", the first, a cross between a tiger and a lioness, and the second a cross between a tigon and a lioness.

Places of Worship

The present **Kalighat Temple**, a hub of activity, dates only from 1809 but an earlier temple, associated with criminals and bloody rituals, had been there from the end of the 16th century. The waterway on which the temple stands was the original navigable channel of the **Hooghly**, and signs of several ancient habitations have been located by archaeologists along its course. This temple is also associated with a form of folk painting known as Kalighat *pat*, originals of which are on display in the museums. The **Armenian Church** off Old China Bazaar Lane was built in 1724. It is remarkable for its architectural style and has a tombstone dated 1628. Four **Jain temples** are located in a pleasant garden on **Badridas Temple Road** in the northeastern part of the city. The principal temple, **Sitalnath**, was built in 1867. The

Above: Creating a goddess. A craftsman working on an image of Durga at Kumartuli.

Parasnath Temple is in **Belgachia**. **Nakhoda** (literally a ship's captain) **mosque** is the city's largest where 10,000 people can pray at a time. Built in 1926, its plan is an imitation of Akbar's tomb at Sikandra but the high red sandstone wall seems somewhat dwarfed in this crowded locality. Another mosque, the **Metiaburz Shiite Mosque** on Garden Reach Road, was built by the exiled Nawab of Oudh.

No textiles are produced in the city now but excellent fabrics woven in the villages can be bought from **Cottage Industries Institute** on Chowringhee and **Handloom House** on Lindsay Street. The only traditional craftsmen working within the city are those who model clay images for the various *pujas*, and they are concentrated in the locality known as **Kumartuli**. *Durga Puja* is the most important festival, held in autumn for three days. It is celebrated with great enthusiasm at 200 or more localities, and culminates with the immersion of elaborate images of the goddess at Babu, Princep and Outram Ghats, along the **Strand**.

CALCUTTA
Accommodation

LUXURY: **Hotel Airport Ashok**, Calcutta Airport, Tel: 569111-29. **Hindustan International**, 235/1 A.J.C. Bose Road, Tel: 442394. **Oberoi Grand**, 15 Jawaharlal Nehru Road, Tel: 29-2323. **Park Hotel**, 17 Park St., Tel: 297336, 297941. **Taj Bengal**, 34 B Belvedere Rd., Alipore, Tel: 283939.
MODERATE: **The Kenilworth**, 1-2 Little Russel Street, Tel: 44-8394/95. **Rutt Deen**, 21 B Loudon St., Tel: 44-3884. *BUDGET:* **Lytton Hotel**, 14 Sudder St., Tel: 29-1875/79. **Shalimar**, 3 S.N. Banerjee Rd., opp. American Library, Tel: 28-5030. **Lindsay**, 8 B Lindsay St., Tel: 24-8639. **Asia**, 11 A-B Jamir Lane, Rash Behari Ave., Tel: 466682.

Museums

Indian Museum, 27 Jawaharlal Nehru Rd, Tel: 239855, 10 am-5 pm, closed Mon. Ancient and medieval sculpture, geological, zoological, botanical and anthropological galleries. **Asutosh Museum**, Centenary Building, College Street, Tel: 347472. Indian objects d'art with emphasis on eastern India. 10.30 am-4.30 pm, closed Sun and university holidays. **Gurusday Museum**, Bratacharigam, Thakurpurkur, 24 Parganas. 11.30 am-4.30 pm, closed Thur. Collection of folklore items. **Victoria Memorial**, 10 am-3.30 pm, closed Mon. **Academy of Fine Arts**, Cathedral Road, Tel: 444205, 3-8 pm. Fine Collection of contemporary Indian art. **Birla Academy of Arts & Crafts**, Southern Avenue.

Post / Telephone

General Post Office, BBD Bagh., Tel: 221451. **Central Telegraph Office**, 8 Red Cross Place, Tel: 234223 (trunk calls). **Overseas Communication Service**, 18 Rabindra Sarani, Tel: 266264. Telex facility available.

Restaurants

INTERNATIONAL: **Trinca's-The Other Room** (closed Thur), 17 B Park Street, Tel: 440788, bar and dancing. **Garden Café**, Oberoi Grand. **Coffee House**, College Street. *INDIAN:* **Nizam's**, 22 -25 Hogg Market. **Shamina** (closed Thur), 17 G Mirza Ghalib Road, Tel: 212674, with bar. **Saqui** (closed Thur), 117 Lenin Sarani, Tel: 264316, with bar. *CHINESE:* **Waldorf** (closed Tue), 1/1 Park Street, Tel: 297514. **Nanking** (closed Thur), 22 Blackburn Lane, with bar. **Golden Dragon**, 40 Park Mansions, Park Street.

Shopping

Handicrafts produced throughout the state are available in Calcutta. Jewelry and carvings from conch shells; decorative gift items in *shola* pith; leather bags and fabric covered with batik work from Shantiniketan are exclusive to the state. Shops in Calcutta stock Darjeeling tea, woolen garments and lightweight wooden masks from this idyllic hill resort.

Excursions

Chandernagore (39 km); Bandel (43 km); Diamond Harbor, (51 km) down the Hooghly river, is a natural harbor from where motor launches run to Sagar Island (135 km). A large fair, the *Ganga Sagar Mela*, is held annually in mid-January. For one-day trips to Digha (185 km) and Bakkhali (132 km), both beaches of great natural beauty, an early morning departure is a must. Other places include Shantiniketan (150 km) and the Sunderbans (131 km); tours are organized by the West Bengal Tourist Dept.

Festivals

The calendar begins with *Makar Sankranti* (mid-January) when devotees gravitate to the holy Ganga for a dip. The blessings of the Goddess of Learning, Saraswati, are sought on *Basant Panchami* (January/February), in particular by scholars and teachers. *Holi* or *Dol Jatra* in Bengal (March/April) is marked by revelry and color. The chariot procession or *Rath Yatra* (July/August) is taken out in honor of the patron deity of Puri. Jagannath is very impressive. However, these celebrations are nothing compared to the fevered pitch of preparations for *Durga Puja* (September/October), the festival to the Goddess Durga. Festivities stretch over five days. During the festival of lights, *Kali Puja* (*Diwali* in north India October/November), images of Kali, another form of Parvati, are installed for worship. Another major event is Christmas, celebrated here more than in any other metropolis in India, due to the colonial influence.

Tourist Information

Government of India Tourist Office, 4 Shakespeare Sarani, Tel: 441402/443521. Information Counter, Calcutta Airport, New Terminal Bldg., Tel: 572611 Extn. 440. **West Bengal Tourist Bureau**, 3/2 BBD Bagh (East), Tel: 238271/3. Information Counters Howrah Railway Station (Tel: 663518).

Access / Local Transport

Calcutta airport services international carriers as well as the two domestic airlines. Howrah and Sealdah are the main railway stations. A network of national highways connects the state capital with major cities and nearby towns.
The metro railway runs on two sectors. Other modes of local transport include trams, horse-drawn carriages, cycle-rickshaws, suburban trains, taxis and even a ferry service across the Hooghly river.

WEST BENGAL

Prior to the partition of India, the state of Bengal was considerably large, encompassing present Bangladesh. Today, as West Bengal it is small in area (87,853 sq.km or 33,920 sq.mi), yet it spans the Himalayan reaches and the deltaic maze at the Bay of Bengal. Coupled with a distinct culture and remnants of a colonial past, this makes West Bengal an interesting experience for the traveler.

Hill Stations

A magnificent sight is Kanchenjunga (8,586 m or 28,169 ft) from **Darjeeling**, a hill station that has been a summer resort since 1837, decades before it was found that the mountain was the world's third highest. Darjeeling's temperature, at its warmest, is 10° Celsius lower than Calcutta's. Built on a narrow ridge jutting

Above: Impressive landscape in Darjeeling, with Mt. Kanchenjunga in the background.

out into the Tista basin, Darjeeling looks across a wide expanse, 1,300 m (4,265 ft) below, to Himalayan peaks stretching along the northern horizon for 96 km (60 mi). Kanchenjunga is only 56 km away. Lesser, but equally striking peaks in that jagged row are the sharply conical Narsingh and the gracefully crested Siniolchu. To appreciate Darjeeling's extraordinary location, one has to take an 8-km (5 mi) ride on the ropeway to **Singla**, a picnic spot at an altitude of 3,000 m (9,843 ft). The surface route is 29 km (18 mi) long and a stiff climb forbids the return journey by any means other than the ropeway. A similar steep drop is the drive to **Tista Bazaar** on the way to **Kalimpong**, 15 km (9 mi) further away.

Darjeeling's most popular rendezvous is the **Chaurasta**, a tiny square occupying the entire width of the ridge and wedged in between the higher points of **Jalpahar** and **Observatory Hill**. **The Mall** leaves the Chaurasta and returns to it after encircling **Observatory Hill**, as do all the promenaders. Darjeeling is conducive to long walks, and they can be interspersed by visits to local institutions. These are the **Lloyd Botanical Garden** established in 1878, and the **Zoo** (specializing in high altitude species), the **Mountaineering Institute**, the house of the late **Tenzing Norgay**, the Sherpa who first climbed Mt. Everest with Edmund Hillary in 1953, the **Shrubbery** which is the residence of the Governor of West Bengal, and the **Natural History Museum**. Orchids at the garden and butterflies at the museum deserve a special mention, for such colorful collections are rare. The exceptional range of orchids and butterflies found in these hills led the Lepchas, a local tribe, to become excellent collectors of specimens and caused their employment as far afield as New Guinea and Borneo.

The **Tibetan Refugee Self Help Center** produces and sells a wide range of Tibetan artifacts and curios. It was established in 1959 to rehabilitate refugees who had fled Tibet with the Dalai Lama in the wake of the Chinese invasion. Csomos de Koros, a Hungarian philologist, who discovered affinities between the languages spoken by Magyars in his country and Magars in Tibet, is buried in the Darjeeling cemetery.

The View from Tiger Hill

Mt. Everest (8,848 m or 20,029 ft), the world's highest peak, is visible from **Tiger Hill** but, being 170 km (106 mi) away, does not stand out as strikingly as the nearer Kanchenjunga. The view from Tiger Hill at sunrise is unforgettable as colors change from gray to pink to a luminous gold. Nearer views of snow peaks are possible from **Sandakphu** (57 km or 35 mi) and **Phalut**. Both places are ca. 3,300 m (10,827 ft) high and favorites with trekkers, although jeeps go up to Sandakphu.

Ghoom, 10 km (6 mi) from Darjeeling, has a **Tibetan monastery** where

manuscripts written on birch bark are carefully preserved. There is also a **Yellow Hat Buddhist temple**, built in 1875. Darjeeling can be used as a base for whirlwind drives to **Mirik** (45 km or 28 mi), **Kurseong** (25 km or 16 mi), **Kalimpong** (38 km or 24 mi) and **Gangtok** (59 km or 31 mi). There is an artificial lake at Mirik. Kalimpong was once on the trade route to Tibet. The **Tharpa Choling Monastery** and the **Bhutanese Monastery** are worth a visit. The town is famous for its cheese.

Darjeeling is a worldwide synonym for the finest flavors of tea. The two earliest plantations were established at **Alubari** and **Lekong**. A visit to **Happy Valley Tea Estate**, 2 km (1.25 mi) from Darjeeling is interesting because you can observe the processing of tea leaves. Darjeeling is also synonymous with the "toy train." Completed in 1881, this 0.60-m gauge track winds from **Siliguri** and **New Jalpaiguri** all the way up to Darjeeling through tea plantations and misty mountains, using such intelligent devices as the Batasia Loop to gain height. The journey takes about seven hours. Siliguri is 80 km (50 mi) from Darjeeling and near **Bagdogra**, the most convenient airport for Darjeeling. The **Jaldapara Sanctuary** 115 km (71 mi) east of Siliguri, has rhinoceros, wild elephant and deer. A permit is necessary for Darjeeling (see West Bengal Guidepost).

Malda and Murshidabad

Roughly halfway to Calcutta lies Malda, which, as English Bazaar, was a trading center for the Dutch, the French and the English. Malda may be used as a base for visits to the nearby ancient capitals of Bengal – Old Malda, Gaur and Pandua. **Gaur** was the capital of the Pala and Sena dynasties (8th to 13th centuries) and was eventually destroyed by the Turks. A new capital was subsequently built at **Pandua** on the remains of Gaur.

Most of Pandua is in ruins; but among the few preserved monuments are the **Barasona Mosque** (1526), the **Feroze Minar** (1486) and the **Chilka Mosque**.

Murshidabad, famous for its silk, became the capital of Bengal in 1705 when the Mughal Viceroy, Murshid Kuli Khan moved his capital here from Dacca. His tomb lies within the **Katra Mosque**. The **Hazarduari Palace**, built in 1837, now houses a rich collection of arms, china and paintings.

Along the Hooghly

The Hooghly river has been used by international shipping from ancient times. As early as 227 B.C. Mahinda, the emperor Asoka's son, set sail for Sri Lanka from Tamluk, a little to the north of Haldia, the recently constructed outport of Calcutta. Imitations in clay of the medallion struck by Augustus (67 B.C. to A.D. 14) have been found on the banks of the river. Later, Chinese junks, Arab dhows and Portuguese naos sailed up this river in succession. The Portuguese established a trading post at Hugli (40 km or 25 mi north of Calcutta) in A.D. 1540. The Dutch followed them in 1625 at Chinsura, the Danes in 1640 at Serampore, the French in 1688 at Chandernagar, and the British in 1690 at Calcutta.

Traveling north from Calcutta, one comes across many places of interest along the Hooghly. **Belur** is the headquarters of the **Ramakrishna Mission**, founded in 1938 by Swami Vivekananda. At **Dakshineshwar** is the famous 9th-century **Kali Temple**. **Serampore** was a center of trading activity for the Danish East India Company for about 50 years until 1845, when the British took over. During this time, William Carey and two other Baptist missionaries established a printing press in 1799 and a college in

Right: A Baul singer, one of the wandering minstrels of Bengal.

1819, now a theological institute. Here, the Danes also built **St. Olaf's Church**. **Chandernagar** belonged to the French from 1673 to 1952 and somewhat retains a French flavor. The **Sacred Heart Church** has a statue of Joan of Arc and a Lourdes Grotto.

At **Chinsurah**, a Dutch settlement from 1625 to 1826, is the Armenian **St. John's Church**. **Hooghly** was founded by the Portuguese in 1580 and named Bandel de Ugolim. The Mughal emperor Shah Jahan destroyed the settlement 50 years later. The **Church of Our Lady of Bandel** was rebuilt in 1690 and continues to draw pilgrims. The town of **Bansberia** is known for its terracotta temples, in particular the 17th-century **Vasudeva Temple**, and the later **Hangeshwari Temple**. **Nawadwip**, 125 km (78 mi) north of Calcutta, was the capital of Bengal in the 11th and 12th centuries. It is revered as the birthplace of the Vaishnav mystic, Chaitanya Mahaprabhu, who taught here in the 16th century. The headquarters of the International Society for Krishna Consciousness (the Hare Krishna people) is nearby, at **Mayapur**. On the east bank lies **Krishnanagar**, where craftsmen specialize in clay modeling.

Downstream from Calcutta is **Achighat**, the place where the first Chinese settlement began in 1840, later giving rise to Calcutta's seething Chinatown. **Budge Budge** is the southern limit of the industrial district, extending from Sahaganj in the north. **Hooghly Point** and **Harwood Point** are bends in the river which broadens into an estuary at **Diamond Harbour** (48 km or 24 mi from Calcutta). **Haldia**, on the west bank, is a new port and industrial center. Beyond this are the lovely bathing beaches at **Digha** on the west bank and **Bakkhali** on the east bank (160 km or 99 mi and 130 km or 81 mi respectively from Calcutta). Bakkhali and Diamond Harbour are on the western fringe of the **Sunderbans**, the deltaic maze of creeks through which

steamers for and from Assam pick their way. The banks are covered with mangrove forests.

The Sunderbans is a reserve with a very large number of tigers, though these are rarely seen. **Gosaba**, headquarters of the reserve, which can arrange an overnight stay, is reached by launch along the Matla from **Canning** (53km or 33 mi). The pelicanry near Gosaba, however, is a place that deserves a visit.

Towards the Uplands

Leaving the river, and the roads beside it, you travel west to the uplands that begin at the industrial town of **Durgapur**. The barrage on the Damodar is a popular picnic spot. Across the barrage are **Susunia Hill** and **Matha** (67 km or 42 mi and 208 km or 129 mi from Durgapur respectively), with graded rock climbs.

Vishnupur and **Bankura** are also located in the uplands. The former is a famous temple town with several carved terracotta temples. It is also associated with a superior quality of silk. The latter is the home of the famous terracotta decorative horses.

Santiniketan (212 km or 132 mi from Calcutta), the university founded by India's famous poet and Nobel Prize winner Rabindranath Tagore, continues to attract writers and artists. The places to visit at Santiniketan are **Uttarayan**, where Tagore lived, the **China Bhavan** and **Kala Bhavan**, the art college and museum, within walking distance of several guest houses and the tourist lodge. Vishnupur and Bankura are best visited by road, while for Santiniketan there is an express train from Calcutta which takes about three hours – a journey offering impressive views of the regional landscape.

Tarapith, 76 km (47 mi) from Santiniketan is a well-known Tantra center where the famous American poet Allen Ginsberg spent several months. **Bakreshwar** (57 km or 35 mi from Santiniketan) has a tourist lodge near hot springs.

Handicrafts and Cuisine

Villages on the banks of the Hooghly earned fame for their silk and cotton fabrics long before the chimneys of the jute mills rose among them. The spinning, weaving, dyeing and printing was all done in villages which lent their names to the texture, weave and design of the fabrics. The best silk is found at **Vishnupur**. It is made from dyed yarn woven into patterns illustrating incidents in the *Mahabharata* and *Ramayana*. The fabric is expensive for it lasts a long time. Murshidabad silk is less expensive.

Bengal's famous cotton fabrics include Baluchar, Santipur, Phuli and Dhaniakhali. There has been a revival of *zardozi* textiles of woven gold thread at the villages of **Ranimati** and **Hakila**. Dhakra brassware is produced by the lost wax process in the villages around **Burdwan**. **Bagan** near **Howrah** specializes in tradi-

tional locksmithery. The town of Krishnanagar is known for its toys. *Pat* painting continues to be a very popular folk art around Santiniketan, Bankura and Midnapur. All these products can be bought in Calcutta but for connoisseurs who want to buy local handicrafts, a visit to the centers of production is not only a must but also a lot of fun.

The prime delicacy of places along the Hooghly is the *hilsa* fish which comes up from the sea each summer to spawn. Some of the restaurants there serve smoked *hilsa*. Bengali sweets are different from preparations elsewhere.

The departure from lentil-based foods to those prepared from milk is due to the Dutch influence which prevailed in Chinsurah for 175 years. This led to the production of a special type of sharp cottage cheese which is still made today and sold in Calcutta's New Market as Bandel Cheese. The sweets are made from casein and evaporated milk and among the popular ones are *sandesh*, *Lady Canning* and *rossogolla*.

Above: A West Bengal scroll painter narrates his story to a rapt audience.

DARJEELING

Accommodation
MODERATE: **Windamere Hotel**, Observatory Hill, Tel: 2397/2841. *BUDGET:* **Bellevue Hotel**, The Mall, Tel: 2129, 2221. **Central Hotel**, Robertson Rd., Tel: 2033, 2746. **Hotel Sinclairs Darjeeling**, 18/1 Gandhi Rd., Tel: 3431/32.

Local Festivals
Lepcha/Bhutia New Year's Day (January). Colorful fairs are held along the Teesta river on *Makar Sankranti* (January). The T*ibetan New Year* (February) is celebrated with folk dances in monasteries. Bengalis celebrate *Durga Puja* (September/October) with the same fervor that is visible elsewhere in the state.

Museums / Galleries
Natural History Museum, near Chourasta, 10 am-4 pm, until 1 pm on Wednesday. Collection: regional fauna. **Himalayan Mountaineering Institute**, Jawahar Parbat, 8.30 am-1 pm, 2-4.30 pm, closed Mon. **Ava Art Gallery**, en route to Ghoom, 8 am-12 noon, 12.30-6 pm, Tel: 2469. **Sain Himalayan Art Gallery** and **Hayden Hall**: The former shows portraits of hill people and landscape paintings, the latter local handicrafts.

Post / Telegraph / Telephone
General Post & Telegraph Office, Laden-La Road, Tel: 2076, 2815. **Bazaar Post Office**, Market Square, Tel. 2634.

Restaurants
Glenary's (Tel: 2055) and **Keventer's** (Tel: 2026) on Nehru Road; **New Dish**, Gandhi Road (Tel: 2861); **Orient**, NB Singh Road; **Snow Lion**, Bellevue Properties; and **Ambassador** and **Chowrasta** at Chowrasta.

Shopping
You can shop for carpets of the Abusson variety with traditional designs, woolen shawls and pullovers, crafts in wood and leather, and table linen. Shopping areas: Chowrasta, Laden-La Road, Market Square, NB Singh and Nehru Roads. Souvenirs can also be bought from Manjusha, the West Bengal emporium, the Tibetan Refugee Self-Help Centre and Hayden Hall.

Tourist Information
Tourist Bureau, 1 Nehru Road, Chowrasta, Tel: 2050. **Tourist Information Counter**, Bagdogra Airport, Tel: 90.

Access / Local Transport
The nearest airport is Bagdogra (90 km). Scheduled services are operated by Indian Airlines to connect it with Calcutta, Delhi, Patna, Guwahati and Imphal. Major express trains terminate at Siliguri/New Jalpaiguri. From here, a narrow gauge "toy" train will take 7/8 hours to reach Darjeeling. Alternately, tourists can hire private taxis,

mini-coaches or board buses. Bus services connect Darjeeling to Calcutta, Durgapur, Patna, Siliguri and Phuntsilong (Bhutan). Regular road routes exist from Darjeeling to Kurseong (32 km), Mirik (43 km), Kalimpong (40 km), Siliguri (80 km) and Gangtok (96 km).

Miscellaneous
Foreign tourists require **Restricted Area Permits** to visit Darjeeling and its vicinity. These are obtainable from Indian missions abroad or Foreigner's Registration Offices at Bombay, Delhi, Madras or the Deputy Commissioner of Police, Calcutta. Darjeeling offers many interesting treks. The routes are: (a) Darjeeling - Manaybharjang - Tonglu - Sandakphu - return, 118 km; (b) same route as above up to Sandakphu. Sandakphu - Phalut and return; (c) Darjeeling - Phalut - Raman - Rimbik - Palmajua - Batasia - Manaybhanjang, 180 km; (d) Darjeeling - Phalut - Raman - Rimbik - Jhepi - Bijanbari - Darjeeling, 153 km Season: April-May, October-December. Arrangements for accomodation, food, equipment and transport can be made by the Tourist Bureau, Tel: 2050.

Further Accomodation

JALDAPARA
Madarihat Tourist Lodge, Tel: Madrihat 30. **Hollong Forest Lodge**. Reservations for both can be made at the Regional Tourist Office in Darjeeling, or WBTDC 3/2 BBD Dagh, Calcutta, Tel: 238271. **Bandari Tourist & Youth Hostel**, Reservations: Divisional Forest Officer, Wildlife Division, P.O. Jalpaiguri. Tel: 838.

MALDA
Government Tourist Bungalow and a few lodges.

MURSHIDABAD
Behrampore Tourist Lodge (12 km away). Reservations: Manager (Tel: 439), or WBTDC, Calcutta (Tel: 235917). Renowned for its silks.

SHANTINIKETAN
Tourist Lodge, Tel: 398, 399. **University Guest House**, Purba Pally, Bolpur, Tel: 651 Extn.87. Also a **Youth Hostel**, and **Inspection**, **Dak** and **Forest Bungalows** in Bolpur (2 km away).

VISHNUPUR
Lali Hotel, Poka Banoh, North Side. **Bharat Boarding**, Gopalganj. **Sri Hotel**, New Court. **Tourist Lodge**. Center for exquisite silk Baluchari and tussar sarees. Scarves and stoles in silk available; ivory and bellmetal-ware is notable.

BANKURA
Bankura, where the decorative terracotta horses are fashioned, is only 21 km from Vishnupur.

SUNDERBANS
Sunder Chital Tourist Lodge, Sajnekhali.

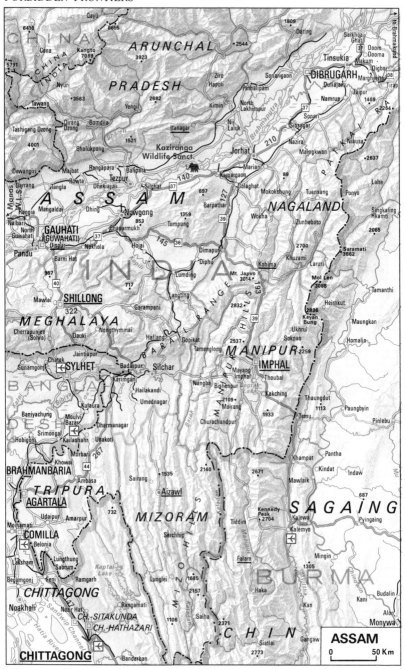

ASSAM

0   50 Km

1	Arunachal Pradesh	7	Assam
2	West Bengal	8	Nagaland
3	Himachal Pradesh	9	Meghalaya
4	Punjab	10	Manipur
5	Haryana	11	Tripura
6	Sikkim	12	Mizoram

FORBIDDEN FRONTIERS

SIKKIM AND THE NORTH-EASTERN STATES

Sikkim and the northeastern states are spread over some of the most beautiful parts of India. However, their proximity to the sensitive border regions poses certain problems for the traveler; some areas are completely closed to foreigners while others are accessible only with permits, which are now easily available.

SIKKIM

Sikkim is a tiny state (7,299 sq. km or 2,818 sq. mi) nestling in the Himalayas, and bordered by Nepal, China and Bhutan on the west, north and east, respectively. Kanchenjunga (8,603 m or 28,225 ft), the third highest peak in the world, is an awesome presence on the western boundary. Kanchenjunga is worshiped as a god who is the presiding deity of Sikkim; and also as the abode of the gods. Endowed with an exciting natural beauty, Sikkim is synonymous with orchids and vast forests of rhododendrons that cover the mountainsides. It is also the world's largest supplier of cardamom.

For a long time, Sikkim was an isolated Buddhist kingdom peopled by the Lepchas and Bhotias of Tibetan origin, and ruled by the Namgyals, also of Tibet.

Preceding pages: Himalayan splendor. A view of Kanchenjunga at sunrise.

In the 18th century, Sikkim had to fight the Bhutanese and the Nepalis. In the early years of the 19th century it was drawn into the Anglo-Nepal wars, after which increasing British interference led to the declaration of a protectorate over Sikkim in 1861. The British also encouraged the influx of Nepali labor into the kingdom; as a result, Nepalis now constitute 75 percent of Sikkim's population. In 1947 the new Indian government recognized Sikkim as an independent kingdom, but retained control of its foreign policy and defense. However, in 1975, monarchy was abolished; the Sikkim National Congress voted for the incorporation of Sikkim into India, and it was annexed amid much controversy.

Gangtok, the capital, is perched on a ridge at the height of 1,520 m (4,987 ft). It is a charming town which retains much of its traditional charm. The most interesting building in Gangtok is the **Tsuk-lakhang**, the royal chapel of the former rulers. The beauty of its traditional Sikkimese architecture is enhanced by the carved and painted woodwork, the murals and wallhangings, as well as the superb collection of Buddhist treasures. This is where royal ceremonies and important religious festivals took place. The *Kagyat* Dance, in celebration of the Sikkimese New Year, and the triumph of

153

good over evil, is still performed here. Nearby is the palace of the former rulers of Sikkim. The **Institute of Tibetology** has one of the finest collections of Buddhist literature and attracts scholars and researchers from all over the world. It also has a vast collection of *thangkas* (painted cloth scrolls), icons and ritual objects. On the mountain slopes near the Institute is an **Orchid Sanctuary**, where it is possible to see almost 500 varieties of orchids. There is also a **Deer Park**. Traditional wood carvings, paintings, textiles and bamboo-ware are available at the **Cottage Industries Institute**. Sikkim is also famous for its liqueur made from the pungent betel leaf.

Sikkim has 194 monasteries situated in secluded mountains, where the ancient religious rituals are still observed. They are also rich repositories of traditional art. **Rumtek** is 24 km (15 mi) from Gangtok and a monastery of significance. The head of the Kagyupa sect of Buddhism was given refuge in Sikkim when the Chinese overran Tibet. He was granted land to build a monastery and finally built Rumtek in the 1960s. It is a replica of the monastery in Tsruphu, Tibet, the residence of His Holiness and also the headquarters of the Dharma Chakra Religious Center. The **Pemayangtse Monastery** is perhaps the most important monastery in Sikkim, and its second oldest, although it has been rebuilt several times. At a height of 2,085 m (6,841 ft), it is an ideal base for exploring the mountains near **Bakhim** and **Dzongri**; the sacred spot of **Yuksom**, where the first Chogyal was crowned in 1642; and the most holy of all monasteries at **Tashiding**, in west Sikkim. The **Tashiding Ningma Monastery** was built in the 17th century.

ASSAM

Assam (78,523 sq. km or 30,318 sq. mi), sprawls across the Brahmaputra valley, south of Arunachal Pradesh and the kingdom of Bhutan. This lush, green land is dominated by the overpowering presence of the immense river and its 120 tributaries, which bring both prosperity and devastation to the land. The silt carried by the river has made the soil extremely fertile. The farmers say that all they have to do is plant the rice seedlings, and come back later to harvest a rich crop. The time in between is spent sleeping. However, the fury of the Brahmaputra in flood can be awesome. The Assamese are said to be a gentle, contented people, whose philosophy of life is *laahe laahe*, or "slowly slowly." They cannot understand the mad rush of city life.

Assam was the ancient Pragjyotishpura (light of the east) of the Kamrupa rulers. However, in the 13th century this kingdom was overrun by the Ahoms, a Buddhist Tai tribe who established their capital at Sibsagar. The Ahoms ruled until the 17th century. Thereafter, Assam was involved in political maneuvers between the Burmese and the British. The British finally took possession of the state, and with further annexations, created the province of Assam in 1874.

In the early 1980s Assam was plagued by agitation, staged against the threatening influx of immigrants, in particular from Bangladesh. The agitation was led by students who were successful in overthrowing the previous government. That problem has been resolved and, today, the state is governed by possibly the youngest political leaders in the world.

Guwahati (Gauhati) is the main city not only of Assam, but of the northeast, to which it is a gateway. It is adjacent to the capital, **Dispur**. Guwahati is located on the banks of the Brahmaputra and offers a magnificent view of the river. The city is famous for its **Kamakhya Temple** on the Nilachal Hills. It is one of the main centers of the Tantric cult and of Shakti worship in the country. The **Umananda Temple** is located on **Peacock Island** in the river, and accessible by boat.

Many visitors spend money here, knowing that it will help the priests who are stranded here during the monsoon months, when it is unsafe to cross the river. Other important temples here include the **Navagraha** (Temple of the Nine Planets) and the **Sulkeswar Janardhan**. Guwahati also has an interesting **State Museum**.

Two hours by road from Guwahati is the silk center of **Sualkuchi**. Here, almost every home is involved in the weaving of silk. Assam is famous for its natural golden colored silk (*muga*), which is the pride of the people. *Pat* and *Endi* are two other varieties of silk.

Assam is also well known for its tea gardens which were established by the British in 1836. Today, Assam contributes to more than half the total output of the country. **Jorhat** is the main town of the plantation district. This is oil country too; 10 percent of India's oil comes from Assam, which also boasts the oldest extant rig, dating to 1867. **Duliajan**, at the eastern end of the state is the center of the oil industry. At **Sibsagar**, 83 km (52 mi) northeast of Jorhat, are the scattered remains of monuments raised by the Ahom kings. Assam is perhaps best known for its **Kaziranga National Park**, home of the Indian rhinoceros. **Manas** is an equally fascinating sanctuary (see section on Wildlife).

NAGALAND

Nagaland (16,572 sq.km or 6,399 sq.mi) lies to the southeast of Assam and borders Burma. There are about 16 major Tibeto-Burmese tribes in Nagaland, collectively referred to by the generic term "Naga." The tribes there are differentiated by their language, sometimes by their hairstyles, and most strikingly by the large colorful shawls that Nagas wear as protection against the cold wind. Each tribe is proud of the distinguishing colors and patterns woven in their shawls.

155

Christian missionaries came to Nagaland in the 1870s, a little before the British took over the administration of the area. About 90 percent of the people are Christians, and they belong mainly to the American Baptist Mission. Education followed the arrival of the missionaries; the first school was built by them in **Kohima**, the capital.

Kohima is particularly known for its exceptionally well-maintained war cemetery which dates to World War II, and an encounter with the Japanese army. Soon after 1947, the Nagas formed the Naga National Council and also demanded autonomy, although some demanded independence for Nagaland. In what is referred to as the "Shillong Accord" of 1975, representatives of the Indian government and the Naga leaders reached an agreement whereby the Nagas accepted the Indian constitution. However, there are still some unsolved political problems that lead to occasional outbreaks of violence and unrest.

The Nagas possess extremely rich cultural traditions of which they are proud and in no hurry to replace with modern values. A visit to the **Mon** district bears testimony to this fact. Here, the ancient institution of tribal chieftainship still exists, with some chiefs claiming jurisdiction over villages as far as Burma. These chiefs are a rare and glorious sight with their huge ivory arm bands, intricate beaded jewelry, feathered headdress and the innate pride of dynastic rulers. Their palaces, which include opium gardens, are fine examples of tribal architecture.

In the past, Naga tribal warfare was often accompanied by ritualistic head-hunting, but this no longer exists. The fighting itself was dramatically executed, for the warriors wore beautiful clothes and used spears and huge swords decorated with tufts of goat hair dyed in madder. Head-hunting, practiced even by the Mizos, was traditionally seen by the Nagas as a means of enriching one's soul. They believed that the soul resided at the nape of the neck, and when the enemy's head was taken the soul escaped to the victorious warrior whose soul, in turn, was then enriched. The warlike nature of the Nagas also expressed itself in a spectacular war dance still performed by warriors today.

MEGHALAYA

The region of **Meghalaya** (22,489 sq.km or 8,683 sq.mi), to the south of Assam, is one of the most beautiful hill areas in India. Made up of gently rolling hills, the exquisite landscape is revered by the local inhabitants. The Laitkor range of mountains around the capital **Shillong** used to be worshiped by the local people who believed that their ancestors descended from heaven on a golden ladder to reside in these forests. The British hunted here and destroyed the traditional beliefs along with a unique method of forest preservation.

This state is known for its matrilineal system whereby women inherit wealth and enjoy considerable power. It is inhabited by three tribes - the Garos in the west, the Khasis in the central region and the Jaintias in the east. Their traditional rulers were the *sieyams*, with independent township kingdoms which the British annexed in the 19th century. However, not far from Shillong there still exists a traditional young *sieyam* living in a palace made of bamboo, thatch and wood, in the construction of which not a single nail is used because it is taboo. Every year in April, young virgins dressed in gold jewelry and silk perform a dance for the king. This is accompanied by feasting. Although the Christian influence in Meghalaya is considerable, local folk dances and traditions persist. The November festival in the Garo hills,

Right: The architecture of this village home is unique to Nagaland.

known as the "200 drum festival", celebrates the end of the harvesting season.
The change of seasons is often symbolized by festivals which keep their
traditions alive.

In the northeast area, it is in **Shillong**
that the British built their beautiful summer bungalows, a golf course and a polo
ground. The climate, very temperate at
the altitude of 1,500 m (4,921 ft), resulted
in the place being called the "Scotland of
the East". Dotted with English-country-
style houses, the present governor's
house, with a lake at the foot of its
sprawling garden, is the best example.
The **Pinewood Hotel** also offers a
country atmosphere with fireplaces lit for
guests each night. For a taste of authentic
local food, tiny restaurants in the **Bara
Bazaar** area are worth a visit. Shillong
was once known for the waterfalls cas-
cading from its hills but these days, due
to the exploitation of the forests, hardly
any waterfalls are seen.

South of Shillong lies **Cherrapunji**
which records the highest annual rainfall
in the world (1,150 mm or 45.25 in).
About 40 km (25 mi) east of Shillong, on
the wide plateau of Mawphlang, are some
giant stone monoliths, believed to have
been part of ancestor worship.

TRIPURA

Tripura (10,477 sq. km or 4,045 sq.
mi) is a small hilly state bordering Bangladesh. It claims to be the most ancient
of all princely states in India, with a recorded history that goes back to the days
of the *Mahabharata*. It was ruled by the
Maharajas for an unbroken period of
1,300 years. These Maharajas were often
at war with their neighbors, especially the
Nawabs of Bengal. Taking advantage of
this, the British intervened and established a protectorate. Tripura acceded to
the Indian Union in 1949. The **Tripura
Palace** in **Agartala**, the capital, is an exquisite piece of architecture set in a Mughal garden. It was built by the most famous ruler of Tripura, Maharaja Bhik-
ram. At the age of 13, he predicted

Rabindranath Tagore's future greatness and later helped him to establish Santiniketan. Tagore's house in Agartala was built by this king and is today an office.

Tripura's original inhabitants were several tribes of Tibeto-Burmese origin. The major tribes are the Reangs, Tamata, Tripuri, Lushai, Halam, and Kukis. Their folk heritage of music, dance, festivals and worship is based on *jhoom* (slash and burn) cultivation. Bamboo has an important role for it is used extensively in the everyday life of the tribes. Instead of worshiping specific deities, they worship the bamboo as a symbol of different gods. Their famous stage setting for marriages and the loom used for weaving are made entirely of bamboo. In recent years, the immense influx of displaced persons from Bangladesh has reduced these ethnic tribes to minorities.

To the south of Tripura lies **Unaikoti**, one of the four places of pilgrimage in the state. The other three are the **Tirthamuk** of **Amarpur**, the **Tripura Sundari Temple** of **Udaipur** and **Brahmakunda** of **Agartala**. The sacred and ancient Unaikoti was built in inaccessible hilly terrain to avoid destruction by non-believing raiders who destroyed religious buildings in West Bengal and Orissa. Magnificent rock figures and stone images dating to the 12th century are found here. Of these, the huge central figure of Siva deserves special mention. Every year, this area comes alive during the Pushmela festival.

MANIPUR

Manipur (22,356 sq. km or 8,632 sq. mi), extending to the south of Nagaland, was formerly a princely state. It is said that the rulers absorbed Hindu influences from neighboring royal houses. This resulted in the major tribe, the Meiteis, embracing Hinduism. The Meiteis, of Tibeto-Burmese origin, who live in the beautiful valleys, form 60 percent of the population. They have established so many cultural institutions, such as the Nehru Dance Academy and the Manipur State Kala Academy, that local people often say that in Manipur culture is an industry! The people are known for their excellence in martial arts, the spear dance and sword fight as well as wrestling. They also perform a graceful drum dance in which young men, clad in white from the waist down, leap into the air as though in flight, while beating elongated drums. However, Manipur is most famous for its *Jagoi* classical dance.

Imphal, the capital, is known for its market, run exclusively by women. Over 16,000 women, both from villages and the town, benefit from this daily market. For them, it is a place of social interaction as well as a commercial venture. Items sold range from gold jewelry and silks to dried mushrooms and snails. The **Matua Museum** houses a rare, private collection of objects from all over the northeast.

Manipur's **Logtak Lake** is the last remnant of a once extensive wetland ecosystem. This wetland area of the Imphal valley, the **Logtak-Keibut Lamjao** complex, is the beautiful home of a fishing community called Thanga-Karang and the only natural habitat of the extremely endangered brow antlered deer, the Sangai of Manipur. Logtak Lake is about an hour's drive from Imphal.

The people of Manipur celebrate the different moods of the changing seasons through dance. *Lai Haroaba*, usually performed between spring and the monsoon, is perhaps the most comprehensive feast of dances. It is believed to be as old as creation and is performed with great pomp before deities who were in existence long before Hinduism came to Manipur, and who are still particularly pleased by this dance. Traditional sports such as hockey, *mukna* or wrestling, and

Right: Konyak tribespeople from Nagaland. The man on the right is a tribal chief.

kang played on mud floors, follow these dance festivals. *Kang*, so named for the lacquer disc with which the game is played, is an ancient game mentioned in the famous Manipur epic called *Khamba Thoibhi*, a tale of a captured princess. *Kang* is a philosophical game, which stresses that the course of life is determined equally by skill and luck, and that happiness and sorrow are both a part of it. It is played only during the Manipuri New Year (Cheiraoba, on 2 April), in the belief that the game has ill effects on people if played at any other time.

MIZORAM

Mizoram (21,087 sq. km or 8,142 sq. mi) lies between Bangladesh and Burma. The Mizos still claim that half their population is in Burma and believe that when they die their souls will enter Burma following the course of the beautiful River Rih. Made up of the Lusei, Hmar and Pawih tribes, the people are termed Mizos. They came to the notice of the British when they began to raid the tea gardens of Assam. During one of these raids a tribal chief kidnapped and brought up as his child the daughter of a tea planter, an act which drew British expeditions into the rugged mountains. The British established control over this area in 1872 and, introducing the Inner Line system, allowed only missionaries to enter. This resulted in 95 percent of the population being converted to Christianity. The spread of education was also rapid and today Mizoram has the second highest rate of literacy in the country.

Mizoram's traditional rulers were the famous Sailos who ruled as chiefs with rights over land and life. The Sailos themselves shared a common ancestor and ruled dynastically. Their rule was abolished when modern politics entered the area in the 1950s. As rulers of an agricultural economy, each chief had within his court an agricultural expert who was well acquainted with those secrets of the forests essential for the slash and burn method of cultivation. The chief was also aided by the elders of the community, a village crier and a priest.

A famine was predicted in 1959 by "those who know, the elders." This warning was felt to have gone unheeded by administrators and the Central Government, and the famine caused numerous deaths in villages. The Mizos, trying to save themselves, organized a volunteer group called Mizo Famine Front which turned political and later became the Mizo National Front (MNF). The MNF went underground; but an accord was established with the Central Government in 1986, after almost 25 years of political turbulence.

The Mizos are also known to be fine weavers and to make beautiful baskets. They are a very musical people who consider singing the best form of relaxation after a day's work. Traditional Mizo society was nurtured on a unique code of behavior based on a philosophy called *tlawmngaihna* or selflessness. Traits of this can still be seen today, although the jostle for modernization can be jarring, especially in the capital, **Aizawl**. To the south of Aizawl is the idyllic second town called **Lungki**, set in a beautiful forested area. In between these two towns is **Serchhip** village. Travelers stop here to enjoy a market where traditional objects, fruits and local vegetables are sold daily.

ARUNACHAL PRADESH

Arunachal Pradesh (83,578 sq. km or 32,269 sq. mi) is the largest state in the northeast. Its capital, **Itanagar,** is a planned town built only in 1982.

Entry is difficult due to its strategic location on the frontier between India and China. The state has some 60,000 sq. km (23,166 sq. mi) of luxuriant and untouched tropical rain forests and an incredible variety of flora including 550 species of orchids alone. The 65 or so Mongolian and Tibeto-Burmese tribes remained uninfluenced by Christianity because the missionaries never reached here. The state is rich in tribal culture not to be found elsewhere in the northeast. In some areas one can still encounter self-sufficient tribes whose lifestyles are still untouched by modernization. The main tribes in this northeastern state are the Apatanis, Miris, Padams, Khamptis and Wangchos. These tribes weave exquisite cloth and baskets. They have a unique tradition of architecture wherein every feature is designed for a precise, practical use. The most famous tribe, the Apatanis, inhabiting the fertile plateau called Ziro, had evolved a high-yielding wet-rice cultivation long before the system was known in other parts of the northeast. This particular area is an anthropologist's paradise, where large villages retain their unique traditional lifestyle.

The holy lake of **Brahmakund** which joins the Brahmaputra in Assam is at the eastern end of the state. Thousands of Hindus bathe here in January on Makar Sankranti day in the hope of being cleansed of their sins.

In western Arunachal at an altitude of 3,050 m (10,006 ft) is **Tawang**, India's largest Buddhist monastery, 350 years old and the birthplace of the sixth Dalai Lama. The monastery is the center of the spiritual life of the Gelupa which is one of the four sects that arose during the growth of Buddhism in Tibet.

The monastery appears like a great fort protecting Tawang valley below it. The strategic location reflects the historical background of the development of Buddhism in Arunachal Pradesh. Its defensive structure, incorporated in the layout of the monastery, is due to past attacks from the Dukpas, another Buddhist sub-sect from Bhutan. Historically so much importance was given to defense that the founder of Tawang lifted all prohibitions against military activities by the inmates of the monastery. A huge library contains many precious scripts.

Restrictions

Restricted Area Permits (RAP) have to be obtained for all the places/states mentioned in this section. Applications should be made at least six weeks in advance to the Secretary, Ministry of Home Affairs (Foreigners Division), Goverment of India, Lok Nayak Bhavan, Khan Market, New Delhi 110003, Tel: 619709.

SIKKIM-GANGTOK
Accommodation
MODERATE: **Tashi Delek**, Mahatma Gandhi Marg, Tel: 2038, 2991. **Tibet**, Paljor Stadium Rd., Tel: 2568, 2523. *BUDGET:* **Nor Khill**, Tel: 3186/87. **Mayur**, Paljor Stadium Road, Tel: 2752, 2825. **Swagat**, Lall Bazar Rd., Tel: 2991.

GUWAHATI
Accommodation
MODERATE: **Brahmaputra Ashok**, M.G. Road, Tel: 32538, 32615. **Samrat**, A.T. Road, Santipur, Tel: 34542. *BUDGET:* **Belle Vue**, M.G. Road, Tel: 28291/92: **Prag Continental**, Motilal Nehru Rd., Pan Bazar, Tel: 33785. **Alka**, M.S. Road, Tel: 31767, 31751. **Expire**, Hem Barua Rd., Tel: 32670, 32211. **Nandan**, Paltan Bazar, G.S. Road, Tel: 32621-29.

Museums
Assam State Museum, Ambari, Tel: 24193, 10 am-4.30 pm, closed Mon and second Sat. **Assam Forest Museum**, South Kamrup Division,10 am-5 pm, Sat 10 am-3.30 pm, closed Sun.

Tourist Information
Government of India Tourist Office, B.K. Kakati Road, Ulubari, Tel: 31381. Information counter at the airport (Tel: 82204), on Station Road (Tel: 24475), and in Ulubari (Tel: 27102).

Access / Local Transport
Air connections (Indian Airlines and Vayudoot) are available to Delhi, Calcutta, Patna and all the capitals of the states/union territories of the Northeast. Several broad and meter gauge trains connect it to the rest of the country. Roads lead to Shillong, Manas, Kaziranga, Dimapur, Kohima, Itanagar, Darjeeling, Gangtok, Imphal and Agartala. Buses run by the governments of Assam, Meghalaya and Arunachal Pradesh ply between Guwahati and all important towns. Deluxe and video coach services also exist. A major tour operator is **Blue Hills Travel**, Paltan Bazaar, Tel: 31427. Modes of local transport are taxis, autorickshaws, tourist cars, jeeps, mini buses and cycle-rickshaws.

SHILLONG
Accommodation
BUDGET: **Pinewood Ashok**, Tel: 23116, 23765. **Alpine Continental**, Thana/Quinton Rd., Tel: 25361. **Broadway**, G.S. Road, Tel: 26996.

Shillong Tourist Hotel, Polo Road, Tel: 24933; **Hotel Godwin**, G.S. Road, Tel: 26516.
Museums
Meghalaya State Museum, State Central Library Building, 10 am-5 pm, closed Sundays and holidays. **Butterfly Museum**, Wankhar Co., Riatsamthiah.
Post / Telegraph Offices
General Post Office, Tel: 22162. Telegraph Inquiry, Tel: 22146.
Restaurants
CHINESE: **Abba**, Lower Lachumiere. **York**, Bara Bazar. *FAST FOOD/CONTINENTAL:* **Ambrosia**, Red Hill Road. **Ee Cee**, Police Bazar, Tel: 24058. *INDIAN:* **Steriling**, Mawkhar, Bara Bazar. **Kiron's**, Police Bazar, Tel: 22626.
Tourist Information
Government of India Tourist Office, G.S. Road, Police Bazaar, Tel: 25632. **Meghalaya Tourism Development Corporation**, Polo Ground, Tel: 26220, 24933. **Director of Tourism's Office**, Crowborough Building, Tel: 26054.
Access / Local Transport
Vayudoot flights serve Umroi airport, 20 km (from Calcutta, Silchar and Guwahati). Though not the nearest, Guwahati's Borjhar airport, 127 km, is convenient as several IA services link it to cities of east India and the northeast.
Accommodation

IMPHAL
Hotel Imphal Ashok, North AOC Point, Imphal Dimapur Road, Tel: 20459; **Hotel Deesh Deluxe**, Near Kali Bari, Khoyathong Road, Thanjal Bazaar, Tel: 20608; **Hotel White Palace**, 113 M.G. Avenue, Tel: 20599; **Hotel Diplomat**, Bir Tikendrafet Road, Tel: 20588.

AIZAWL
Hotel Shangrila, Bora Bazar. **Embassy Hotel**, Chandmari. **Tourist Bungalow & Lodge**, Chaltlang; **Hotel Chawlka**, Zarkawt, Tel: 2292.

KAZIRANGA
Forest Lodge and two **Tourist Lodges** (Tel: 29).

NAHARLAGUN (ITANAGAR)
An **Inspection Bungalow** and **Field Hostel** (Tel: ITN 275). Reservations: Chief Engineer, CPWD, Naharlagun.

AGARTALA
Broadway Guest House, Colonel Chowmohini, Palace Compound, Tel: 3122; **Hotel Meenakshi**, Khush Bagan, Tel: 5721; **Royal Guest House**, Kunjaban, Tel: 3826. Several hotels are located on H.S. Basak Road.

KOHIMA
Japfu Ashok, Tel: 272126. Both government-run lodges and private hotels.

1	Arunchal Pradesh	7	Assam
2	West Bengal	8	Nagaland
3	Himachal Pradesh	9	Meghalaya
4	Punjab	10	Manipur
5	Haryana	11	Tripura
6	Sikkim	12	Mizoram

WHERE FANTASY REIGNED

RAJASTHAN

GUJARAT

MADHYA PRADESH

RAJASTHAN

Rajasthan, more than any other state in India, brings to life enduring images of the exotic east, and in a way that surpasses the fancies of the most fertile imagination. Fairy-tale like forts and palaces in fairy-tale like settings dot the landscape, bearing witness to the increasingly opulent lifestyle of the rajas who ruled for several centuries. At the other end of the scale is a vigorous, thriving folk culture. It expresses itself in an explosion of color, in exuberant celebrations, in haunting music and an extraordinary delight in beauty, and is all the more remarkable in a people for whom existence itself is a continual struggle.

A Brief History

The great Thar Desert sprawls across western Rajasthan, covering more than half of the 342,274 sq. km (132,152 sq. mi) which comprise the state. Its scattered population consists largely of semi-nomadic peasants. Further east, the shifting sands are stalled by the Aravalli ranges - the oldest in India - which harbor river valleys and still, gleaming lakes.

Preceding pages: Scene at Pushkar fair. Left: A loyal retainer of a maharaja.

The bardic tradition is so strong in Rajasthan that it is often difficult to separate history from legend, as its history is so similar to the romance of legends. But there were settlements in Rajasthan long before the era celebrated in song. Archaeological finds have proved **Kalibangan** contemporaneous with the Indus Valley sites of Mohenjodaro and Harappa (3000 B.C. to 1500 B.C.), and as advanced. A pattern of tribal organizations survived through the turn of the millennium, during which time foreign tribes such as the Huns and the Scythians infiltrated through the northwest and mingled with the local population.

A change occurred around the 7th century A.D., when warrior clans called Rajputs (*rajputra*, sons of kings) carved out kingdoms for themselves in this region. Their origin is still a matter of debate, but it is known that these warrior clans confirmed their superiority through a purification by fire, which accorded them Kshatriya status, and by claiming mythical descent from the sun and the moon. They perpetuated this through their social status, profession and above all by a rigid code of honor. The latter included such hair-raising rites as the *jauhar*, a collective voluntary immolation which is performed by women in the face of defeat, in preference to the enemy's

165

harem. While the Rajputs never exceeded 8 percent of the population, they became the undisputed rulers of the land, though often at war with one another. For almost 1000 years they controlled the destiny of this desert state, governing their kingdoms through *jaghirdars*.

During the years of the Sultanate, the Rajputs were constantly at war with the Sultans of Delhi, not least of all because Rajasthan was on an important trade route to the ports of Gujarat. Fortunes seesawed for almost 400 years. It took all the shrewdness of Akbar, the Mughal Emperor, to resolve the situation. He recognized that the support of the Rajputs was essential for the realization of a stable empire. He won them over, not with battle, but through matrimonial alliances. Thus Rajput princesses entered the Mughal harem, but in keeping with Akbar's policies, were not converted to Islam. In fact, temples were built within

Above: The magical Hawa Mahal, the Palace of Wind in Jaipur.

the palaces for their worship. In exchange for acknowledging his supremacy, Akbar granted Rajput rajas positions in his court and army, as well as lavish incomes. Defiance, however, incurred the relentless employment of the Mughal army; Chittor remains the outstanding example, Rana Pratap the outstanding hero.

With the gradual decline of the Mughal Empire in the 18th century and the absence of allegiance to a single ruler, the Rajputs once again succumbed to infighting. They eventually found themselves as protectorates of the British, with a British Resident in each state. In fact, they supported the British during the Revolt of 1857 and, during the years of the freedom struggle, became the "Pillars of the Empire." They were pampered with titles and *durbars* and the formation of the "Chamber of Princes." Independent India offered these princes the option of merging with India or Pakistan, making it clear that the government would not relish the existence of independent Rajput states within the Indian union. Since partition was largely based on religion, it was inappropriate for Hindu rulers to merge with Pakistan.

Rajasthan after Independence

On 31 March 1949, the United State of Greater Rajasthan was created as an administrative unit, with the merger of 22 princely states, and the rulers of Udaipur and Jaipur as the acknowledged heads. Ajmer conceded a few years later and on 1 November 1956, the state of Rajasthan came into being. The Rajput rulers enjoyed a Privy Purse and other privileges until 1970, when these were abolished at the instance of Indira Gandhi.

Apart from the states of Jaipur and Bikaner, which were blessed with some extraordinary rulers, the Rajput era did not encourage economic progress. While the subjects enjoyed the protection of their ruler, little else was done for them. The rulers themselves, however, maintained lavish courts which, in turn, nurtured the development of art and crafts. Painting, in particular, flourished in the late medieval era. Beginning in the 16th and 17th centuries Mewar, Bundi, Kota, Kishangarh, Marwar and Bikaner were the thriving centers of miniature painting. Rajasthan still has an extraordinarily rich tradition of crafts even though it reflects new patronage. Folk traditions, which have proved to be as resilient as the people of the desert, are centered around legendary heroes, such as Pabuji, Ramdeoji, Tejaji, Jambhoji and Gogaji. They are believed to possess supernatural powers and are propitiated for the well-being of the community. The scattered settlements of rural Rajasthan led to the establishment of numerous fairs, which are held in accordance with the lunar calendar, at locations often sanctified by ancient myth. These fairs combine the celebration of a religious festival with commercial transactions, and, best of all, express the vitality of the desert folk.

Rajasthan harbors a great ethnic variety: among the more prominent tribes are the Bhils, the Meenas, the Garasiyas, Meghwals and Kalbeliyas.

Since independence, considerable progress has been initiated, especially in the spheres of industry, water supply, education and irrigation. The Indira Gandhi Canal is bringing Himalayan waters into the heart of the desert. Whether it can successfully bring about the transformation of peasants into agriculturists remains to be seen. Large areas of the state remain backward and many tribal communities, for better or for worse, are resistant to change.

While the major cities of Rajasthan are connected by air and rail, there also exists an enticing network of roads; one of the most pleasant ways to discover this state is by road, and in winter.

Jaipur

Jaipur, the capital of Rajasthan, is also one of its most fascinating cities. It was established in 1728 by Raja Jai Singh II, and its very inception was propitious. Jai Singh was no ordinary man. He came from the wealthy house of Amer, whose rulers had served four successive Mughal emperors with fierce loyalty.

In building Jaipur, Jai Singh's vision incorporated more than architectural splendor; for with the help of the chief architect, Vidyadhar, he gave India her first planned city in the sprawling plains 11 km (7 mi) from Amer. The growing population is taking its toll, and it may be difficult to discern a plan in the prevailing chaos, but from the heights of **Nahargarh Fort** it is still clearly visible.

The city is divided into nine squares, each signifying a treasure of Dhanpati, the god of wealth. The regal spaciousness of the **City Palace** at the center gives way to markets and residences set out on a grid and contained within the crenelated walls that once marked the boundary

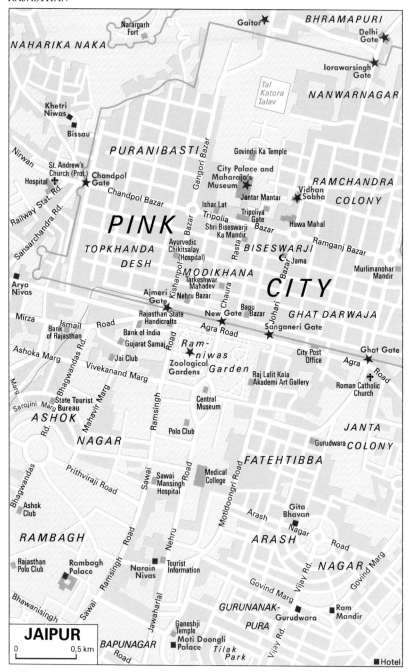

NARARGARH Fort

Gaitor

BHRAMAPURI

Delhi Gate

Iorawarsingh Gate

NAHARIKA NAKA

Tal Katora Talav

NANWARNAGAR

Khetri Niwas

Bissau

PURANIBASTI

Gangori Bazar

Govindji Ka Temple

City Palace and Maharaja's Museum

RAMCHANDRA COLONY

Nirwan

St. Andrew's Church (Prot.)

Chandpol Gate

Jantar Mantar

Vidhan Sabha

Hospital

Chandpol Bazar

Ishar Lat

Tripolia

Tripoliya Gate

Railway Stat. Rd.

PINK

Bazar

Shri Biseswarji Ka Mandir

Bazar

Hawa Mahal

Ramganj Bazar

Sansarchandra Rd.

TOPKHANDA

DESH

Ayurvedic Chikitsalay (Hospital)

Kishanpol

Rasta

BISESWARJI

Jama

Murlimanohar Mandir

Arya Nivas

MODIKHANA

Tarkeshwar Mahadev

Chaura

CITY

Mirza

Ajmeri Gate

Nehru Bazar

Bazar

Johari

Bank of Rajasthan

Rajasthan State Handicrafts

New Gate

Bapu Bazar

GHAT DARWAJA

Ismail

Road

Bank of India

Agra Road

Sanganeri Gate

Ghat Gate

Ashoka Marg

Bhagwandas Rd.

Gujarat Samaj

Ram-niwas

City Post Office

Agra

Road

Marg

Jai Club

Vivekanand Marg

Zoological Gardens

Garden

Raj Lalit Kala Akademi Art Gallery

Roman Catholic Church

Sarojini Marg

State Tourist Bureau

Mahavir Marg

Ramsingh

Central Museum

JANTA

ASHOK

NAGAR

Polo Club

Gurudwara

COLONY

Bhagwandas

Prithviraji Road

Sawai

Road

Medical College

FATEHTIBBA

Motidoongri Road

Ashok Club

Sawai Mansingh Hospital

Gita Bhavan

RAMBAGH

Ramsingh

Nehru

Arash

Nagar

ARASH

Road

NAGAR

Rajasthan Polo Club

Rambagh Palace

Narain Nivas

Tourist Information

Govind Marg

Vijay Rd.

Govind Marg

Bhawanisingh

Sawai

Jawaharlal

Govind Marg

GURUNANAK-PURA

Gurudwara

Ram Mandir

Ganeshji Temple

Moti Doongli Palace

Tilak Park

BAPUNAGAR

Road

Vijay Rd.

JAIPUR

0   0,5 km

■ Hotel

which was pierced by seven gateways. The buildings are characterized by balconies, tiny windows, courtyards, cupolas and arched entrances. The city was given a wash of pink for the visit of Prince Albert in 1876 (though there is some debate about this) and the color has since been maintained. Bazaars were planned along the main street and the number of shops on each side was specified, as was the layout of houses above. Areas were allocated according to professions and this kind of zoning survives. Generations of dyers, jewelers, stone carvers, miniature painters and hand block printers, to name a few, have inhabited the same localities for over 200 years.

A Sustained Vitality

Being the shrewd man that he was, Jai Singh made it obligatory for nobles to build houses within the city, which led to Jaipur becoming prosperous very fast. Many of these miniature palaces, such as **Bissau House** and **Khetri Niwas** near **Chand Pol**, are hotels today. The gods were not forgotten either; the religious fervor that prevailed in Amer overflowed into Jaipur, attracting Vaishnavs and Jains to build temples. While north India reeled under Nadir Shah's invasion, Jaipur remained an untouched haven. Traders, jewelers and bankers fled the bloodbaths at Delhi and Agra, and found refuge in Jaipur. So, from its very start Jaipur was a commercial hub.

Today, Jaipur is probably one of the fastest growing cities in India, and it has spread far beyond the pink crenelated walls. It presents a fascinating picture of a city where remarkable growth, evolution and change are sustained by tradition. Its magnificent forts and palaces, now thrown open for a glimpse of erstwhile splendor, are among its major attractions. A contemporary vitality also pervades the city which is the largest emerald cutting center in the world. Jaipur is

also renowned for its enameled jewelry and other precious stones. (**Gem Palace** on M.I. Road is a recommended jewelry store.) In the process of satisfying princely demands, Jaipur was a place where no craftsman ever sat idle. The city is particularly well known for its textiles, hand block printed and tie dyed, its blue pottery, carpets, miniature artists and puppets. Entrepreneurs have excelled in adapting ancient skills to modern designs (see **Anokhee** on Yudhishtir Marg). Antique shops abound, and many are outside the gates of the City Palace.

To explore the depths of the old city is also to explore the overwhelming profusion of traditional crafts. At **Khajane Walon Ka Rasta** there are marble carvers; **Rangwalon ki Gali** specializes in tie and dye craftsmen; at **Maniharon Ka Rasta** craftsmen make lacquer bangles; at **Johari Bazaar** and **Gopalji Ka Rasta** there are jewelers at work.

Royal Splendors

Part of the **City Palace** is still the residence of the ex-Maharaja; part of it is a **museum**. It warrants an extended visit, displaying some of the treasures of the wealthiest rulers of Rajasthan. The palace itself bears witness to an era of extravagance. There is the famous **Peacock Courtyard**, above which rises the **Chandra Mahal** where the Maharaja lives; there one can find gorgeous carpets, gilded thrones, finely worked doors, windows and a plethora of regal accessories. The last include two giant silver urns made specially for Maharaja Madho Singh to carry Ganga water to England, where he went to witness the coronation of Edward VII.

Just outside the City Palace is **Jantar Mantar**, the largest stone observatory in the world, built between 1728 and 1734 by Jai Singh II. The nearby spectacular **Hawa Mahal,** or Palace of Wind, was built by Maharaja Pratap Singh in 1799.

The façade of this quaint five-story structure is marked by 953 niches and windows. It is likely that the Hawa Mahal was used by royal ladies to observe the outside world.

Across Ajmer Road, between **Ajmeri Gate** and **Sanganeri Gate**, are the famous **Ram Niwas Gardens**, laid out by Ram Singh II in 1868. The **Central Museum** is housed here in the **Albert Hall**, whose foundation was laid by Prince Albert. Ram Singh also built the **Rambagh Palace**. Until a few decades ago Rambagh was the fabulous residence of the late Maharaja Man Singh II, but like many other palaces in Rajasthan it is now a hotel (see Nostalgia Tour).

No trip to Jaipur is complete without a visit to **Amer Fort** (11 km or 7 mi), the original seat of the ruling house. Amer is one of the most beautiful palaces in Rajasthan. Raja Man Singh I (1586-1614), among the first Rajputs to serve

Above: In the temple of Karni Mata at Deshnoke. Right: Camels in the Thar desert.

the Mughal emperor Akbar, gave shape to Amer Palace. His royal residence (at the far end) is stark in comparison to the palaces added later by Mirza Raja Jai Singh and Jai Singh II. In the short span of a few decades Mughal influences permeated the Rajput courts. These are evident in the ornate **Sheesh Mahal**, the **Hall of Private Audience**, the **Sukh Mahal**, in the painted **Ganesh Pol** and the **Suhag Mandir**. At least half a day should be kept aside for Amer Fort.

Behind it are the eerie remains of a ruined city; down below, in the valley, is the ancient city of Amer. The ramparts of Amer are linked to the higher, rugged **Jaigarh Fort**, built in 1726, and recently opened to the public. Jaigarh is supposed to contain an enormous treasure, which led to what was perhaps the largest treasure hunt in modern times. Nothing, however, was found, but the stories multiplied. The road to Jaigarh also links **Nahargarh**, a pleasure resort for the queens built by later Maharajas. Nahargah offers superb views of Jaipur, revealing the spread of the modern city almost to the sand dunes in the far west.

Alwar and the National Parks

The history of **Alwar** (150 km or 93 mi northeast of Jaipur) dates back to 1500 B.C., but it emerged as an independent state in the 18th century, under Pratap Singh. Often bypassed by travelers for the greater attractions of Jaipur, Alwar is not without its charms, and typifies the capital of a comparatively small Rajput state. The **Bala Fort** rises 300 m (984 ft) above the city (visitors must obtain permission). The immense **City Palace** is partially occupied by some government offices, but the **Alwar Museum** has a fine collection of sculpture, armory, manuscripts and paintings. At **Sillisehr** (8 km or 5 mi) is a secluded summer palace (now a hotel) by the edge of a lake nestling in the midst of the Aravalli hills.

Bharatpur has the historic **Lohagarh Fort** and **Museum**, but is better known for its bird sanctuary. For details of the sanctuaries at Bharatpur, **Ranthambhore** and **Sariska**, see the article on "Wildlife."

Shekhavati

North of Jaipur lies an area (starting from Sikar) known as **Shekhavati**, where *marwari* businessmen built their country houses in the 18th and 19th centuries. Shekhavati is now renowned for its murals and for these former financial wizards of Rajasthan.

The Marwaris, the indigenous traders of northern Rajasthan (Marwar) were said to be gifted with a rare business acumen. They evolved a unique tradition of trading and business management which, guarded by strong community ties, has seen their recent transformation from small-time traders to the industrial giants of modern India. Today, a large percentage of India's industrial houses are owned by Marwaris who manage to keep pace with the times without losing the distinctive characteristics of their community. Their country homes in Shekhavati are traditional *havelis*, multi-storied, with complex architectural plans that often incorporate two or more courtyards. They are particularly fascinating for the murals that enliven their façades, and for their ornately carved doors and windows. These murals depict a wide range of images – from vivid equestrian figures and *shikars*, to details of life of the nobility, and gods and goddesses.

Sikar is 110 km (68 mi) from Jaipur; en route is **Samod,** known for its glittering palace where part of *The Far Pavilions* was filmed. Sikar has a fort and the Biyani *havelis*. From here, within a range of 150 km (93 mi), are several of the renowned Shekhavati homes. They are to be found at **Nawalgarh**, which also has a fort; **Dundhlod** (guests may stay in a part of the fort); **Mandawa** (where there is the Castle Hotel and the even more exotic Desert Camp in the midst of sand dunes);

Fatehpur; **Mahansar** (here, the Soney Chandi ki Haveli is particularly exquisite); **Jhunjunu**, and **Churu**.

Bikaner

Bikaner is a desert outpost that was a major trading center on the old caravan route from Central Asia even before the Rathor prince, Rao Bika, the second son of the founder of Jodhpur, captured it in 1486.

The immense **Junagadh Fort** was begun in 1587 by Raja Rai Singh, a contemporary of Akbar's. It comprises 37 palaces with pavilions, mosaic courtyards, carved balconies and temples. Though it is used by the erstwhile royal family only for ceremonial occasions, the fort is in a fine state of preservation and a section of it is opened to visitors. The **Shish Mahal**, the **Grand Durbar Hall**, the 17th-century **Karan Mahal** and the **Phool Mahal** bring to life the grandeur of a bygone era. Daily worship is offered by hereditary priests at the **Har Mandir**. The fort **museum** has a rare collection of Sanskrit and Persian manuscripts, and miniature paintings. On the outskirts of the city is the **Lalgadh Palace**, designed in the last decade of the 19th century by Sir Swinton Jacob for the Maharaja Ganga Singh. Lalgadh is partly occupied by the ex-Maharaja (who is an Olympic marksman), and has been partly converted into a hotel managed by the Welcomgroup. With its hunting trophies, its billiard and smoking rooms and library, it remains a fine example of the lifestyle of the later, westernized Rajputs.

Two museums are located in the city - the **Rajasthan State Archives** and the **Bikaner Museum**. The old city, especially the area around **Kot Gate,** is in lively contrast to the serenity of royal enclosures. The bazaars abound with local handicrafts – camel-hide water bottles, slippers, purses and lampshades, camel-hair blankets, durries and carpets. In fact,

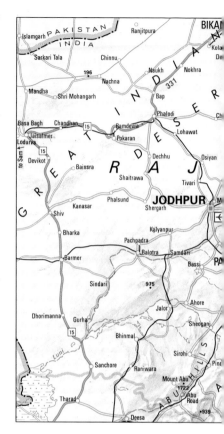

camels are very much a part of the scene here; a visit to the camel breeding farm, 10 km (6 mi) from Bikaner makes an interesting outing. At **Deshnoke** (30 km or 19 mi south), there is a temple to the miracle-working Karni Mata. The temple of this titular deity of the Rathors of Bikaner is well known for its rats, which scuttle unharmed and free all over the place.

Kishangarh, Ajmer and Pushkar

Kishangarh (100 km or 62 mi from Jaipur on the Ajmer road) was founded in 1611 by Kishan Singh, brother of the Raja of Jodhpur. It is renowned in the world of art for the superb miniatures painted here in the 18th century. The

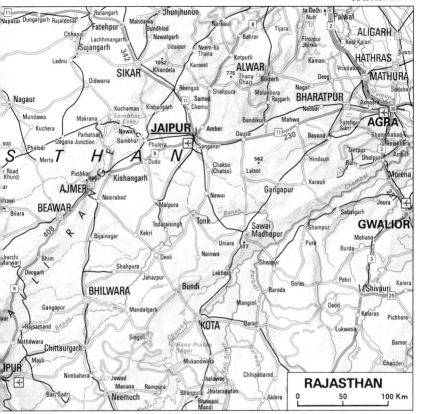

flourishing studios were further enriched by the influx of famous artists, including Surat Ram and Nihal Chand, who fled the puritanism of Aurangzeb's court. The love of Krishna and Radha, portrayed in a courtly rather than the usual, pastoral setting was the theme of most of the paintings, now known as the Kishangarh school. Modern Kishangarh is an important wholesale market for red chillies, but the old city, about 3 km (1.5 mi) away, retains its medieval ambience, though not its art.

Ajmer, 30 km (19 mi) further west, is situated in a picturesque valley surrounded by the Aravalli range. It was founded in the 7th century by Ajaipal Chauhan. He named it Ajaimeru, the "in-vincible hill," because here he built **Ta-ragarh**, India's first hill fort. The importance of this city rests in the **Dargah Sharif**, where the Sufi saint Khwaja Muin-ud-din Chishti is buried. The saint was born in Sanjar, Persia, in 1142 and probably came to India with the army of Muhammad Ghur, in 1191. He died in 1236, by which time he was recognized as a saint and protector of the poor. Today, his devotees extend beyond the pale of Islam. Throughout the year, a steady stream of pilgrims visit the Dargah, which is situated in the heart of the old city. Taragarh, which provides a backdrop to the shrine, is accessible by road via Nallah Bazaar. Adjacent to the shrine is the **Adhai din ka Jhonpra**, an

173

ancient Sanskrit college which was converted into a mosque in 1198 and remains one of the finest monuments of medieval India. Ajmer also has the excellent **Government Museum**, a 19th-century **Jain Temple** and the **Anasagar Lake** which was built in 1150. The beauty of this lake, situated between hillocks, is enhanced by the marble pavilions and embankments created by Shah Jahan.

Pushkar is situated just 11 km (7 mi) northeast of Ajmer. Sacred to the Hindus, it is associated with Brahma, who is believed to have slain a demon with a lotus. The petals fell at three spots, where lakes emerged. Pushkar is one of the very few places where there is a temple dedicated to Brahma. The town itself has over 400 temples, and the sacred lake there is surrounded by 52 *ghats* (embankments) built by kings and nobles. For most of the year, Pushkar is a sleepy town, absorbed in religious activities. But for 12 days prior to the November full moon it becomes the venue for the Pushkar fair, which is the largest camel fair in the world. A scene, almost Biblical in character, begins to unfold on the silent dunes west of the town. Villagers from all over Rajasthan converge here to buy and sell camels, camping out in the open. Three days before the full moon, the women come in their exotic finery. They bathe in the lake and offer worship, and they partake of the delights of the fairground. The Pushkar fair, which attracts several thousand people, is one of the most spectacular sights of Rajasthan, overwhelming in its magnitude and its visual impact.

Jodhpur

Jodhpur, the former capital of Marwar State is the gateway to the Thar Desert. The maharajas of Jodhpur belong to the Rathor clan. In 1453, Rai Jodha con-

Right: View of the blue quarter of Jodhpur, behind Mehrangarh Fort.

quered the area that is now Jodhpur and which takes its name after him.

In 1459, he raised the majestic **Mehrangarh Fort** which towers above an isolated rock, 130 m (427 ft) above the modern and bustling city. The sheer, soaring walls, topped by cupolas and balconies, enclose palaces, barracks, stables, temples and gunpowder magazines. These are reached via several imposing gateways along a circuitous ascent. Each of the gateways commemorates an historic victory or deity. **Loha Pol**, the Iron Gate, bears the handmarks of several women who became *satis* by immolating themselves on the funeral pyres of their husbands. (The last *sati* in the Jodhpur royal family was as recent as 1953.)

Loha Gate gives way to the **Nagnechiji Temple** dedicated to the family deity of the Rathors of Jodhpur. The wide and commanding ramparts of the fort, on which there is an array of cannons, offers spectacular views of the city below.

The royal palaces built by successive rulers have been converted into a **museum** which houses some superb treasures. Among these are gold and silver elephant *howdahs*, and a portable Mughal tent which was elaborate enough to serve as the emperor's hall of private audience at camp. The 19th-century **Takhat Vilas**, the Maharaja's bedroom, has some exquisite paintings. At the **Chokhevala Rang Mahal** (the Garden Palace), dinner is organized by prior arrangement, and guests are entertained by so called Langas, traditional folk musicians of the desert.

On the way to the Fort is the **Jaswant Thada**, the elegant marble cenotaph of Jaswant Singh II (1899) as well as those of other maharajas cremated here. Jodhpur city dates to the 16th century. **Jalori** and **Siwanchi Gates** are the nerve center. Those interested in shopping can look out for Jodhpur's specialties – embroidered leather shoes at **Mochi Galli**, tie and dye fabrics, lacquerware and puppets. Not far

from the modern air force base extends Jodhpur's other claim to fame – the **Umaid Bhavan Palace** (see Nostalgia Tour). There are several antiques shops along the approach to the palace.

All the major hotels in Jodhpur organize a "desert safari," which offers a close up view of rural Rajasthan. It also includes several villages of the Bishnois, who have been active environmentalists since the 15th century. The founder of this sect, Jambeshwar, was born in 1451 at Papasar village. He grew to be exceptionally aware of the cycle of nature and formulated the 29 (*bis-noi*) principles. Some of these principles deal with social and moral codes, but the most interesting are involved with the environment, and are rigidly followed even today.

There are other places of interest near Jodhpur. **Mandore** (9 km or 6 mi) has remains of the old capital, elaborate cenotaphs, and a hall commemorating folk heroes and numerous Hindu gods. **Balsamand** (7 km or 4 mi) has an artificial lake, a summer palace and a bird sanc-

tuary. At Osiyan (60 km or 37 mi) are Hindu and Jain temples dating to the 8th and 9th centuries.

Bundi and Kota

Though off the beaten track, **Bundi** (200 km or 124 mi south of Jaipur) is one of the enchanted spots of Rajasthan. **Bundi Palace** rises from the verdant shores of the **Naval Sagar Lake**, in a setting that brings to mind the delicacy of a miniature painting. The interior of the palace is mostly in disrepair, except for the **Chitra Shala** which has exquisite murals of the Bundi school of painting which thrived under Rao Bhao in the second half of the 17th century. Above the palace is **Taragarh Fort** where there are large reservoirs, and from where there is also an excellant view of **Sukh Sagar**, the other lake. The erstwhile Maharaja lives in **Phool Mahal**, on the shores of **Phool Sagar**. James Tod, the indomitable chronicler of Rajasthan's history, lived here as guardian to the young

Bishen Singh. His *Annals and Antiquities of Rajasthan* is a vivid portrait of 19th-century Rajasthan.

Kota, 37 km (23 mi) southeast of Bundi, is on the banks of the turbulent Chambal river. It has a far more imposing palace and fort, maintained by the Rao Madho Singh Museum Trust. But it lacks the charm of Bundi, with which it formed part of Haravati, the "garden" of the Hara clan. Kota became a separate state in 1624 and was also an important center for miniature painting. Today it is one of the most industrialized towns in Rajasthan, and still famous for its gossamer-fine *Kota doria* sarees.

Udaipur

Udaipur was founded in 1567 by Rana Udai Singh II after the third sack of

Chittor by the Mughal army of Akbar. The Ranas of Udaipur belong to the Sisodia clan of Mewar, a dynasty that has ruled for 1400 years. The Sisodias trace their ancestry to Bapa Rawal (A.D. 728) and are the oldest of Rajasthan's ancient dynasties. They also offered the fiercest resistance to the Mughals; in this connection, Rana Pratap was a legend in his lifetime. No princess of Chittor, their earlier capital, ever entered the Mughal harem.

Udaipur has the air of a tranquil pleasure resort, far removed from the vigor of Rajput heroism. The skyline is dominated by the **City Palace**, the largest palace complex in Rajasthan. Despite numerous additions architectural unity has been maintained within the sheer walls that overlook **Pichola Lake**. Much of the glitter and dazzle of the City Palace is preserved as a **Museum**, the **Mor Chowk**, the **Ruby Palace**, the **Krishna Vilas** and the **Osara** being particularly elaborate. The former royal guest house, the **Shiv Niwas** is now one of the most luxurious hotels in Udaipur.

Above: City Palace, Udaipur. Right: Performing a daily chore in good spirit, Jaisalmer.

Outside the City Palace is the **Jagdish Temple** (1651) dedicated to Vishnu as Lord of the Universe. There is a fine image of the Garuda (half man, half bird), Vishnu's mount. To wander through the bazaars is one of the greatest delights of this city. In **Bara Bazaar** and **Bapu Bazaar**, both near the palace, one can watch craftsmen at work. Udaipur specializes in *lahariya bandhani* (a tie and dye method which patterns waves of color), *pichwais* (paintings on cloth traditionally hung behind the image of Krishna at Nathdwara), enameled jewelry, gorgeously attired puppets, wooden toys, figures of animals studded with beads and mirrors, and copper and silverware.

Lake Pichola

Lake Pichola has two islands; on one is the 16th-century **Jag Mandir**, famous for having provided refuge to Prince Khurram before he became Shah Jahan. On the other is the **Jag Niwas Lake Palace**, today a fabulous hotel (see Nostalgia Tour). Among the other attractions of this city are the Rose Garden at **Sajjan Niwas**; the **Machchalaya Magra** hill which offers a spectacular view of the lake and city; the **Bhartiya Lok Kala Mandal** which has done outstanding work in preserving and documenting folk traditions; and the **Saheliyon ki Bari**, a garden enlivened by a complex network of fountains. A recent attraction on the outskirts of the city is **Shilpgram**, a rural arts and crafts "village," where craftsmen and performing artistes of rural Gujarat, Goa, Maharashtra and Rajasthan pursue their professions.

Chittor (112 km or 70 mi) has witnessed all the blood, battle, chivalry and heroism associated with Rajputs. Once capital of the Mewars, from the 7th to the 16th century, **Chittorgarh** is one of the most spectacular forts in Rajasthan. It crowns a 180-m (591 ft) high hill and covers some 280 hectares (692 acres).

The town was sacked three times – by Alauddin Khilji in 1303, by the Sultan of Gujarat in 1535 and by Akbar in 1567.

Thousands of women committed *jauhar* and even more men lost their lives. Some of the most romantic legends are associated with Padmini, the beautiful queen whom the Khilji Sultan desired. Within the fort are several palaces, a victory tower visible from miles away, and many temples including one where Mirabai, the 16th-century mystic, worshipped.

Mt. Abu and Ranakpur

Mt. Abu and **Ranakpur**, situated west and north of Udaipur, respectively, have the finest Jain temples in Rajasthan. Mt. Abu also affords another glimpse of the state's varied landscape, for here the forested Aravalli hills rise to their highest point at Guru Shikhar (1,721 m or 5,646 ft), creating a picturesque hill resort in the heart of the desert. **Gaumukh Temple**, 4 km (2.5 mi) below Mt. Abu has a shrine dedicated to Vishnu in his Rama and Krishna incarnations. This is believed to be the location of the ancient fire purification ceremony which bestowed Kshatriya status on warrior clans who then claimed to be Rajputs born of fire. Richly associated with myths and long revered as a sacred place, Mt. Abu is best known as a Jain pilgrim center.

The fine marble temples of **Dilwara** (*devalvara*, province of temples) dating from between the 11th and 13th centuries, represent the richest phase of Jain temple architecture. While these temples are as profusely carved as their Hindu counterparts, they are in essence different. The difference stems from the Jain view of life.

The world, according to the Jain belief, is not illusion; nor does it represent the myriad aspects of a Supreme Being. In fact, it is constituted of full and heavy matter, from which the spirit must seek to escape by asceticism. Even the gods, though they may be of a more subtle substance, belong to the material realm. The spirit alone is luminous. It is this belief that determines the "ponderous inflexibility" of Jain sculpture.

Another characteristic is the rigid depiction of the *Tirthankara* (one who has made the crossing through the torrent of rebirth). The Jains believe that there were 23 *Tirthankaras*; the twenty-fourth was Mahavira, a contemporary of the Lord Buddha and the founder of Jainism. These Jain saviors alone have reached the state of absolute perfection. In doing so they have purged themselves of all idiosyncrasies which color life; they are released, perfect and aloof. This spiritual aloofness is indicated by the rigid symmetry and immobility of their stance.

The impressive **Rishabhnath Temple** was built by the banker Vimala Sha of Gujarat and consecrated in 1031. The plan of this sanctuary incorporates several chapels and 232 columns. Opposite

Right: A piece of silk from Rajasthan, bright and colorful.

178

this temple is the **Neminath temple** dedicated to the twenty-second *Tirthankara*, and built in 1232 by two brothers, Tejapala and Vastupala. In the immense **Hall of Donors** are the carved figures of donors behind monumental elephants. In both these temples the marble has been worked to a shell-fine, translucent thinness, not by chiseling, but by rubbing. It is said that the workers were paid according to the quantity of marble dust they produced. Also at Mt. Abu are the **Raj Bhawan Art Gallery and Museum**, the popular **Nakki Lake** and, some distance away, **Trevor's Tank**, a pool encircled by a bird sanctuary. **Abu Road** (27 km or 17 mi) is the railhead, and the medieval town abounds in shops selling ritual offerings.

Ranakpur, on the banks of the Magai, is a serene and secluded place, nestling at the foot of the Aravallis. The **Adinath Temple** was completed in 1432. It was raised by a Jain merchant, Dharna Saha of Dhanera. This three-storied marble temple is one of the largest Jain temples in India and as profusely carved as the Dilwara temples, though its plan is *chaumukh* (four-faced). The temple has 29 halls and 1,444 pillars, and its sculptures incorporate various figures from Hindu mythology as well. Evening worship is particularly interesting here. There is a smaller **Parasnath Temple** as well as a **Sun Temple**. The beauty of Ranakpur is enhanced by its remoteness; nothing exists there apart from the temple and amenities for pilgrims.

Jaisalmer

Jaisalmer, connected by road, rail and air, should feature on the itinerary of travelers who wish to experience the splendor of the desert. Here, about 800 years ago, an awesome citadel was raised on **Tricuta Hill**, which overlooks a vast and barren plain. In 1156, a Bhatti Rajput prince named Jaisal decided to move his

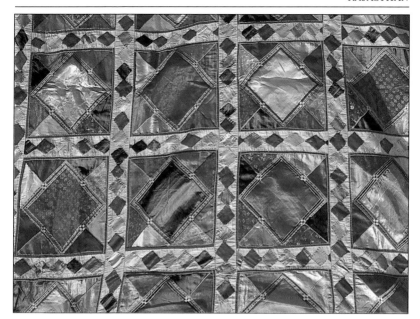

capital from Lodurva (16 km or 10 mi). He consulted the hermit Eesul, who told him of Lord Krishna's prediction that a descendant of his lunar clan would rule from Tricuta. Since the Bhattis belonged to this lineage, Jaisal saw himself as the one chosen to fulfil this prophecy.

Jaisalmer was on the spice route until the 18th century, when it was bypassed by the opening of Bombay port. Its history is somewhat akin to that of other Rajput states; only the Bhattis were particularly feared as marauders, ready to inflict violence for the smallest gain. They were constantly at war with neighboring clans, especially those of Jodhpur and Bikaner. But they had to change their tactics with the Sultans, agreeing to pay tribute in order to preserve their independence.

Even so, the mighty fort was attacked twice by the Muslims. Alauddin Khilji's army laid siege for seven years; eventually the Rajput women committed *jauhar* and the men rode out to certain death. Another, but less prolonged attack was launched by Firuz Shah Tughlaq. Relations with the Mughals were far more amicable, while in the British era Jaisalmer remained on the periphery, all but forgotten.

Though a modern township is gradually emerging at the foot of Tricuta Hill, **Jaisalmer Fort**, built of golden Jurassic stone, is still vividly medieval in character, all the more because it continues to be inhabited. For this reason it has been called a "living museum." Wandering through the fort and the old town is a fascinating experience. A winding road leads through the quaint bazaar (where, among other things, are sold the famous woven blankets and shawls, silver jewelry and block printed textiles) to **Manek chowk**, where laden caravans once halted. Entrance to the fort is through a steeply inclined path, marked by four towering gateways. The last, **Hava Pol**, gives way to an open space, where the rite of *jauhar* is known to have been performed. Visitors are allowed within certain parts of the **palace**, including the

during the 18th and 19th centuries, and it is most elaborately expressed on the intricate façades of *havelis*, the erstwhile mansions of rich merchants. **Patwon ki Haveli**, for example, belonged to a brocade merchant who was known for his wares from Afghanistan to China. Consisting of five units, it was started in 1800 and took 50 years to build. **Nathmalji ki Haveli** belonged to the prime minister of the state. It dates to the late 19th century and is still occupied by his descendants. **Salim Singh Haveli**, on the other hand, conspicuous for its upper storey, was built in the 18th century. These *havelis* are unique architectural treasures.

Badal Mahal is the "city" palace and present home of the erstwhile royal family. **Garhsi Sar**, on the fringes of the fort, is an artificial lake created in a catchment area as a source of water for the fort. From **Sunset Point** near the Tourist Bungalow there is a beautiful view of the "golden" citadel.

Some interesting trips can be made out of Jaisalmer – **Bara Bagh** has royal cenotaphs; **Lodurva** has the ruins of the ancient capital as well as an ornate **Jain Temple** where worship is still offered; **Akaal** (18 km or 11 mi) is a **fossil park** which bears witness to the fact that 180 million years ago this area was covered with luxuriant forests.

The most interesting visit is to **Samm**, 40 km (25 mi) southwest of Jaisalmer, beyond which foreigners are not allowed. There are sand dunes at Samm, and all the barren splendor of the desert. A popular "sunset point" (camel rides, musicians, and hordes of people), Samm is perhaps better visited in the early hours of the morning. An annual "Desert Festival" is held here in February. The area around Jaisalmer is known for the haunting music of the Manganiyars. They live in neighboring villages, some of which may be visited on camel safaris organized from Jaisalmer by enterprising hoteliers.

Rang Mahal which is covered with paintings. It is far more interesting to wander through the lanes within the fort. The architecture is mostly traditional, and generations of families have lived within the encircling bastions. They are remarkably tolerant of outsiders; some allow visitors to their rooftops, from where spectacular and unforgettable views are had, especially at sunset. (There are small hotels and lodges within the fort, too.) Three Jain temples, dating from the 12th to the 15th centuries, are known for their carvings – the **Ashtapadi Mandir**, the **Rishabdevji Temple** and the **Sambhavnath Temple**. The last is supposed to contain a number of ancient Jain manuscripts.

The true expertise of the famous *silavats*, the stone carvers of Jaisalmer, can be seen in the old town, in the vicinity of Manek Chowk. This art was at its peak

Above:The exquisitely carved balcony of a haveli at Jaisalmer. Right: Business transactions at a camel market.

JAIPUR
Accommodation
LUXURY: **Rajputana Palace Sheraton**, Kaiser-I-Hind Rd., Atal Ban, Tel: 62031. **Rambagh Palace**, Bhawani Singh Rd., Tel: 0141-75141. **Clarks Amer**, J.N. Marg, Tel: 822616-619. **Jai Mahal Palace Hotel**, Jacob Road, Civil Lines, Tel: 0141-68381. **Mansingh**, Sansar Chand Rd., Tel: 78771. *MODERATE:* **Jaipur Ashok**, Jai Singh Circle, Bani Park, Tel: 75171, 75121. **Meru Palace**, Ram Singh Rd., Jaipal, Tel: 61212. **Khasa Kothi**, M.I. Road, Tel: 75151. **LMB Hotel**, Johari Bazar, Tel: 565844. *BUDGET:* **Broadway**, Agra Rd., Tel: 41765. **Khatri Palace**, Chandpol Gate, Tel: 69183. **Mangal**, Sansar Chandra Rd., Tel: 75126. **Narain Newas Palace Hotel**, Kanota Beach, Narain Singh Rd., Tel: 563448. **Arya Niwas**, Sansar Chandra Rd., Tel: 73456.

Museums
City Palace Museum, Inside Tripolia Gate, Tel: 48146, 49035, 9.30 am-4.45 p.m., closed on five public holidays. **SRC Museum of Indology**, Nilambara Prachya Vidya Path, 24 Gangwal Park, Tel: 48948, 10 am-5 pm. **Central Museum**, Ram Niwas Garden, 10 am-15 pm, closed Fri.

Restaurants
VEGETARIAN: (Rajasthani): **Chanakya**, *INTERNATIONAL:* **Kwality**, M.I. Road, Tel: 72275; **Niros**, M.I. Road, Tel: 74493; **Handi**, Maya Mansions, M.I. Road, Tel: 69020.

Tourist Information
Government of India Tourist Office, State Hotel, Khasa Kothi, Tel: 72200. Also a counter at Sanganer Airport (16 km; Tel: 82222). **Rajasthan Tourism Development Corporation**, Usha Niwas, Kalyan Path, Tel: 72345. **Department of Tourism**, 100 J.L.N. Marg, Tel: 74875. Information bureau at the railway station (Tel: 69714) and Amer (Tel: 86264).

Shopping
Shopping areas: M.I. Road, Nehru Bazaar, Chaura Rasta and Johari, Tripolia and Bapu Bazaars. **Rajasthan Arts and Crafts** near City Palace. **Anokhi**, 2 Yuddistra Marg (Tel: 67619).

Local Festivals
Gangaur (March/April). Celebrated exclusively by women, it commemorates the ideal match of Shiva and Parvati. The *Elephant Festival* (March /April) is in honor of the elephant headed god Ganesha. *Teej* (July/August) celebrates the monsoon and is also devoted to Parvati for the bestowal of marital bliss. Of the non-local festivals and fairs of Rajasthan, the Pushkar (October/ November) and the Merta-Nagaur fairs (cattle fairs), Baneshwar fair (February) and the Ramdeoji Fair

(August/September) at Pokhran near Jaisalmer are worth taking in as is the *Desert Festival* (February/March) at Jaisalmer.

Access / Local Transport
Air connections to Delhi, Bombay, Agra, Aurangabad, Ahmedabad, Bikaner, Jodhpur, Udaipur and Jaisalmer. Jaipur is also well connected by rail to the rest of the state and the country. The Pink City Express makes it possible to travel Jaipur from Delhi and return the same day. It also serves Udaipur three times a week (via Jaipur). Modes of local transport: tourist and unmetered taxis, cycles, auto-rickshaws and buses.

JAISALMER
Accommodation
RTDC's **Moomal Tourist Bungalow**, Tel: 92, 192. **Jawahar Niwas Palace**, Tel: 108. **Narayan Nivas Palace**, Tel: 97. **Jaisal Castle**, Fort, Tel: 62. **Neeraj Hotel**, Tel: 142.

BIKANER
Accommodation
Hotel Lalgarh Palace, Tel: 3263. **Gajner Palace Hotel** (32 km), Tel: 3263. RTDC's **Dhola-Maru Tourist Bungalow**, Poonam Singh Circle, Tel: 5002. **Anand Hotel**, Station Road, Tel: 3521.

Local Festivals
Gangaur (March/April). Devotees congregate at Junagarh Fort and in the Old City near Kote Gate. An *annual fair* is held in November at Kolayat (on the Bikaner-Jaisalmer highway), an ancient pilgrim center dedicated to a sage. The two-day *Desert Festival* (November) organized by the Tourism Department presents local performing arts and a spectacular fire dance show.

Museums
Ganga Golden Jubilee Museum, 10 am- 5pm, closed Fri. **Sadul Museum**, Lalgarh Palace.

Shopping
Shopping areas: Kote Gate, Mahatma Gandhi Road (in the modern market).

Tourist Information
Tourist Information Bureau, Junagarh Fort, Poonam Singh Circle, Tel: 5445. **Information Center**, Ginani Area, Tel: 4595. Also a counter at the Dhola-Maru Tourist Bungalow, Tel: 5445.

UDAIPUR
Accommodation
LUXURY: **Shivniwas Palace**, City Palace, Tel: 28239-41. **Lake Palace**, Pichola Lake, Tel: 23241. **Laxmi Vilas Palace**, Fateh Sagar Road, Tel: 24411-13. **Shikarbadi**, Goverdhan Vilas, Tel: 83200-4. *MODERATE:* **Anand Bhawan**, Fatch Sagar Rd., Tel: 28957. **Chandralok**, Saheli Marg, Tel: 29011. **Lakend**, Fatesagar Lake, Tel: 23841.

BUDGET: **Hilltop Palace**, 5 Ambavgarh, Fatehsagar, Tel: 28708-09.

Local Festivals

Hariyali Amavasya Fair (July/August) on the banks of Fatehsagar; Amarakhji fair on *Raksha Bandhan* day (August) at Amarkhji, 15 km away; *Dev Jhoolni* or *Ekadashi* Fair (September); Rishabdeoji fair (Jan-Feb) at the shrine named after this Jain saint; Eklingji fair in honor of Shiva on Shivaratri (March); a tribal fair (in March) at Ahar (3 km) where the Bhils congregate; *Pratap Jayanti*, the birth anniversary of the region's warrior-king, Maharana Pratap Singh.

Museums

City Palace Museum, 9.30 am-4.30 pm. **Bharatiya Lok Kala Museum**, NN Acharya Marg, near Mohta Park, Tel: 24296, 9 am-6 pm. **Ahar Museum**, Tel: 26104, 10 am-5 pm, closed Fri.

Restaurants

INTERNATIONAL: **Kajri**, Tel: 25122. **Apsara**, Tel: 23400. **Berry's**, Tel: 25132. **Kwality**, Tel: 25104.

Shopping

Areas: Chetak Circle, Bapu Bazaar, City Market, Hathi Pole, Palace Road, Clock Tower, Shastri Circle, Delhi Gate, Sindhi Bazaar.

Tourist Information

Tourist Information Bureau, Kajri Tourist Bungalow, Tel: 23605. Also information counters at Mohta Park (Chetak Circle, Tel: 24924), at the railway station (Tel: 23471) and Dabok Airport (24 km, Tel: 23420).

JODHPUR

Accommodation

LUXURY: **Welcomgroup Umaid Bhawan** Palace, Tel: 22316, 22516. *MODERATE:* **Ratananda Polo Palace**, Residency Rd., Tel: 31910-14. *BUDGET:* **Ajit Bhawan**, near Circuit House, Tel: 20409. **RTDC's Ghoomar Tourist Bungalow**, High Court Road, Tel: 21900. **Shanti Bhawan Lodge**, near Railway Station, Tel: 21689. **Youth Hostel**, 96 Polo I, Tel: 21628.

Local Festivals

Festivals of the region: *Marwar Festival* (an organized festival); the *Cattle Fair* at Nagaur (135 km), *Dhulandi* at Navsati (near Bhilara, 78 km), *Shitlamata* (at Kaga on the outskirts, April) and *Kesariya Kanwarji* (at Umaid Nagar, 42 km).

Museums

Government Museum, Tel: 25753, 10 am-4.30 pm, closed Fri, publ. holidays. **Umaid Museum**, Umaid Bhawan, 9 am-5 pm. **Old Fort Museum**, 8 am-6 pm (summer); 9 am-5 pm (winter).

Restaurants

INTERNATIONAL: **Vama**, Tel: 22061. **Pankaj**, Tel: 24974. **Tourist Bungalow**, Tel: 21900.

Shopping

There are several antique stores near the Umaid Bhawan. Other shopping areas: Sojati Gate, Station Road, Sardar Market, Khanda Falso, and Tripolia, Mochi and Lakhana bazaars.

Access / Local Transport

Ratanada Airport, 5 km from the city.

Accommodation

ALWAR

Alankar Hotel, Tel: 2027. **Ashoka Hotel**, Tel: 21780. **Tourist Hotel**, Tel: 22727 and **Alwar Guest House**, Tel: 20012, on Manu Marg. **Silisehr Palace Hotel** (8 km), Tel: 3764.

SHEKHAVATI

Roop Niwas, Nawalgarh. **Castle Mandawa**, Mandawa, Tel: 24. **Hotel Rath Mandawa**, Dhigal Road, Tel: 40, 59. **Dundlod Fort**, Dundlod, Tel: 90 (Reservations: Dundlod House, Jaipur, Tel: 66276).

AJMER

Khadim Tourist Bungalow (RTDC's), Savitri Girls College Road, Tel: 20490. **Bikaner Hotel**, Prithviraj Marg, Tel: 20580. **Hotel Anand**, Jaipur Road, Tel: 23099. **Hotel Mansingh Palace**. At **Pushkar**: RTDC's **Sarovar Tourist Bungalow**, Tel: 40. Several lodges/inns. Alternately, stay in Ajmer (11 km).

MT. ABU

MODERATE: **Abu International**, Polo Ground, Tel: 177. **Hotel Hilltone**, Tel: 137. **Hotel Palace**, Delwara Rd., Tel: 21, 23. *BUDGET:* **Connaught House**, Rajendra Marg, Tel: 260. **Hillock**, Tel: 367. **Samrat International**, near bus stand, Tel: 53, 73. **Mount Hote**l, Dilwara Rd., Tel: 55. **Savera Palace**, Sunset Rd., Tel: 254.

BUNDI

Circuit House, Tel: 2336. **Dak Bungalow**, Tel: 2336. **Sukh Mahal Rest House**.

BHARATPUR

Bharatpur Forest Lodge, Tel: 2260. RTDC's **Saras Tourist Bungalow**, Agra Road, Tel: 2169, 3700. Circuit House, Tel: 2366. **Golbagh Palace Hotel** Tel: 3349.

CHITTORGARH

Sanwariya Hotel, near Railway Station, Tel: 2597. **Panna Tourist Bungalow**, Tel: 2273. **Janta Avas Grihl**, Tel: 9. **Natraj Tourist Hotel**, Tel: 2509.

KOTA

RTDC's **Chambal Tourist Bungalow**, Tel: 26527. **Brij Raj Bhawan Palace Hotel**, Tel: 23071.

RANTHAMBHORE

RTDC's **Castle Jhoomar Baori Tourist Bungalow**, Sawai Madhopur, Tel: 2495. **Jogi Mahal**, National Park, Tel: 2223. Also private hotels.

GUJARAT

Gujarat, south of Rajasthan, (195,984 sq. km or 75,670 sq.mi) is surrounded by desert on the north, forests on the east, the Satpura mountains on the south and the Arabian Sea along a 1,600 km (994 mi) coastline on the west. The state can be broadly divided into three parts: Kutch; the semi-arid peninsula of Saurashtra; and the verdant plains of Gujarat where the major cities are located and numerous rivers facilitate the growth of groundnuts, cotton and bananas. An immigrant tribe called the Gujjars came to India in the first century A.D., hence the name Gujarat. Saurashtra, the only region that never succumbed to British rule, means "the good nation" and, as the land of the Kathi community, is also known as Kathiawad. Kutch (pronounced Kachchha) is derived from the Sanskrit *Kachchapa* meaning tortoise, because its shape is somewhat like one. In the monsoon, when the salt marshes of the Rann are inundated by the sea, Kutch is almost isolated from the mainland.

Ahmadabad

Travelers often bypass Gujarat. In fact it is a dynamic state with an ethnic variety expressed most richly in the traditions of craft. Gujarat is synonymous with enterprise, whether in the fields of business, cooperative ventures or voluntary organizations. Progress has not subverted traditions, identity or culture, a fact that in many ways is unique to Gujarat. This culture has emerged from a mixture of influences that include both a maritime aspect and the broader involvement of this area with historical changes in the rest of India over the past millennia. **Gandhinagar**, a planned administrative township 26 km (16 mi) from Ahmadabad, is the capital of Gujarat.

Ahmadabad truly encapsulates the spirit of Gujarat. The old and new cities are linked across the Sabarmati river, which flows between. Ahmadabad was founded in 1411 by the Muslim Sultan Ahmed Shah. As a result, the city has some of the finest examples of Indo-Saracenic architecture. Ahmed Shah built the **Juma Mosque** in 1423. It is among the best in India, although more famous for its shaking minarets which collapsed during the earthquake of 1818. Two vibrating minarets still exist at the **Mosque of Sidi Bashir**, and another at the **Rajpur Bibi's mosque**. The **Sidi Saiyad Mosque,** constructed by an Abyssianian in 1572, is renowned for its exquisite stone tracery. This mosque is on Relief Road, one of the city's busiest areas. Other mosques worth visiting are the **Rani Rupmati** and **Rani Sipri**.

The foremost religious tenet of non-violence prevented the Jains from engaging in warfare and agriculture. Trade and business were viable options, and as a community their success has contributed enormously to the prosperity of Gujarat. Ahmadabad has several Jain temples and foremost among these is the **Seth Huthisingh Jain temple**, built in 1848. It is made of marble and graced with exquisite carvings. The idol of the fifteenth Jain Tirthankar, Dharmanath, is within.

Quite apart from specific monuments and temples, the maze-like lanes of the old city are lined by traditional homes known as *havelis*. These have beautifully carved wooden façades. The best *havelis* may be seen around **Doshiwada-ni-Pol**. Alongside traditional design, Ahmadabad can also boast of excellence in modern architecture. The **National Institute of Design** and the **Indian Institute of Management**, both premier institutions, are good examples.

Memories of Gandhi

Associated with austerity and dedication, the **Gandhi Ashram** is on the banks of the river. When Gandhi returned to

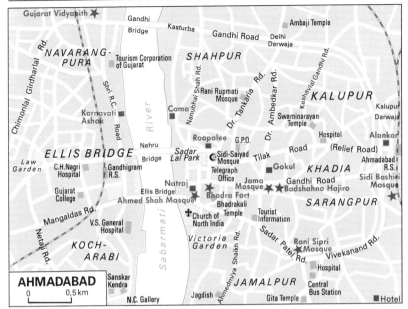

AHMADABAD

0   0,5 km

India in 1915 from South Africa, he established his ashram at a place called Kocherab, outside Ahmadabad. Due to an epidemic in Kocherab he then moved the ashram to its present site. "Hridayakunj" is a hut in this ashram built by Gandhi himself. He lived in this unpretentious home from 1918 to 1930, conducting India's freedom struggle. In 1930 he left for Dandi, for the famous *Salt Satyagraha,* with a vow that he would not return until India won her freedom. Some of his personal effects, including a spinning wheel, are at Hridayakunj. The ashram has a library, a fine museum and a sound and light show in Gujarati, Hindi and English that brings alive the life and times of the Mahatma. A school started by Gandhi still caters to the needs of the underprivileged. The **Gujarat Vidyapeeth** University was also established by Gandhi in 1929 and today the **Navjivan Press**, specializing in Gandhi's works, is here.

The deserted area of those days is now the modern commercial hub of **Ashram Road**. **Manek Chowk** is at the center of the old bazaars where Gujarat's traditional crafts are available in abundance – specially woven, handblock-printed, tie and dye and embroidered fabrics, silver jewelry and antiques shops. The Sunday pavement bazaar below Ellis Bridge is also interesting.

Museums

The best of the varied arts and crafts of this region are preserved in several museums in Ahmadabad. Visits to the **Calico Museum (Shahibag)** and the **Shreyas Folk Art Museum (Ambavadi)** are a must. The former has in its collection some rare textiles from the 17th century onwards. A large variety of exquisite fabrics and garments, brocades and embroideries is on display. The neighboring **Pichchwai Museum** of temple hangings is also excellent. Ahmadabad was once known as India's Manchester. Since the 17th century textiles of satin, voile, brocade and silk have been exported from here. The first textile mill

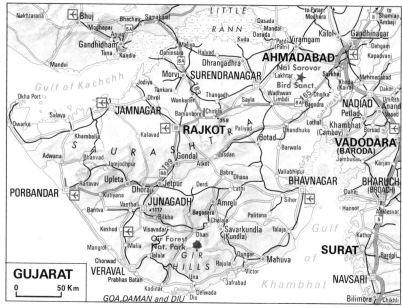

was established in the city in 1859 and even today 25 percent of India's textiles are manufactured here.

The Shreyas Folk Art Museum has a collection of items that testify to the creative genius of the artisans of Gujarat. Their innate understanding of form, color and design transformed the most functional objects into works of art. Some of these, in wood and metal, have a remarkably contemporary flavor. Women, too, play an important role in the craft tradition, particularly with their intricate and colorful embroideries. The **Tribal Museum** on Ashram Road affords a glimpse of the rich and varied ethnic lifestyles. A fascinating array of traditional metal utensils is permanently on view at the **Vechaar Museum**. It is part of the Vishalla Environmental Center for Heritage of Art, Architecture and Research, a 15-minute drive from the city. The collection includes metal pots and pitchers, nut

Right: Shopping at the local grocery store in a village in Gujarat.

186

crackers, locks and dowry boxes. In the same complex is the **Vishalla Restaurant** serving excellent Gujarati vegetarian food in rustic surrounds enlivened by folk music and puppet shows. A rare collection of Indian miniature paintings can be seen at the **Sanskar Kendra** (Paldi).

Excursions

Step-wells, known as *Vaava* in Gujarati, are unique to this region. Consideration for others was the prime motive behind these complex structures which comprise steps and platforms descending to the water tank. Thirsty and fatigued travelers could rest on the cool, paved, wide steps. These step-wells, which are often two or three storys deep, have beautifully carved pillars and lintels. **Dada Harini Vaava** is a 16th-century step-well at **Sarkhej** (18 km or 11 mi) on the road linking Ahmadabad with Saurashtra. At Sarkhej there is also a 15th-century tomb of Mahmud Shah Begra, known as **Sarkhej Roja**. Sultan Ahmed Shah's spiritual master, Ahmed Khattu Ganj Baksh, is also buried here. Sarkhej was used by the rulers as a place for leisure and retreat.

Adalaj Vaava (17 km or 11 mi) was built in 1499 by Queen Rudabai of the Waghela dynasty. It is a five-storeyed structure with decorative motives and intricate geometric and floral patterns carved on stone pillars and archways.

Kankaria Lake was laid out by Sultan Qutubuddin in 1451. There is a small summer palace with a garden in the middle of the lake, which, it is said, was used by the Emperor Jehangir and his queen Nur Jahan. About 65 km (40 mi) from Ahmadabad is a bird sanctuary at **Lake Nalasarovar**. Migratory birds like the rosy pelican, flamingo and stork come between the months of November and February. There is a temple of a local goddess in the center of the lake.

Lothal, 90 km (56 mi) from Ahmadabad, has excavated remains of the port city dating as far back as the 2nd millennium B.C. Lothal was a part of the Indus Valley civilization. Later, Gujarat traded with West Asia from this port.

North Gujarat boasts of a famous Sun temple at **Modhera** (106 km or 66 mi from Ahmadabad) built in A.D. 1026 by King Bhimadev I of the Solanki dynasty. He also built the step-well **Ranaki Vaava** with its exquisite carvings. During the solar equinoxes the first rays of the sun light up the image of the sun god in the *sanctum sanctorum*. **Patan** is famous for its **Rudramala Temple** and a tie and dye fabric known as *patola*. The **Sahastralinga Lake** is here, with 1000 Shiva temples around it, built by King Siddharaj Jaisingh. **Shamlaji**, **Kesariyaji** and **Ambaji** are other places of pilgrimage en route, with carved temples.

Vadodara and Surat

Vadodara (Baroda) is a city of the erstwhile princely state, once ruled by the Gaekwads. Here the **Nazarbag Palace**,

Makarpura Palace, **Pratap Vilas Palace**, **Laxmi Vilas Palace** and **Bhadra Palace** are worth seeing for their collections of art and antiquities. **Kirti Mandir** commemorates important persons of the Gaekwad family. It is also known for its murals created by the late Nandalal Bose. **Vadodara Museum**, the **Planetarium** and **Surasagar Lake** are other places of interest. The city is also known for its University of Fine Art.

Surat, a port on the Tapti river, has housed Portuguese, Dutch, French and British colonials in the past. It was also a gateway to Mecca between the 15th and 17th centuries. It has a fort built in the 16th century and graveyards also dating to that time.

At present, it has a flourishing textile industry and is also the center for the manufacture of *zari*, fine threads of pure gold and silver used in weaving and embroidery. Surat is also a busy center of diamond cutters, and famous for its cuisine. *Undhiyum* (vegetables cooked in an earthen pot buried in the ground),

187

ponk (green grains of barley), and sweet-meats like *ghari* and *nankhatai* are some of the specialties. *Utaraana*, the famous kite festival celebrated all over Gujarat on 14 January is particularly popular in Surat.

Bardoli, an important center of activity during India's freedom struggle, is located in the Surat district. It has the **Sardar Vallabhbhai Patel Museum**. Dandi, of the salt *satyagraha* is also nearby. The **Badripada Wild Life Sanctuary** and a hill station, **Satpura**, are located in the Dang forest.

Saurashtra

On the way from Ahmadabad to **Saurashtra** is **Tarnetar**. A most colorful fair is held here for three days between August and September, at the temple of Shiva. People break into joyous folk songs and folk dances to the rhythmic accompaniment of folk instruments. This is a superb chance to see the color and richness of rural Gujarat.

Palitana is at the foot of the Shatrunjay Hill, covered by 863 magnificent Jain temples built over a period of 900 years, the earliest dating to the 11th century. The **Temple of Adishvarnath**, the first Jain Tirthankar is considered the most important of this spectacular temple city. The temples are built of marble with fine carvings. The treasury of this temple city has precious and unique jewels, which are possible to view on special request. No human being is allowed to stay on the hill at night. Even the temple priests have to climb down the 602-meter (1,975 ft) high hill as soon as the sun sets. The night is only for the gods.

At **Prabhas Patan** stands the famous Shaivite temple of **Somnath**, sacked by Muhammad of Ghazni and said to have been destroyed and rebuilt seven times.

Above: We cannot show our faces! Tribal women at the Tarnetar fair, Gujarat. Right: The 11th century temple at Modhera, dedicated to Surya, the Sun God.

Somnath is one of the 12 most important Shaivite temples of India. Near Somnath is **Bhalka Tirth** where Lord Krishna was killed by the arrow of a hunter. **Chorwad** is a tranquil beach resort.

Porbandar, the birthplace of Mahatma Gandhi, is also a place of pilgrimage for many. It is an old port from which India traded with the Arabs, Africans and Persians. Gandhi was born here in 1869 in the house that is now called **Kirti Mandir**. It has personal effects and photographs of Gandhi, a library and a big hall for hand spinning.

According to legend, **Dwarka**, a city of great religious importance, was built by Lord Krishna. It is believed to have been destroyed five times. The ornately carved **Dwarkadish Temple** is dedicated to Lord Krishna and its main entrance is still revered as the gateway to heaven. Krishna's birthday, in the month of August, is celebrated with great enthusiasm. Dwarka was an ancient port, and traces of a submerged city have been found off the coast. Descendants of the stone carvers who built the temples of Dwarka and Somnath may be seen pursuing the same profession in the town of **Wadhwan**.

Jamnagar is famous for its tie and dye fabrics and woolen shawls. The **Lakhota Palace** now houses a fine museum. Jamnagar also has a **solarium** which was built in 1933. **Junagadh**, in the foothills of **Mt. Girnar**, is on record as far back as 250 B.C., the time of Emperor Asoka. Today it is known for the temples on Mt. Girnar, an important place of pilgrimage for the Jains. The 16 marble shrines can be reached after climbing 2000 steps. The oldest temple is that of Neminath, who was the 22nd Jain Tirthanker. There is also a Muslim shrine.

Nearly 54 km (34 mi) from Junagadh is **Sasan Gir** forest where a sanctuary has been set up spreading over 1,295 sq.km. It is the only place in India to view lions in their natural surroundings, close to wild boars, spotted and barking deer, four-horned antelopes, hyenas, foxes, jackals and a large variety of birds. Guided jeep trips are available.

Kutch

Kutch, though lacking a tourist infrastructure, has a rich variety of semi-nomadic pastoral communities whose lifestyles have remained virtually unchanged for centuries up to today. Their dress is colorful and ornate and the women are often laden with jewelry. Their unique and beautiful mud houses have walls decorated with interesting textured patterns and tiny mirrors. The **Banni** area in particular has an exuberant tradition of craft. Collectors and connoisseurs have come here from all over the world in search of embroideries.

Bhuj is the main town of Kutch. The **Ayanamahal**, the fanciful palace of mirrors, was built in 1865. **Bhuj Museum**, established in 1877, has a large collection of Indo-Scythian inscriptions. Near-by **Bhujodi** has a community of weavers who produce colorful traditional blankets

Above: Bhil tribespeople step out in their finery to celebrate the spring festival of Holi.

known as *dhablas* and woolen durries. Kutch is also famous for its **Flamingo Sanctuary** and **Wild Ass Sanctuary**.

Festivals

The richness of Gujarati culture is best seen during festivals and fairs. *Navaratri*, *Diwali* and *Bestun Varsh* are celebrated all over Gujarat. *Navaratri* is observed for nine nights and devoted to the goddess of Shakti. Rhythmic dances are performed to the accompaniment of devotional *garba* songs. This festival is observed in September to October.

On *Diwali*, the festival of lamps, Gujaratis worship their account books, as this is the last day of the Hindu calendar. The goddess of wealth, Lakshmi, and the goddess of learning, Sarasvati, are both propitiated on this festival. Most of the businessmen in Gujarat open new account books on the day after New Year's Day, and distribute tempting sweets. This festival falls during October to November.

GUIDEPOST GUJARAT

AHMADABAD
Accommodation
MODERATE: **Cama Hotel**, Khanpur. Tel: 25281. *BUDGET:* **Rivera**, Khanpur Road, Tel: 24201. **Panshikura**, beside Town Hall, Ellisbridge, Tel: 402960. **Ambassador**, Khanpur Rd. Tel: 24201. **Karnavati**, Ashram Road, Tel: 402161. **Kingsway**, GPO Road, Tel: 26221.
Museums / Art Galleries
Shreyas Folk Art Museum, 10 am-12 noon, 3-6 pm, closed Mon, Tel: 68172. **Museum of Textiles**, Shahibag, Tel: 51001, 10am-12.30 pm, 2.30-5 pm, closed Wed. **National Institute of Design Showrooms**, Paldi, Tel: 79693, 4.30-5.30 pm, closed weekends. **N.C. Gallery**, Sanskar Kendra, Paldi, Tel: 78369, 76507.
Restaurants
INTERNATIONAL: **Volga**, Ashram Road, Tel: 78533. **Neelam**, Lal Darwaza, Tel: 461445.
REGIONAL: **Vishala Village**, Sarkhej.
Tourist Information
Tourism Corporation of Gujarat, H.K. House, Ashram Road, Tel: 449683. Regional Manager, **Tourism Corporation of Gujarat**, Airlines House, Lal Darwaza, Tel: 390326.

VADODARA
Accommodation
LUXURY: **Welcomgroup Vadodara**, R.C. Dutt Rd., Tel: 323232. *MODERATE:* **Express Hotel**, R.C. Dutt Rd., Tel: 323131. **Express Alkapuri**, 18 Alkapuri, Tel: 325960. **Surya**, Sayajiganj, Tel: 328282. **Hotel Utsav**, Prof. Manek Rao Road, Tel: 551415. *BUDGET:* **Aditi**, Sayajiganj, Tel: 32-7722. **Rama Inn**, Sayajiganj, Tel: 329567. **Surya Palace**, Sayajiganj, Tel: 329999.
Museums / Art Galleries
Maharaja Fatehsingh Museum, Laxmi Vilas Place Compound, Jawaharlal Nehru Marg, Tel: 56372, April-June 9 am-12 noon, 3.30-6.30 pm; July-March 9 am-12noon, 3-6 pm, closed Mon. **Museum & Picture Gallery**, Sayaji Bag, Tel: 67489, 9 am-7 pm daily, except public holidays.
Tourist Information
Tourist Office, Vadodara Municipal Corporation, Khanderao Market, Tel: 51116.
Accommodation
SURAT
BUDGET: **Dhawalgiri Guest House**, Dhawalgiri Apartments, Athwalines, Tel: 40040. **Dreamland**, Sufi Baug, opp. Railway Station, Tel: 39016. **Rama Regency**, Ambica Niketan, Athwalines, Tel: 87167. **Palazzo**, Ring Road, Tel: 623018-21.

JAMNAGAR
Hotel President, Teen Batti, Tel: 70283. **Hotel Aram**, Pandit Nehru Marg, Tel: 78521-24.

CHORWAD
Palace Beach Resort, Tel: 567, 556, 558.
JUNAGADH
Hotel Vaibhav, near S.T. Stand, Tel: 21070/71; **Hotel Girnar** (Gujarat Tourism), Majwadi Darwaza, Tel: 21201, 21203.
GIR RESERVE
Lion Safari Lodge, (TCGL), Tel: 21, 28.
DWARKA
Hotel Guru Prerna, near Bhadrakali Mandir, Tel: 385. **TCGL's Dormitory**, Near Vishranti Grah, Tel: 313. **Hotel Meera**, near Power House. **Somnath**, Prabhas Patan. **Holiday Home** (TCGL's), Veraval, Tel: 20488.
PORBANDAR
Toran Tourist Bungalow, Chowpatty, Tel: 22745, 21476. Several beach villas overlooking the Arabian Sea.
PALITANA
TCGL's Hotel Sumeru, Station Rd., near Oberoi Naka, Tel: 227. Several guest houses, lodges and *dharamshalas*.
BHAVNAGAR
Welcomgroup Nilambag Palace, Tel: 24241, 21337, 29323. **Hotel Apollo**, opposite Central Bus Station, Tel: 25251.
BHUJ
Hotel Aram, Tel: 23397. **Hotel Prince**, Tel: 20390-92. (western style).
Festivals
At *Makar Sankranti* (January), keen rivalry is in the air as kiteflying enthusiasts overtake the sky. Gujarat wears a most festive look during the *Navratris* (September-October), a nine-day long festival in honor of Amba, the mother goddess. *Garba* and *Dandiya Ras*, performed by gaily dressed dancers, are a delight to watch. Close on its heels is *Dussehra*. The Tarnetar (August-September), Dang Durbar (March), Dakor, Pavagadh and Madhavrai (March-April) fairs are especially colorful.
Access / Local Transport
Nine locations in Gujarat, Ahmedabad, Bhavnagar, Bhuj, Jamnagar, Keshod, Porbandar, Rajkot, Surat and Vadodara, with Bombay as a common link feature on the domestic air map. Western Railways connects Ahmedabad to Bombay and nearby towns and with Delhi and cities in Rajasthan. Both national and state highways provide a network of convenient routes leading to tourist destinations within the state and outside.
Shopping
Textiles top the list of handicrafts. Block prints and tie and dye work equal woven material (of silk cotton and gold) in quality and design. There is a florishing trade in antiques, too.

191

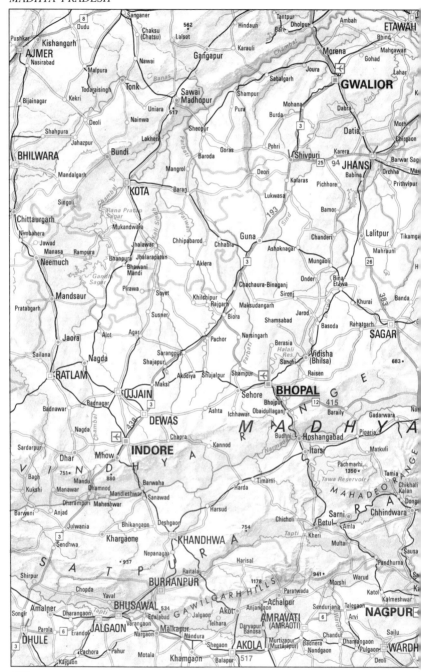

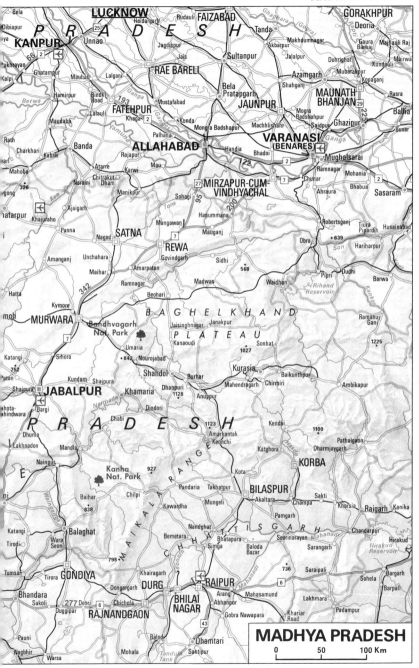

MADHYA PRADESH

0   50   100 Km

MADHYA PRADESH

Unlike many other states in India, mention of Madhya Pradesh does not evoke a single image, partly because it does not possess typical attractions such as the mountains or the sea, and partly because its immensity and the astonishing variety of what it does have to offer do not permit its confinement to a stereotype. Geographically, Madhya Pradesh is located in the heart of India. Spending time in the state is experiencing the essence of India – the pristine magic of its forests, the magnificence of its monuments, the exuberance of festivals, and the great peace that solitude and silence bring. Madhya Pradesh is the largest state in the country, sprawling over 443,000 km. It has one-third of India's forests and hence numerous natural parks and sanc-tuaries, including **Kanha** and **Bandhavgarh** which are among the fi-

Above: "A pearl in the necklace of the castles of Hind". The Fort of Gwalior.

nest in the country. Apart from forests, there is also the vast plateau, the hill ranges of the Vindhya and Satpura and the great rivers flowing across it – the Narmada, Tapti, Chambal, Sone, Betwa, Mahanadi and Indravati. Its climate is, by and large, moderate, and its people are warm and gentle: their catholicity has enabled all the major faiths to flourish – Hinduism, Islam, Jainism and Buddhism. Vast areas of the state are enriched by the unique and precious culture of its tribes.

Close to nature, sometimes surrounded by it, and often competing with it in magnificence, stand the monuments of Madhya Pradesh. Being located in the center of India, all trade routes across the country, and from north to south, had to pass through Madhya Pradesh. The resultant commerce, together with the wealth of its soil and the rivers, brought great prosperity to the area. While it had contact with all parts of India, it was fortunately just south of the region that suffered constant invasions. The rare combination of wealth and absence of depredations has left the state with over 1000 monuments, and many antiquities in a perfect state of preservation, ranging in time from the paleolithic to the colonial, and in size from a single figure to a city.

Gwalior

Gwalior is regarded as Madhya Pradesh's gateway, and guarding and dominating the city is its fort astride a large hill, brooding, masculine, described by the Emperor Babur as "the pearl in the necklace of the castles of Hind."

The two temples in the fort, **Sas Bahu Mandir** and **Teli Ka Mandir**, are worth seeing, but the place one can spend hours at is **Man Mandir**, the 15th-century palace of Raja Man Singh Tomar. Its amazingly efficient systems of lighting and cooling are fascinating, so, too, are the exquisite blue enamel tile work, the subterranean chambers where royal prisoners were chained, and the huge tank of fire into which the women of the palace leapt when the fort was taken by an enemy.

Just below the fort is **Gujari Mahal**, a palace built by Man Singh for his consort Mrignayani, which is now a museum that houses what is perhaps the finest collection of medieval sculptures in the country. Close to the museum is the **tomb of Tansen**, one of India's greatest singers, who adorned the court of Emperor Akbar. Even today, Gwalior is a major center of classical Indian music.

Modern Gwalior was also the capital of the martial Scindia dynasty, whose wiry Maratha soldiers conquered territory from the west of India right up to Delhi. The palace of the Scindia dynasty, **Jai Vilas**, is a majestic white structure combining Tuscan, Italian and Corinthian styles of architecture. In its *darbar* or audience hall is a massive chandelier and its numerous chambers have exquisite carpets and a large collection of rare art objects and antique furniture.

Shivpuri and Chanderi

The town of **Shivpuri**, to where the Scindias and Chanderi moved in summer, is an ideal pleasure resort with its game sanctuary, lake and palaces. The national park, which now has several varieties of deer, was earlier the forest where Viceroys went with Maharajahs to bag their tigers. A rather unique ceremony, held in the **cenotaphs** of the Scindias in the evenings, is when musicians of the Gwalior gharana (school of music) sing before statues of the rulers, dressed for the occasion by ceremonially attired retainers. Shivpuri certainly does retain the flavor of a regal past.

Another town with a medieval ambience is **Chanderi**, the traditional weavers city, with cobbled streets and period architecture, known all over India for its very finely woven sarces. The place to stay is the **Rest House** built by the Scindias, located on a hill with a number of open verandahs commanding splendid views of the city, especially at dawn or dusk. Close by is the 16th-century city of **Orchha** on the Betwa river. The many **temples** and **palaces** here are beautiful examples of Bundela architecture. The **Jahangir Mahal palace**, converted into a hotel, has narrow stairways, numerous chambers, terraces and windows providing framed views of the spired city.

Bhopal

Bhopal, the capital of Madhya Pradesh, also has the dubious distinction of being the centre of the world's worst industrial accident. On December 2, 1984, Methyl Iso-Cyanide gas leaked from theUnion Carbide Corporation's plant outside the city, and within a few hours an estimated 10,000 people had died (4000 by official figures), and nearly 500,000 were left with some form of permanent disability. Though a settlement of US$ 470 million has been arrived at be-

tween the Indian Government and the Union Carbide Corporation in the USA, distribution of aid has been held up due to endless litigation and red tape, and the misery of the hapless victims continues. Though Bopal has much to offer the tourist, it will be many more years before this city can overcome the depressed mood of a large section of its population.

Bhopal's mosques, especially the **Tajul-Masajid**, the **State Archaeological Museum** and the **Bharat Bhawan** are worth a visit. The last is a uniquely designed art complex, merging with the banks of the great lake, with an art gallery, a workshop for fine arts, a repertory theater, libraries of Indian poetry, classical and folk music and the largest collection of tribal art in the world.

About an hour's drive from Bhopal is the great **Shaivite temple** at **Bhojpur**, said to have been built by the legendary Raja Bhoj (1010-53), warrior, scholar

Above: A woman collects dried cow-dung cakes which she will use as fuel.

and patron of the arts. On entering the temple you see the gigantic *lingam*, the symbol of life-force. Outside are incomplete sculptures, the earthen ramp used to lift stones to the *sikhara* (spire) of the temple, and designs of the temple engraved in the rocks. It appears as if the workers have just broken off from work – a scene that has remained frozen for 900 years. Forty minutes' drive away are the hills of **Bhimbethka** which house one of the richest groups of rock shelter paintings in the world, and the remains of 100,000 years of civilization – styles ranging from the Upper Paleolithic to the Early Historic.

Sanchi and Udaigiri

Less than 50 km (31 mi) away from Bhopal is **Sanchi** which has, apart from the celebrated **Great Stupa**, a great variety of architectural forms called *chaityas* (prayer halls), temples, pillars, monasteries and toranas (carved gateways) – which constitute, according to Marshall, the finest examples of Buddhist architecture in India. Around the Great Stupa, in contrast to the peace flowing from its gentle hemispherical curve, is the bustle of life itself frozen for posterity by the fine carvings on the toranas by the ivory workers of **Vidisha**. Close by is the **pillar of Heliodorus**, a unique monument proclaiming the conversion of a Greek Ambassador to Hinduism, and the **Udaigiri caves** containing superb specimens of the Gupta period – the classical age of ancient Indian art.

Less than 200 km (124 mi) from Bhopal is **Indore**, in the heart of **Malwa**, "Therein is neither exceeding heat nor exceeding cold and the nights of Malwa, are they not famous from ancient days? Even as men say "The dawn of Banaras, the evening of Oudh, the night of Malwa." So Ahmad-ul-Umri Turkoman put it in 1599. In Indore, **Lalbagh**, the well-preserved palace of the Holkars, **Kanch Mandir**, the quaint Jain shrine of glass, and the **Central Museum** with its very rich collection of coins and medieval sculpture, should all be seen.

Mandu

While at Indore, also spare time to read about **Mandu** and those who dwelt in it - about Hoshang Shah the great warrior, Sultan Ghiyath-ud-Din with his harem of 15,000 women, of the visits of the Emperor Jehangir, and of the exquisite and sad tale of Baz Bahadur and Rupmati - a Sultan who gave up his kingdom for a singer, and she her life for his memory. If one invests one's visit to Mandu's palaces, tombs, mosques and pavilions with memories of all that occurred there, it is simply the most romantic place in the world. These are not isolated and desolate monuments, but the remains of **Shadiabad** - an entire city built for joy. Emperor Jehangir who journeyed all the way from Delhi to spend time here wrote, "I know of no place so pleasant in climate

and so pretty in scenery as Mandu during the rains." Visit **Rupmati's pavilion** at dusk – the windswept terrace where she sang her sweetest songs, gazing at the Narmada flowing through the plains below, will bring back vividly its sad and poignant past. The next day or two can be spent in seeing Mandu's monuments. Two buildings intimately associated with medieval romance are **Jahaz Mahal**, the pleasure palace built to resemble a ship between two lakes, and **Hindola Mahal**, the "swinging palace" in whose subterranean chambers the mistresses of Ghiyath-ud-Din spent their summer days. **Hoshang Shah's Tomb**, which retains the masculinity and majesty of the ruler, is one of the finest examples of Afghan architecture and was visited by Shah Jahan's master craftsmen before they started work on the Taj Mahal. Other structures that also must be seen are the **Jami Masjid**, **Asharfi Mahal**, **Rewa Kund**, **Baz Bahadur's palace**, **Nilkanth** and the **Caravanserai**.

Omkareshwar and Maheshwar

Omkareshwar and **Maheshwar** can be visited on the way back to Indore. Maheshwar, the ancient city of "Mahishmati", is famous for its sarees, introduced 250 years ago by the remarkable Rani Ahilyabai who also planned and built Indore. The **Rajwada** has interesting heirlooms of the Rani and the stately ghats on the Narmada seem to bear her saintly spirit. Also on the Narmada is the sacred town of Omkareshwar, whose fine **temple** houses one of the 12 jyotirlings.

Ujjain

One of India's most sacred cities is **Ujjain**, less than 50 km (31 mi) from Indore. Ujjain has a large number of temples including the famous **Mahakal,** visited by millions during the Simhasta every twelve years. Apart from the

temples the city has memories of a great cultural past, for it was governed by Asoka and Vikramaditya and here, Kalidas wrote the finest poetry of India.

Khajuraho

Legend has it that 1000 years ago, Hemvati, the lovely young daughter of a Brahmin priest, was seduced by the Moon God while bathing in a forest pool, and from their union was born Chandravarman, founder of the Chandelas, a dynasty that built 85 temples in **Khajuraho** in the short span of 1000 years, between A.D. 950 and A.D. 1050. Only 25 temples survive. These are, however, architectural masterpieces – masses of carved stone whose peaks soar in prayer to the skies. The sculpted panels are some of the most perfect creations of man. Unfortunately, the most publicized are the erotic sculptures, but if these are seen not

Above: The beautiful medieval temples of Khajuraho attract many tourists.

in isolation, but with the 800 other creations, one cannot but feel awe and reverence for what is a celebration of the human form, a depiction of man in his myriad moods – in battle, in prayer, longing and loving, in movement and in sublime repose. Contrasting with the extravagance of the activity outside is the stark simplicity and sublimity of the *garba grihas* (*sanctum sanctorum*) inside. The temples and sculptures should be seen at leisure, for seldom has stone been worked so perfectly. The **Khandariya Mahadev Temple** is the most famous. It also becomes the venue for a dance festival held every year, in March.

It is difficult to do justice to Madhya Pradesh, for there is much more to see than what has been described here. There is the entire tribal world of **Chhatisgarh** and **Jhabua**, and the numerous and magnificent sanctuaries and national parks, places of great solitude like **Tamia**, **Pachmarhi** and **Amarkantak**; and the superb craftwork in bell metal, terracotta, beads and textiles.

BHOPAL
Accommodation
MODERATE: **Jeha Numa Palace**, Shamla Hills, Tel: 540100. **Ramsons International**, Hamidia Road, Tel: 75298. *BUDGET:* **Lake View Ashok**, Shamla Hills, Tel: 541600. **Nalanda**, Ibrahimpura, St. No. 2, Tel: 77035. **Pagoda Hotel and Restaurant**, Hamidia Rd., Tel: 77157.

Museums / Art Galleries
State Archaeological Museum, Banganga Marg, Tel: 63207, 10 am-5 pm, closed Mon and public holidays. **Tribal Research Development Institute**, Tel: 4492, 10.30 am-5 pm. **Birla Museum**, Vallabh Bhavan, Tel: 64387, 10 am-5 pm, closed Mon and public holidays.

Tourist Information
M.P. State Tourism Development Corporation, Gangotri, IVth Floor, T.T. Nagar, Tel: 554340-43; Information counters at the airport and railway station.

GWALIOR
Accommodation
MODERATE: **Welcomgroup Usha Kiran Palace**, Jayendraganj, Lashkar, Tel: 23453, 22049. *BUDGET:* **Metro**, Gansh Bazar, near Gandhi Market, Tel: 25530. **Motel Tansen**, 6A Gandhi Marg, Tel: 21568. **Vivek Continental**, Topi Bazaar, Lashkar, Tel: 27016-17-18.

Museums
Archaeological Gujari Mahal Museum, Gwalior Fort, Tel: 8526, 10 am-5 pm, closed Mon and public holidays. **Maharaja Jivaji Rao Scindia Museum**, Jai Vilas Palace, Lashkar, Tel: 22290, 9.30 am-4.30 pm, closed Mondays.

Restaurants
Volga, **Regal** and **Gujari Mahal**.

Tourist Information
Motel Tansen, 6 Gandhi Road, Tel: 21568, 26742.

SANCHI
Accommodation
Traveller's Lodge, Tel: 223. **Buddhist Guest House**, Tel: 239. **Railway Retiring Rooms**, Tel: 225.

Museum
Archaeological Survey of India Museum. 9 am-5 pm daily, Tel: 227.

Accommodation
INDORE
MODERATE: **Shreemaya**, 12/1 R.N.T. Marg, Tel: 34151. **Indotel Manor House**, Tel: 31645, Agra-Bombay Rd. *BUDGET:* **Central**, 70-71 M.G. Road, Tel: 32041-43. **Kanchan**, Kanchan Baugh, Tel: 33394-97. **Lantern**, 28 Yashwant Nivas Road, Tel: 35327.

SHIVPURI
Chinkara Motel, Agra-Bombay Road, Tel: 297. **Tourist Village**, near Bhadaiya Kund, Tel: 2600 (both MPSTDC). **Shivpuri Lodge**, Madhav Chowk.

KHAJURAHO
LUXURY: **Hotel Chandela**, Tel: 2054. **Hotel Jass Oberoi**, Bypass Road, Tel: 2085-88. *MODERATE:* **Hotel Khajuraho Ashok**, Tel: 2024. **Hotel Payal**, Tel: 2076. **Hotel Rahil**, Tel: 2062. **Tourist Village Complex**, Tel: 2062. **Tourist Bungalow**, Tel: 2064.

ORCHHA
MPSTDC's Hotel Sheesh Mahal, Tel: 224.

MANDU
MPSTDC's Travellers Lodge, Tel: 221 and **Tourist Cottages**, Tel: 235. Also a few guest/resthouses.

UJJAIN
MPSTDC's Shipra Hotel, University Road, Tel: 29628-29. **Grand Hotel**, **Adarsh Gupta Lodge**, **Taj** and **Sher-i-Punjab** hotels.

Shopping
The list begins with textiles - cotton and silk blended sarees from Chanderi and Maheshwar; vegetable dyed handprinted material; tussar silks from Raigarh Bastar and Jagdalpur; and cottons with *zari* (gold thread embroidery) from Bhopal. From Indore come leather toys and glass bangles while the quaint votive lamps, rice measures and animal figures in bell-metal are made by tribespeople using a lost wax method of casting.

Festivals
Marrhai is a tribal festival, and celebrations in Bastar and Chhatisgarh are particularly impressive. Folk dances and theater are offered at the *Bhagoriya festival* (in Jhabua). Classical arts are celebrated at the annual *Khajuraho dance festival* (March) and the *Tansen festival* at Gwalior. Worth a mention are *Mahashivaratri* in March (Khajuraho/Ujjain/Maheshwar); *Buddha Jayanti* in May (Sanchi); *Ram Navmi* (Chitrakoot); *Kartik Mela* in November (Maktagiri, Nohta) and last but not least, the *Kumbha Mela*, celebrated once every 12 years at Ujjain.

Access / Local Transport
Bhopal, Gwalior, Jabalpur, Indore, Khajuraho and Raipur are linked to the rest of the country by Indian Airlines. Tourist destinations are also accessible by rail. There is an extensive network of motorable roads. In the cities, coaches, cars, unmetered taxis, metered scooter rickshaws, mini buses and tempos facilitate local travel. However, in smaller locations like Sanchi and Mandu, visitors have to rely upon *tempos, tongas* and bicycles (available for hire) for sightseeing.

TO THE SOURCE OF THE GANGA

(Note: this article refers to Route 5 in the map on page 215.)

The **Gangotri Temple**, 200 km (124 mi) from **Rishikesh,** is seen as the spiritual source of Hinduism's most sacred river. Every Hindu aspires to make the pilgrimage to pray here for his ancestors. The physical source is another 19 km (12 mi) southeast along the retreating course of the **Gangotri Glacier**. The ice cave of **Gaumukh**, the Cow's Mouth, marks the present snout of the glacier, one of the longest and widest in the Himalayas.

Starting from **Rishikesh**, or more accurately **Haridwar**, 25 km (16 mi) to the south where the Ganga leaves the mountains for the plains, the pilgrim road winds up to **Narendranagar**, a small summer seat of the former Maharaja of Tehri-Garhwal, custodian of a priceless collection of Pahari miniature paintings.

Preceding pages: Dusk. Naga sadhus at the Kumbh Mela, Haridwar. Above: An ascetic.

Chamba (60 km or 37 mi) on the ridge has a road to **Mussoorie**, a lively hill resort (55 km or 34 mi). The road spirals down to the old capital of **Tehri** (20 km or 13 mi) a small town due to be flooded when a new and controversial dam scheme takes place.

The Road to Gangotri

The road to Gangotri runs west along the River Bhagirathi which is joined in Tehri by the Bhilangana, flowing from the peak of Thalay Sagar (known as Sphetik Prishtwan, 6,904 m or 22,650 ft). On the way to **Uttarkashi** you pass through Dhunda, a beflagged village where nomadic herdsmen from the border area with Tibet have settled. This is the home of Bachendri Pal, the first Indian girl to climb Mount Everest.

Uttarkashi has many *ashrams* (retreats for Hindu holy men). It also has in the temple at **Barahat,** a magnificent standing trident which is considered the most outstanding work of art in Uttarakhand. It is more than 1000 years old. Across the river stands the **Nehru Institute of Mountaineering**. From Uttarkashi an excursion can be made to **Dodital** (3,307 m or 10,850 ft) where a small lake surrounded by dense jungle is a favorite with fisher-men. **Bhatwari** (30 km or 19 mi) is the base for the old pilgrim bridle-way east to **Budh Kedar** and the seven lakes culminating in **Sahastra Tal**.

Across the Himalaya

Now the main road cuts across the main range of the Himalayas, where the angry river recently swept away 20 km (13 mi) of its length. **Gangnani** has some hot springs. The climb to **Sukhi** (2,744 m or 9,003 ft) reveals the other side of the mountain: lush conifer jungles and the broad river flowing over silver sand. **Harsil** (75 km or 47 mi) has a large wooden mansion built by the English self-styled "Raja" Wilson over 100 years ago. This man became so rich from lumber contracts that he minted his own rupee coins. He also married a local woman and introduced apples to the area.

Near Harsil is the village of **Mukhba** where the Goddess Ganga spends the winter. The river now curves east round the northern aspect of the Himalaya. At **Lanka** (10 km or 6 mi from Gangotri) the Jad Ganga joins the Bhagirathi in a deep gorge. When the first bridge over the 350-m (1,148 ft) drop was built by Wilson he had to ride his horse over to prove to the pilgrims it was safe.

With the arrival of the motor road the small village of **Gangotri** (3,048 m or 10,000 ft) has been transformed into a major pilgrim center. Hindus go first to pray at the **Bhagirathi Sheel**, the stone on which the king (whose prayers moved the Goddess to descend to earth) did penance. The Gangotri temple dates back about 250 years. The most beautiful ceremony is the evening *aarti*, the waving of lights in offering to the roaring river

whose waters wash away your sins. The surroundings, amid thick cedar groves, are inspiring, and the strange behavior of the river adds to the sense of mystery. From a broad stream it suddenly narrows and, after coursing over a thunderous waterfall (**Surajkund**), it narrows further to pass through a meter-wide gorge it has carved out of the smooth rock.

The Photo Swami

Near Surajkund can be found the huts of holy men. One of the best known is the artistic cottage of Sunderananda (better known as Photo Swami). Other holy men meditate on the rocks, observing a vow of silence. Some go naked, with ash rubbed into the skin to keep out the cold, others enjoy creature comforts. The bazaar consists of a few tea shops and all supplies need to be brought from Uttarkashi.

The trail to **Kedar Tal** base camp for Thalay Sagar and Brighupanth (6,722 m or 22,054 ft) starts from Surajkund, where the Kedar Ganga joins the Bhagirathi. Follow the river to its source along the steep and narrow track, a two-day trek which often sees big herds of wild blue sheep *(bharal)* above the tree line.

The path to **Gaumukh** is open from May to October and some pilgrims complete the 38-km (24 mi) round trip in only one day. However, at altitude this speed is very dangerous. It is better to camp at **Chirbas** (10 km or 6 mi) at 2,600 m (8,530 ft), or spend the night at **Bhojbas**, another 6 km (4 mi), at the uncomfortable altitude of 3,792 m (12,441 ft). Here is the famous *ashram* of Lal Baba, a holy man who provides free food and shelter to pilgrims – but who also enjoys a reputation for a fiery temper. As many pilgrims are suffering from mountain sickness (for which the only known cure is to lose altitude), the anger of the holy man may be a blessing in disguise. The approach to the source is dry and stony, more sacred than beautiful.

Gaumukh and Beyond

The snow peaks in the background hint at hidden glories awaiting discovery. The beautiful pyramid peak of Sudarshan (6,516 m or 21,387 ft) can be seen from the doorway of the Gangotri temple. At Chirbas the Bhagirathi Sisters come into view, the highest of the three peaks rising to 6,857 m (22,497 ft). This elegant trio fills the background as you approach the source. However, once round the last bend the startling lines of Shivling (6,543 m or 21,467 ft) emerge from the other flank of the glacier and it is this peak that presides proudly over the **Gaumukh cave** as you draw near. From the *ashram* the last 3 km to the source are almost level but the path is lost in a tumble of boulders and you have to pick a way through to the most holy part of the sacred river.

Most pilgrims bathe in the icy torrent that roars out from under the glacier, already a full-blown river at birth. It is also the custom to fill water bottles for use in religious rites in the home. To the religious pilgrim the arrival at the snout of the glacier is his goal. For the mountain lover, however, further treats are in store if you climb on to the glacier and work your way along the edge for another few kilometers. Then you will come upon the world's most sublime collection of snow peaks, a scene of unspeakable grandeur. The sides of the glacier are steep and unstable and are best negotiated early in the morning before the sun loosens the ice. Two routes can be followed, to **Nandanvan** on the same side as Gaumukh, or to **Tapovan** across the glacier. An ideal day's trip is to do them both. Start up the muddy side of the snout then pick a way along the rubble at the edge. The center of this 3-km (1.5 mi) wide glacier is dangerously crevassed. Nandanvan is 6 km

Right: Sadhus, a common sight near Gaumukh, the source of the Ganga.

(4 mi) of very hard going along the edge. At 4,337 m (14,229 ft) some claim this is the real source of the Ganga because you can see the river flowing. Nandanvan is the base camp for the Bhagirathi peaks but its chief beauty is that it stands right in front of Shivling and reveals the whole mountain, from its 10-km (6 mi) wide base up to the spectacular sweep of its winged summit.

A Jewel Among Peaks

This jewel among peaks stands only 4 km (2.5 mi) across the glacier and is used as a marker for picking a way through the crevasses to the other side. The steep walls on the edge of the glacier are very loose and require skill and concentration to climb. The meadows at Tapovan are unbelievably beautiful and circle the base of Shivling like a garland. Early in the season before the snow has melted they are temporarily turned into a lake. This season has the advantage that you can cross the river opposite **Bhojbas** by a snow-bridge. (The rule is to test its safety by hurling heavy boulders into the middle of the snow.)

To get to **Tapovan** (4,463 m or 14,642 ft) from Gaumukh you have to cross the snout of the glacier which means climbing up the side and using the ice cave as a bridge. Having crossed the green ice the path follows a shepherd's trail diagonally across a shale slope which leads out at the meadows of Tapovan. In summer holy men live here in underground chambers. You can walk for miles up the edge of the **Gangotri Glacier** (which runs for 24 km or 15 mi to the Chaukumbha massif, 7,138 m or 23,419 ft). However the going is very tough. On the way you will pass the base of Kedarnath and Kharchakund. Numerous side glaciers also lead to striking unnamed peaks. This is the ultimate mountain scenery and gives those who see it a sense of being a privileged pilgrim at the source.

IN THE FOOTSTEPS OF THE BUDDHA

To many people India is the land of the Buddha, and a visit to the country means a pilgrimage to those places sacred to the memory of the Enlightened One. The story of his life, his message of compassion and his profound understanding of the human predicament had a deep and widespread influence throughout all Asia and are relevant even today, more than 2000 years after his time.

The Buddha's first journey from his home at Kapilavastu was at the age of 29 to Vaisali, Rajgir and ultimately Bodh Gaya, where he spent six years, and finally attained his Enlightenment. He then went to Sarnath, where he delivered his first sermon or, in religious language, set in motion the Wheel of Law. From Sarnath he returned to Rajgir and then visited Sravasti and Kapilavastu, having been absent from home for 12 years. He undertook his last journey at the age of 80, from Rajgir to Nalanda, Patna, Vaisali, Pava and Kusinagar. During the 40 years that followed his Enlightenment he traveled often but he never revisited Bodh Gaya. Yet on the day before his death he included it among the four places that he thought deserved to be sacred to his followers.

The other three were Lumbini (Lord Buddha's birthplace, in the Nepal *terrai*), Sarnath and Kusinagar where he attained the Nirvana. Bodh Gaya's claims to be a place of pilgrimage seem to have gone by default until Asoka's first pilgrimage in the eighth year of his reign (253 B.C. to 226 B.C.). The Emperor's second pilgrimage was undertaken twelve years later when he erected shrines at Lumbini, Kusinagar, Vaisali, Bodh Gaya and Sarnath. The first Buddhist Council was convened at Rajgir, soon after the Buddha's death in 483 B.C., the second at Vaisali one hundred years later, and the third at Patna during Asoka's reign.

Sarnath, where several Buddhist structures were raised from the 3rd century B.C. through till the 11th century A.D., presents to the visitor the most extensive ruins, followed by Nalanda and Sravasti. What has escaped destruction remains impressive. Buddhist iconography emerged in the first century B.C., with symbols such as the Bo tree, footprints, the wheel, parasol and the stupa representing the Buddha. The very first sculptures of the Buddha were made in the 2nd century A.D. More Buddhist sculptures than architecture survived, and can be seen preserved at the sites or in museums.

While the Buddha was alive groves, pools and hills were sacred, and the best examples of these are the *sal* copse by the pool at Lumbini; the *Bo* tree (*Ficus religiosa*, locally known as *pipal*) and the lotus pond at Bodh Gaya; the Deer Park at Sarnath; the orchard by the lake at Nalanda; Jeeta's wood at Sravasti; Ambapali's orchard and pond at Vaisali; and the *sal* trees at Kusinagar.

Rajgir

Rajgir had more of these landmarks than other centers: **Venuvana**, the bamboo brake where the Buddha and his disciples lived; **Karnada Tank**, where the Buddha used to bathe; **Jivakamarvana**, the orchard presented to the Buddha by the physician Jivaka; **Griddakuta Hill** (the hill of vultures) from where the Buddha delivered his sermons and the **Sattapani Cave**, where the First Buddhist Council was convened.

The first Buddhist structures at Rajgir were raised when Ajatsatru built a monastery and a stupa over his share of the Buddha's ashes. That reliquary is now a mound used as a graveyard. Treading the paths that the Buddha took is becoming a pilgrimage for world peace. Much later the Japanese built the **World Peace Stupa**, with gilded images of the Buddha. Adjacent to the hilltop where the

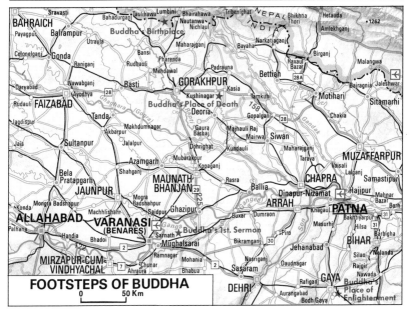

FOOTSTEPS OF BUDDHA
0   50 Km

Buddha used to deliver sermons, the stupa is visible for miles around. Access is by an aerial rope-way. The association of Buddhism with peace goes back to 250 B.C. when Emperor Asoka became a convert to it out of revulsion at the carnage in his conquest of Kalinga.

Rajgir also has the **Nipponzan Myohoji**, the Japanese temple, and the **Centaur Hokke Club** which offers some traditional facilities to Japanese pilgrims. The Burmese, too, have built a temple. There are also hot springs at Rajgir, around which Hindu and Jain temples have been built.

Nalanda

The site of **Nalanda** was one of the greatest monastic universities of the ancient world. Established in the 5th century B.C., it remained a live center of learning till the 12th century A.D. when it was destroyed by the invader Bakhtiar Khilji. Lord Mahavira and the Buddha both taught here for years. Hsuan Tsang,

the Chinese traveler studied here in the 7th century A.D. and there is a monument in his memory. He was one among many of those from East and Southeast Asia who came here to study logic, metaphysics, medicine, prose composition and rhetoric. The university of Nalanda offered free educational and residential facilities to as many as 10,000 students and 2000 teachers, for it was supported by a number of villages. Its library, Ratna Sagar, is believed to have contained nine million volumes. It is not surprising, then, that the destruction of this university dealt a crippling blow to Buddhist education in India.

Excavations have revealed nine levels of occupation. Spread over 15 hectares (37 acres) stand the ruins of six temples, eleven monasteries, the **Sariputra Stupa** built by Asoka to honor the Buddha's first disciple, Ananda, and scattered *chaityas* or prayer halls. Sculptures, bas reliefs and frescoes can still be seen. In 1951 an international center for Buddhist studies was founded. Another modern in-

stitution is the **Nava Nalanda Mahavira Research Centre** treasuring many rare manuscripts. There is also a museum and a Thai temple.

Bodh Gaya

For the Buddhists, **Bodh Gaya** is the most sacred of the sacred cities, for it is here that the Buddha attained Enlightenment beneath the famous Bo tree. The present tree is only a "successor" of the original. Beneath the tree is the **Vajrasana**, the **Diamond Throne**, which marks the place where the Buddha meditated. Nearby is the **Mahabodhi Temple** with a gilded image of the Buddha. Originally raised in the 2nd century, it has been damaged and restored over the centuries. Hsuan Tsang, who visited this temple in A.D. 635, records that he saw

700 gilded images of the Enlightened One. There is also a massive **Dharma Chakra**, the **Animalesh Lochan Chaitya**, and the **Lotus Tank** in the midst of which is a statue of the Buddha protected by a cobra. The **Archaeological Museum** contains statues of the Buddha in gold, bronze and stone. There are Burmese, Thai, Tibetan, Chinese and Japanese monasteries at Bodh Gaya. The river Niranjana flows past this tranquil place.

Vaisali

In **Vaisali** (birthplace of Lord Mahavira) there are ruins of two stupas which were built to commemorate the Second Buddhist Council. The impressive Lion Capital was built by Asoka to commemorate the Buddha's last sermon. There are also Jain temples and a museum.

Kusinagar and Lumbini

Kusinagar is where the Buddha finally attained Mahaparinirvana. Among

Above: Ruins of the ancient Nalanda University, where the Buddha and Mahavira taught. Right: Pilgrims at dawn near Kusinagar, one of Buddhism's sacred cities.

the ruins are the **Mukutbandhan Stupa** and a beautiful statue of the reclining Buddha.

At Gorakhpur, en route to Kusinagar, there is the **Rahul Sankritayan Museum** with a collection of *thangka* paintings. An inscribed relic casket was dug out of the ruins of a stupa at **Piprahwa**, now identified as **Kapilavastu**.

Lumbini, the birthplace of the Buddha, was located in 1890 after being untraced for 1,500 years. At the excavation site in the **Maya Temple** are the ruins of a monastery and a pool. There are ruins of a stupa at **Sravasti** as well.

Sarnath

Sarnath, where the Buddha preached his first sermon in the **Deer Park**, contains the most impressive remains, as well as a modern temple. The **Dharmarajika, Chaukhandi** and **Dhamek stupas** are outstanding. There are also the remains of a monastery, and the beautifully polished Lion Capital of Asoka.

Sarnath contains an excellent library and at the Mulagandha Kutir Vihara there are excellent frescoes by Kosetsu Nosu. The **Sarnath Museum**, not far from the site, contains some of the finest specimens of Buddhist sculpture.

At all centers of Buddhist worship, the *Vaisakha* (April-May) full moon is observed as the anniversary of three important events – the Buddha's birth, Enlightenment and death – while the *Asadh* (July-August) full moon is observed as the anniversary of his first sermon.

Within the last 20 years, facilities have improved greatly for pilgrims and travellers. The Vaisali Express, with its air-conditioned coaches, runs past railheads for Sravasti, Kapilavastu, Lumbini, Kusinagar and Vaisali.

The Ganga at Patna is now crossed by a road bridge, at whose northern end the express halts at Hajipur. Nalanda, Rajgir and Bodh Gaya are within 191 km (119 mi) of Hajipur on the same road. Hourly buses run to Kusinagar from Gorakhpur and to Lumbini from Naugarh.

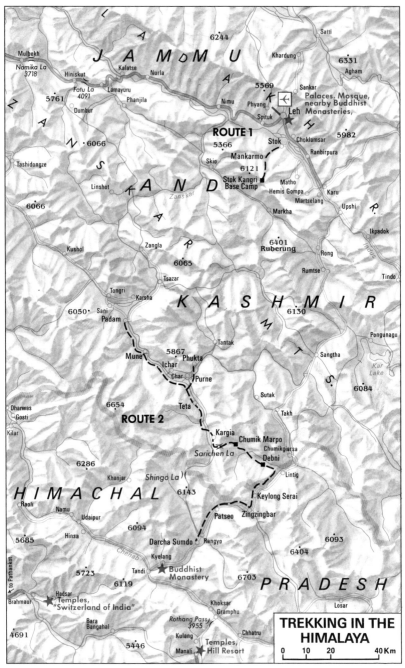

TREKKING IN THE
HIMALAYA

0   10   20   40 Km

TREKKING IN THE HIMALAYA

The most important thing in trekking the Himalayas is to appreciate the scale and match your destination with your ability. Everyone acclimatizes differently and caution in these mountains can save your life. The best trekking seasons are pre-monsoon (June) and post-monsoon (September-October). But flower-lovers have to go in the rainy months of July and August. North of the main ranges in **Lahaul** and **Ladakh,** on the other hand, monsoon months are ideal for trekking because heavy rain rarely penetrates over the passes (in theory at any rate!). As your water intake is a critical factor, the pre-monsoon visitor may have a problem finding enough. It is crucial at altitude to force yourself to eat and drink, and for this reason it is vital that you take only food that you like. This, in turn, has to be bought well in advance of your arrival. Hill towns have very little to offer and the prices are high. (Optimism is a luxury you cannot afford in these mountains.) Bring instead the will to survive and the willingness to improvise. If you are fit enough, porters are not always necessary. You can do without a tent most of the time. Allow for wildly fluctuating temperatures which require woolens in the morning, cotton during the day and waterproofs in the evening.

Himalayan weather has set patterns but it is dangerous to believe in predictability in the realms of the unpredictable Lord of the Snows. A sampling from five treks in different regions – from the easy to the definitely tough – will indicate the wide range of possibilities.

Kashmir

This is an easy monsoon trek with religious interest. You can join the three-day trek to the cave at **Amarnath,** which starts at **Pahalgam** passing lush mead-ows to reach some stunning peaks. Camp at Lake Sheshnag (3,700 m or 12,140 ft) then cross a 4,500 m (14,764 ft) pass to arrive at the vast cave containing a small *lingam* (pillar) of ice, worshipped by the devotees as Shiva, Lord of the Snows.

Ladakh

A fairly easy high-altitude trek with the promise of wildlife sightings. This three-day trek from **Stok** village (across the Indus from **Leh**) to the base camp for **Stok Kangri** (6,316 m or 20,722 ft) follows the Stok River through a canyon with intriguing rock formations. Camp on a shepherd's threshing floor at **Mankarmo** and try to sleep amid the cacophony of goats, donkeys and yaks bedded down all around you. Turn towards the peak in the west and climb for 10 km (6 mi) to base camp keeping a look out for wild blue sheep. Your campsite is surrounded by rugged rock pinnacles that make excellent yodeling points. The third day gets you back to Stok and Leh. This trek is best done in July and August unless you are equipped for cold weather (see Route 1 in the map on page 212).

Zanskar

A tough nine-day trek over the Himalayas with horses. The horses are not only needed for your luggage but to help with the dangerous river crossings. These can be deadly and should never be attempted on your own. Always try to cross as early as possible and use a rope. Make sure your money is carried high on the body and in a waterproof wallet. Horsemen can be found in **Manali,** though the trek starts from **Darcha,** a day's bus journey into the interior. By sharing a horse you can travel cheaper. Once across the Himalayas in **Zanskar** – the first village of **Kargyiak,** is four days from **Darcha** – you can backpack down the Luna Valley to **Padum,** provided you are very tough.

Between the villages of **Darcha** and **Purna** there is nothing in the way of supplies or even tea shops. The trekker is entirely alone. The shortest route is over the **Shingo La Pass** and the safe months are July and August. All of the passes are over 5,000 m (16,400 ft) and need to be taken seriously. Early starts avoid the bad weather that can turn nasty by evening. Once over the top the empty gray valleys lined by *mani* walls (to guide the traveler and invoke the protection of the Buddha) give way to scattered green fields and the white villages of **Zanskar** (Route 2 in the map on page 212).

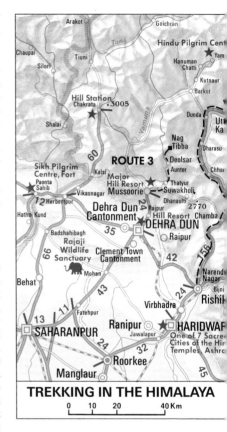

Garhwal

Easy three-day trek from **Mussoorie** and back – any time of the year. To the north of Mussoorie can be seen the black forested mountain of **Nag Tibba** called "the snake peak." It is best approached by an 11-km (7 mi) march along the **Tehri** motor road to **Suwakholi** then down through pine jungle to **Thatyur** on the Aglar River (on returning you can catch a bus back to Mussoorie). A 7-km (4 mi) walk north along the stream issuing from Nag Tibba leads to the village **Aunter** at its base. The forest bridle-path runs on the eastern side of the stream and goes to the forest bungalow at **Deolsari** (3 km or 1.5 mi from Aunter.) The bungalow stands next to a wooden pagodastyle temple set in a dense conifer forest. By contrast the temple in Aunter is a tall, narrow stone tower with a massive foundation because, the villagers tell you, in the old days the gods walked tall! The climb to Nag Tibba is 5 km (3 mi) by the forest path but the jungle is so thick it is safer to take a village guide. Wild animals like bears, barking deer and wild pig are common and villagers refuse to go about at night out of fear of them. A tiny temple to the snake god stands to the west of the summit (3,038 m or 9,967 ft) where the ruins of an old forest bungalow

mark another exit route to the Yamuna Valley. The view from the top gives an exhilarating all round survey of Garhwal (Route 3 in the map on page 215).

Kumaon - Pindari Glacier

This trek is a famous Himalayan classic (see Route 4 in the map on page 215). The eight-day walk provides a fabulous mix of culture and scenery. It has verdant river valleys, resplendent snow peaks, dense jungles, majestic waterfalls and a dazzling glacier to crown your efforts. Best of all there are bungalows all along the route. The ideal season is probably October when the range is clear. The River Pindar rises on the east of Nanda

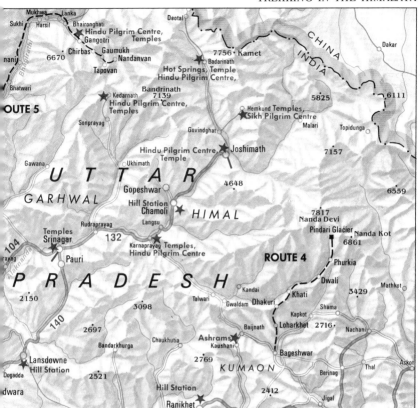

Devi Sanctuary issuing from the impressive tumble of ice known as "Traill's Pass" after an early British administrator who was led over by a villager called Malak Singh. The great grandson of the villager still lives in **Khati** (along the way) and will show his visitors' book containing the names of distinguished travelers over the last 150 years. The trek begins near **Loharkhet** (39 km or 24 mi north of Bageshwar). You can climb to **Dhakuri** to be rewarded with a thrilling view of Nanda Kot (6,861 m or 22,251 ft), one of the most peerless peaks in the whole Himalayas. From this point, the path dives down to Khati.

From this village, a breathtaking trail goes to the **Sunderdhunga Glacier**, a much more difficult trek that takes you up to the base of **Maiktoli** (6,803 m or 22,320 ft). From the bungalow of **Dwali** another trail goes to the **Kafni Glacier** near the base of Nanda Kot. The jungles are a magnificent mix of fern and bamboo and bird life is equally rich. From Loharkhet the Pindari Glacier is 45 km (28 mi) and the bungalows are conveniently spaced every 6-8 km (4-5 mi). The last bungalow is at **Phurkia** above the tree line. This was built near the snout but the glacier has retreated so much – 3 km (1.5 mi) in a century – that now you have to walk to see the ice fall from **Zero Point** (3,353 m or 11,000 ft).

(Route 5 in the map below refers to the article To the Source of the Ganga.)

215

THE NOSTALGIA TOUR

In India nostalgia comes easily, for here past and present coexist with fascinating ease. This is continually obvious at many levels, from the purely visual to the more abstract areas of beliefs and attitudes. In preceding centuries the western world looked upon India as the land of maharajas and even that image has survived. In recent years, film and literature have created an increasing interest in the British Raj. Despite fundamental changes the lifestyle of this bygone era may still be glimpsed.

Palace Hotels

India's palace hotels offer a taste of this legendary past. In the decades just before Independence in 1947, and indeed for a while after, India's palaces surged with royal life and bubbled with cham-

Above: The romantic Lake Palace Hotel set in the shimmering Pichola Lake, Udaipur.

pagne. Because many are hotels today it is actually possible to sleep in a room that was occupied by a maharaja or a viceroy.

Starting in western Rajasthan, the **Lake Palace** in **Udaipur** is unique, and certainly one of the most luxuriously appointed hotels in the world. Set like a jewel in the center of Pichola Lake, surrounded by rugged hills, it is approachable only by boat. Professionally run since 1971, the hotel has over 80 rooms including lavish suites like the Khush Mahal (the Palace of Happiness). They are complemented by rich interior decor: opulent furniture, both traditionally Indian and antique European, stained glass, wall paintings with hunting scenes and dancing girls, and several ponds interlaced in the architectural layout. Known as Jag Niwas Palace, it was formely used as a summer residence by the rulers of the erstwhile Rajput state of Udaipur.

The view from the Lake Palace is in itself enchanting: an expanse of water , the old city and its sprawling palace rising off the waterfront, encircled by the dark rolling hills. Few hotels in the world could have a more romantic location than this one.

Jodhpur Palace

If you go northwards to **Jodhpur**, a variety of experiences will be on offer. **Umaid Bhawan Palace**, built between 1929 and 1942 to create employment during a severe drought, is still the residence of the former Maharaja of Jodhpur. This palace does not have the fairy-tale charm of Udaipur but is imposing and ponderously grand, with over 300 rooms, 55 of which form part of the hotel. Antique paraphernalia, ranging from furniture and carpets to armor, portraits, chandeliers and stuffed tigers, is blended with art-deco interiors. The Regal Suites are particularly lavish. Choice cuisine can be enjoyed at the Marwar Hall and the more select Chamber of Princes. The palace has a basement swimming pool as well as an interesting museum. The outstanding exhibits include a room full of antique clocks and a fine selection of miniature paintings. In the nicely landscaped garden, where peacocks roam, there is a cool marble pavilion which offers a grandstand view of the awesome Mehrangarh Fort in the distance. Folk dances and traditional wandering minstrel shows are regularly seen in the palace, while parties can be organized in the fort. By special arrangement, hotel guests can travel in the Maharaja's saloon on the overnight train to Jaisalmer.

An Informal Royal Home

A short drive away from the Umaid Bhawan is **Ajit Bhawan**, another royal home, less grand and more traditionally Indian, with all the accessories of Indian royalty. The service here is welcoming casual and friendly, with the owners (who are a part of Jodhpur's royal family) at hand to provide company and conversation. Meals are taken in the central courtyard to the sound of Indian classical music. Away from the main building a charming traditional village environment has been recreated with great success. In this hotel one feels like a guest of the family. A safari to villages (organized by both hotels) provides some interesting glimpses of the countryside surrounding Jodhpur and should not be missed.

The Ram Bagh of Jaipur

The city of **Jaipur** also takes you back into the past, and here you can stay at two palace hotels, **Jai Mahal** and the 19th-century **Ram Bagh Palace**. At one time Ram Bagh Palace was the only private residence in the world with its own polo ground. In a city that is perhaps richer than any other in Rajasthan in its palaces and forts, the opulence of princely India can be experienced firsthand at these two hotels.

Before leaving Rajasthan, one other hotel deserves mention: the **Royal Castle** at **Khimsar**, 90 km (56 mi) en route from Jodhpur to Bikaner. Somewhat like Ajit Bhawan, this is a rambling building, part ruin, part contemporary, which for 21 generations has belonged to the numerous family of the former feudal chiefs of Khimsar. Today Khimsar is a tiny unobtrusive town, and in the 14-roomed hotel you will feel more like a visiting friend. Khimsar gives you the atmosphere and setting that fuels nostalgia. The atmosphere is enhanced by the silence, the remoteness of the setting and the discreet but attentive service. Close to the hotel, blackbuck roam free over flat fields and rough stony scrub land that often turns into desert. (See Rajasthan Guidepost for addresses of palace hotels. Bookings via any Welcomgroup hotel.)

There are other palace hotels across the country, such as the grand **Lalita Mahal** in **Mysore**. In the lower Himalayas of Himachal Pradesh is **Chail** (2,250 m or

7,382 ft), the summer palace of the Maharaja of Patiala. Chail is 45 km (28 mi) from Shimla and the hotel affords a spectacular view of the mountains. (Reservations through Himachal Tourist Information Office, Chandralok Bldg. Janpath, New Delhi. Tel: 3325320.)

Forest Bungalows

At the other end of the scale you will find the little forest bungalows, mostly a legacy of the British rule in India. Scattered all over India, often in forgotten but wildly beautiful settings, they are often period buildings.

Most of these comfortable bungalows were built for hunting expeditions and forestry. Today they are used mostly by government personnel, but the ordinary public can stay at them with written permission. Their atmosphere makes up for any hardship one may encounter. There, in dusty corners or ancient sideboards, you will find a visitors' book dating back 50 years or more, or quaint government notices and tattered pre-war editions of travel books left behind by foreigners.

Back to Nature

In most of these bungalows the conditions are primitive; but they are usually clean and amazingly inexpensive. There is no electricity and though a kitchen is provided one must do one's own cooking which means taking provisions along. Advance booking is necessary, and there is usually an old watchman or caretaker-cum-general factotum who will arrange bedclothes and hot bath water for you.

Most often you will feel that you have been transported through some time warp into the last century. All around is the silence of the forest, broken perhaps by the gurgle of a nearby stream, or the distant chugging of a steam engine on a narrow-gauge track, as at **Motichur** in U.P., where one of these bungalows is situated

between Haridwar and Rishikesh, on the fringe of the Rajaji National Park. Although some of these bungalows are accessible only along fair-weather roads, Motichur is just off the main highway, though hidden by a belt of trees. Bookings at Motichur can be arranged by writing to the Director of Rajaji National Park at Dehra Dun. Similarly, most of these bungalows are booked through the main forest department or the wildlife protection official of the district.

A grander version of the traditional forest bungalow is the **Kabini River Lodge** at **Nagarahole**, two hours by road from Mysore. Famous for its elephants and its lake, Nagarahole is a rich forest dominated by teak, and the former Maharaja's hunting lodge is today a tourist retreat. Here, under a thatched shelter on the banks of the huge Kabini river reservoir, you may enjoy a log fire (even in summer). The accommodation is a little old fashioned, with large rooms and broad verandahs conducive to comfort.

Colonial Clubs

Also sprinkled across India are those other legacies of the British - clubs. The small golf and country clubs in the hills of the northeast and south are the most charming, because the way of life among the tea and coffee planters of these areas has remained virtually unchanged since colonial times. One of the more famous clubs is at **Ooty** (**Uthagamandalam**), a small town with a lake set among green, rolling hills near Mysore, in the area that used to be called the "Scotland of the East." In the **Ooty Club**, fox-hunting records are still up on the walls on wooden panels, and a comfortable air of antiquity surrounds you. The atmosphere of the Ooty Club is duplicated many times in small towns across India and indeed in some of the larger Indian cities as well; **Calcutta** for instance, has the Bengal Club and the Tollygunge Club.

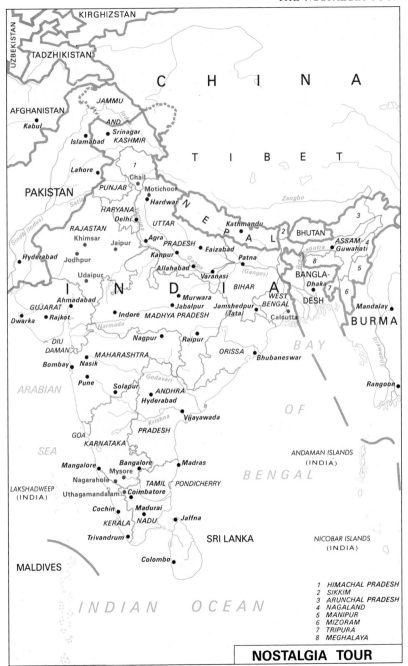

1 HIMACHAL PRADESH
2 SIKKIM
3 ARUNCHAL PRADESH
4 NAGALAND
5 MANIPUR
6 MIZORAM
7 TRIPURA
8 MEGHALAYA

NOSTALGIA TOUR

THE SEVEN SACRED CITIES

Life from the Hindu point of view is a magical abundance of energy, an overflowing of the Divine. Certain places are credited with possessing sacred powers which, when visited by the pilgrim, bestow on him immediate blessings and also immunize his soul from further suffering. During the classical age of Hinduism (c. 4th century A.D.) several of these lists were compiled in rhyming Sanskrit so that they could be easily remembered. For example, merely reciting the list of the seven sacred rivers could be considered the equivalent of having a bath. Thus anyone traveling need not be prevented from performing holy tasks out of fear of impurity. Essentially these lists were practical aids to help in the salvation of the seeker.

Currently (because tradition has changed since the 4th century), the seven sacred cities (*Saptpuri*) of Hinduism are Ayodhya (birthplace of Lord Rama), Mathura (the birthplace of Lord Krishna), Haridwar (the most auspicious spot for the immersion of one's ashes), Varanasi (which is said to give instant salvation by bathing in the River Ganga), Kanchipuram (where Hindu scholarship and culture have flourished for millennia), Ujjain (where Sanskrit poetry and drama reached its peak), and Dwarka (the ancient coastal kingdom where Lord Krishna ascended to heaven).

Nowadays, several unlisted towns attract more dev-otees than the old places. The town of Gaya in Bihar was once listed among the seven famous cities as the place where Hindus remembered their ancestors.

Rama's Birthplace

Today, **Ayodhya** is very popular and possesses rustic charm in the hundreds of small temples where the virtuous deeds of Rama and Sita (the hero and heroine of

Above: It takes all kinds to make the world! An ascetic performing penance.

the epic scripture, the *Ramayana*) are re-membered. **Mathura** and **Dwarka**, on the other hand, attract many Vaishnavas of other sects who worship Radha and Krishna. Hinduism caters for all the psychological nuances in human relationships, being more concerned with the subtle layers of life than the gross. While Rama and Sita represent the courtly example of virtuous rulers, Radha and Krishna typify the bliss of village lovers caught in the passion of love.

Krishna's Domain

Near Mathura is **Vrindavan** where the divine lovers met, and each Holi festival explodes in colorful memory of their divine romance. By contrast the mood at Dwarka is more restrained and reflects Lord Krishna's mature nature as adviser to the legendary heroes of the *Mahabharata*. Dwarka also happens to be one of the four spiritual cardinal points of Hinduism. It was founded by the philosopher Shankaracharya as the westernmost temple where pilgrims bound for the circuit of the subcontinent could take their bearings and find inspiration from the hereditary line of teachers he had installed at these four points.

The Gates of God

Haridwar is one of the most popular places of pilgrimage thanks to the beauty of the Ganga which flows by at considerable speed. Those who bathe here have to cling to chains lest the current should sweep them away. The evening worship at Harki-Pauri is one of the most entrancing religious spectacles in the world. Leafboats filled with flowers and bearing a lit oil lamp on top are set in the river's evening light to float at the tug of destiny. The symbolism is extraordinarily moving and enables the visitor to overlook the importuning crowd of beggars, priests, con men and cranks who infest all holy places where simple people gather armed only with faith. Haridwar means "the Gates of God" and refers both to the Ganga escaping from the hills into the plains and to the liberation of the soul when the body is burnt.

Actually, the main river at Haridwar is now the Ganga Canal and the old course can be seen in the southern suburb of Kankhal where the orthodox pilgrim must start his *yatra* (pilgrimage). Haridwar is one of the four sites of the Kumbh Mela which occurs every 12 years and is attended by millions of Hindus eager to bathe on the auspicious day of the (traditional) celebration of the winter solstice.

The Kumbh Mela

Three cities rotate the Kumbh Mela between them – **Prayag**, at the confluence of the Ganga and Yamuna rivers at Allahabad, **Nasik** in Maharashtra, near the source of the Godavari river and **Ujjain**. Owing to the popularity of the Kumbh, every six years an Ardh (half) Kumbh is held which whets the appetite of the devotee for the real thing. These Melas (fairs) date back to the 13th century and reflect Hinduism's love of pageantry and hierarchy.

The various sects of holy men gather in encampments on the river bank and range in their behavior from the most scholarly and retiring of recluses to the vulgar gymnastics of the bed-of-nails type of yogi. The latter Naga (naked) orders were raised to defend Hinduism from the onslaught of foreign beliefs. The precedence in bathing of these various orders is of crucial importance for the smooth running of the Mela and in the past there have been violent quarrels over protocol. As the greatest religious show on earth the Kumbh Mela is also a marvel of Indian administration.

Continuing down the Ganga brings the pilgrim to the most sacred city of all, **Varanasi**, which is every bit as magical as

221

its reputation. It draws its life from the river and it is to the *ghats* (stepped embankments) that the pilgrim goes to fulfill his deepest longings.

Like Hinduism itself Varanasi takes everything in its stride. The ancient Sarnath stupa, the medieval mosque and the modern railway bridge all merge into the body of the world's oldest continuously inhabited city. Serene amid the throng, sitting on the steps at Dasasvamedh Ghat, one can sense that these stones have witnessed not just the river, but the essence of all life flowing past. Widely known as "Kashi," the City of Light, the **Vishvanath Temple** contains one of Saivism's 12 *jyotirling* (pillar of light). Scattered over north and west India these temples constitute another list of pilgrimages for the extra-devotional.

By any reckoning the town of **Ujjain** (which also appears on the list of *jyotirling* temples) must be among the most

sacred as it occurs in so many itineraries. However, its glory is reserved in modern times for scholars who recall the golden age of Hinduism under the Gupta dynasty when it was called Ujjaini. Sited on the Sipra, one of the most westward of the tributaries of the Ganga, modern Ujjain is a clean and well laid out town, something that cannot be said of the sacred cities of U.P. The refinement that Ujjain conjures up is best caught in the peerless poetry of the Sanskrit dramatist Kalidas whose colorful descriptions of the courtesans still have relevance even after 1500 years. Their modern counterparts recently organized themselves into a union!

The seventh in the list of sacred cities of Hinduism is **Kanchipuram**, the lone representative from the south, and in the *Saptpuri Yatra* the most spectacular from the viewpoint of temple architecture. It is said that Kanchi combines the learning of Ujjain, the devotion of the Vaishnav cities and the ascetic tradition of Shankaracharya who is believed to have left his body here.

Above: Pilgrims bathing in the River Ganga at the sacred city of Varanasi.

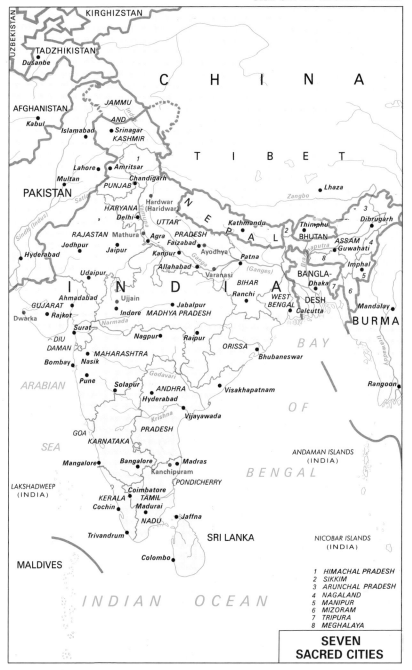

SEVEN
SACRED CITIES

WILDLIFE

India has a virtually unmatched diversity of forest wildlife. Although effective forest cover has shrunk alarmingly, protected areas are now many and widespread, covering a complete range of habitats. These areas have varying ground conditions and degrees of accessibility, often dependent on seasonal weather.

The **Dachigam National Park** (21 km or 13 mi from **Srinagar**, Kashmir) is a pristine alpine ecosystem extending, from 1,700 to 4,300 m (5,573-14,108 ft). It harbors a highly endangered species, the Kashmir stag or *hangul* (*Cervus elaphus hanglu*), a relative of the European red deer. Dachigam also has a sizable population of Himalayan bears, both black and (higher up) brown, which are most visible in summer. Musk deer, foxes, marmots and bird life can be observed, but luck and bush-craft are needed for good views. Winter is the best time to observe *hangul*, when they gather in Lower Dachigam, Upper Dachigam being almost completely snowbound. This is one of the few National Parks in India where walking in the forest is allowed, and it is safe and exciting.

Corbett National Park

Corbett National Park and Project Tiger Reserve is in Uttar Pradesh, 300 km (186 mi) east of New Delhi. India's oldest national park is one of her most beautiful, set in the verdant foothills of the Kumaon Himalayas. With its mixed deciduous forest dominated by *sal* (*Shorea robusta*), grassy meadows and a perennial submontane river coursing through it, this habitat is rich in tigers, herbivores and a substantial summer population of wild elephants, migrants from neighboring forest tracts. Corbett National Park is at the heart of the area in which Jim Corbett hunted most of his

man-eaters. Elephant rides are available for visitors, and a fairly good road network makes it possible to drive within the park. *Chital* (*Axis axis*), *sambar* (*Cervus unicolor*, India's largest deer), barking deer (*Muntjac*), wild pig, monitor lizard, *gharial* (fish-eating crocodile) and over 500 bird species including partridge, jungle fowl, pheasants, hawks, buzzards, eagles, and paradise flycatchers are easily spotted. Breathtaking sightings of tiger and leopard have increased recently.

Dudhwa, Manas and Kaziranga

Southeast of Corbett stretches the **Dudhwa National Park**. This is the famous *terrai* area, the thick, often swampy jungle of the Indo-Nepal border at the feet of the Himalayan system. Dudhwa is famous for its *barasingha* or swamp deer (*Cervus duvauceli*) which are found in large numbers here. The tiger population is sizable and herbivores are abundant, while bird life is astonishing in its variety. Rhinoceros existed in Dudhwa many decades ago before being wiped out by humans, but a small nucleus population has in recent years been translocated from Kaziranga in Assam.

Up against the Bhutan border, 176 km (109 mi) from **Guwahati**, Assam, extends **Manas Tiger Reserve**. Here the jungle is tropical monsoon, a deep lush green. The Reserve is named after the Manas River which flows through it and is the only known habitat of the unique and beautiful golden *langur* (*Presbytis geei*). Manas has a larger population of tigers, wild buffalo and elephants, and its colorful bird life ranges from the endangered great Indian hornbill to the tiny scarlet minivet. It is difficult to observe tigers in the open near Manas, but buffalo and elephant are more easily seen. Sloths, barking deer, wild pig and *sambar* are regularly sighted. Insect life is spectacular. A boat trip down the river is an unforgettable experience. Rhino and *gaur* (*Bos*

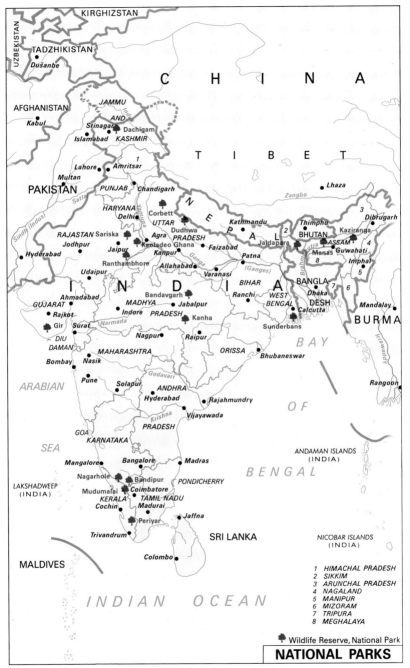

KIRGHIZSTAN

UZBEKISTAN

TADZHIKISTAN

Dušanbe

C   H   I   N   A

AFGHANISTAN

JAMMU

Kabul

AND

Srinagar Dachigam

Islamabad *KASHMIR*

T   I   B   E   T

Lhaza

Lahore *Amritsar*

Multan

PAKISTAN *PUNJAB* *Chandigarh*

Zangbo

3

Dibrugarh

N *HARYANA*

Delhi Corbett

UTTAR Dudhwa

E *Kathmandu* *Thimphu* *Dibrugarh*

2 BHUTAN Kaziranga

RAJASTAN Sariska *Agra*

Jodhpur Keoladeo Ghana

P *Faizabad* Jaldapara *ASSAM* *4*

Manas *Guwahati*

Jaipur *Kanpur* *Patna*

Hyderabad Ranthambhore A *8* *Imphal*

Udaipur Allahabad *Varanasi* *5*

I N D *BIHAR* A *7* *6*

Ahmadabad Bandavgarh *Ranchi* BANGLA-

GUJARAT *MADHYA* *Jabalpur* *WEST* *Dhaka* DESH

Rajkot *Indore* *PRADESH* *BENGAL* *Calcutta* *Mandalay*

Gir *Surat* Kanha

DIU *Narmada* Sunderbans BURMA

DAMAN *Nagpur* *Raipur*

MAHARASHTRA *ORISSA* BAY *Irrawaddy*

Bombay *Nasik* *Bhubaneswar*

Godavari

Pune *Solapur* *ANDHRA*

Hyderabad OF

Krishna *Rajahmundry*

ARABIAN *Vijayawada*

PRADESH

GOA

SEA *KARNATAKA* ANDAMAN ISLANDS

(INDIA)

Mangalore *Bangalore* *Madras*

Nagarhole BENGAL

LAKSHADWEEP Bandipur *PONDICHERRY*

(INDIA) Mudumalai *Coimbatore*

KERALA *TAMIL NADU*

Cochin *Madurai*

Jaffna

Periyar NICOBAR ISLANDS

Trivandrum SRI LANKA (INDIA)

MALDIVES *1 HIMACHAL PRADESH*

2 SIKKIM

Colombo *3 ARUNCHAL PRADESH*

4 NAGALAND

5 MANIPUR

I N D I A N   O C E A N *6 MIZORAM*

7 TRIPURA

8 MEGHALAYA

🌲 Wildlife Reserve, National Park

NATIONAL PARKS

gaurus, the world's largest wild ox) inhabit these jungles in small numbers and are extremely shy of humans. Foreigners need a permit from Delhi to visit Manas.

The wildlife of **Kaziranga** (221 km or 137 mi from Guwahati) is abundant. Rhino, water-buffalo and small herds of swamp deer dot the grassy meadows and swamps, red jungle fowl strut about, ospreys, fishing eagles and harriers majestically course the skies. Wild elephants are often found in or near the many sluggish watercourses. Bordered on one side by the great Brahmaputra river and on the other by the Guwahati-Jorhat highway, Kaziranga is the last stronghold of the great Indian onehorned rhinoceros.

The winter brings migrant ducks, bar-headed geese and other water birds, and on a clear day the Himalayas are visible on the horizon. Walking is dangerous in Kaziranga, but one can get very close to rhino on elephant-back or in a vehicle and sightings are frequent. By contrast, the rhinos of **Jaldapara** in north Bengal (their only other substantial population) are shyer, as are the *gaur* of Jaldapara.

The Sunderbans

The **Sunderbans**, vast mangrove swamps, are now a National Park and Project Tiger Reserve, with the largest single population of tigers in India, and the closest to a major city: Calcutta is only 70 km (44 mi) away. This area, more than any other, strikingly demonstrates the amazing adaptability of tigers. They are known to swim 10 km (6 mi) across brackish estuarine rivers on their territorial beat. At first glance the Sunderbans appear to be merely wide expanses of water and low jungle. A closer look reveals fascinating life forms: fiddler crabs, mudskippers, crocodiles, turtles and tigers, though the latter are rarely

Right: Graceful and alert. Chital stags at the Sariska wildlife sanctuary, Rajasthan.

seen. *Chital* and wild pig are easily sighted in the evening and an interesting water bird colony is located at Sajnekhali. The only way to travel the Sunderbans is by boat, through tiny streams that crisscross the mangroves.

Ranthambhore, Ghana and Sariska

The tigers of **Ranthambhore** are far more relaxed in the proximity of humans than those of Corbett, Dudhwa or the Sunderbans. Here the Project Tiger Reserve and National Park consists of semi-arid rock, thorn and scrub jungle interspersed with patches of startling green where water courses flow through depressions. Because of the open nature of the jungle and the situation of water sources, animals including the tiger are easily sighted. In Ranthambhore, large *sambar, chital* and crocodile are concentrated around a system of three small natural lakes which in winter also attract migratory water birds. *Chinkara* or Indian gazelle, an attractive, delicate and endangered animal, can be seen, with some patience, as can *nilgai* (blue bull) and wild pig. An ancient fort broods over the reserve.

Located between Ranthambhore and the Sariska Tiger Reserve, 176 km (109 mi) from Delhi by road, lies what is probably the world's best known bird sanctuary, the **Keoladeo Ghana National Park**. Initially a man-made swamp, the Ghana (as it is commonly known), is now a 29 sq. km (11 sq. mi) lake system crisscrossed with cycle paths and dirt tracks and interspersed with patches of dry land which are host to *sambar, nilgai*, wild pig, *chital*, pythons and a variety of birds. Water birds, however, are what the Ghana is famous for. In September, if the rains have been good, painted storks, spoonbills, egrets, ibises, herons and others convert the *babul* trees into squawking, flapping, shrieking chick nurseries. Close on the heels of the nest-

ing season come migratory birds from the C.I.S., China, and India's extreme north: thousands of duck and geese (bar-headed and greylag) are among these. In November the star attractions arrive: the western flock of the rare Siberian crane, which naturalists from all over the world come to see. For a bird lover, the Ghana in midwinter, after a good monsoon, is truly paradise.

Sariska, 200 km (124 mi) southwest of Delhi, is a large Project Tiger Reserve, the most accessible from Delhi. Sightings of pig, *sambar*, *chital*, *nilgai* and monkeys are common but tigers are entirely a matter of luck. "Hides" built at strategic water-holes in this dry deciduous forest area facilitate sightings and an interesting drive leads to a small, ruined fortress.

Kanha and Bandavgarh

Two outstanding sanctuaries, **Kanha** and **Bandavgarh**, are located in Madhya Pradesh. Both are excellent for exciting tiger viewing, second after Rantham-bhore, and both elephants and vehicles are used. The tiger is top predator here as in Ranthambhore and Sariska, undisturbed by the other large mammal, the elephant. The jungle is mixed deciduous, with bamboo and open meadows in Kanha, frequented by *chital* and the central Indian subspecies of the swamp deer, *barasingha* (*Cervus duvauceli branderi*). Kanha is famous for successfully retrieving this deer from the brink of extinction. Two antelopes, the *chousingha* or four-horned, and the handsome blackbuck, and wild dogs are also visible. Bandavgarh also has a fort and ancient caves.

Gir Forest

The Indian lion, plentiful until the 17th century, now survives only in the **Gir Forest** in Gujarat. Scrub jungle not unlike African bush, the Gir does not have any tigers. Lions are the top predators, although remarkably tolerant of humans. These majestic, tawny great cats are literally the last handful of their breed.

227

URBAN MIGRATION

According to a recent document issued by the National Institute of Urban Affairs, India's urban population is roughly 160 million. This virtually equals the urban population of the U.S.A. (161 million) and is only a trifle lower than that of the Soviet Union (169 million). In terms of its share in the total population, India's urban population is 23.7 percent.

The distinguishing feature of India's urbanization is that it goes back nearly 5000 years when the Indus Valley civilization saw the birth of some of the earliest urban settlements in human history. However, India's urban pattern today is a mosaic of the pre-British, colonial and post-independence periods. This is best represented in the form and lifestyle of most of the Indian cities which are composed of traditional cores to which civil lines, cantonment areas and railway colonies were added in the British period, and to which residential, industrial, institutional and other extensions have been added since 1947. The cities with over one million population represent a certain degree of uniformity in the process of urban migration. Most of them are industrial centers and many of them are also provincial capitals.

While some of the migration to urban areas has occurred as a consequence of planned processes of industrial and administrative developments (such as the steel city of Durgapur) much more migration continues to take place in a completely unplanned manner. The big cities act as magnets for the underemployed rural poor who come in search of jobs in industry, construction sites and in the informal service sector. In fact it has been argued that the true indicator of rural poverty lies in the urban slums. Since much of the migration to cities is chaotic,

civic amenities and housing cannot keep pace with the population inflow. This results in large shanty towns in and around cities. In the larger urban centers like Bombay there are even middle-class slums where doctors, lawyers and other professionals are forced to reside.

Squatting and illegal encroachments are not uncommon. It takes tremendous political will to undo the ad hoc settlements that tend to spring up in cities. It is not surprising, therefore, that while governments often threaten to act, they eventually do not like to incur unpopularity, especially as they do not have either concrete alternatives or immediate solutions to offer for rural poverty and general unemployment. However, it has been observed that the migration into Calcutta, which is Bengal's capital and also its largest industrial center, has slowed down ever since the agrarian policies of the West Bengal government have sought to provide the rural poor with some guarantee of economic livelihood.

As elsewhere in the developing world, unchecked urbanization in India leads to unhygienic conditions of existence which threaten not only the slums but also the rest of the city. Yet migration to urban areas does apparently provide some relief to the low caste rural poor because they can get away from obligatory labor, and in some instances from their own debts which they can rarely dream of ever repaying. The long term solution to India's problem of rapid urban migration lies in the setting up of satellite townships around the bigger centers with medium to small-scale industries that will provide employment for the semi-skilled and unskilled work-force in search of jobs, and will also ease the pressure on the big cities. Attempts in this direction are being made in some parts of the country, but such satellite townships are always slow to attract investment as they lack the kind of service infrastructure which the urban centers already have.

Preceding pages: Indian ladies watching a procession at Pushkar.

COMMUNAL STRIFE

In India, communalism has come to stand for political antagonism based on religious identities. It does not have any of the positive connotations that the root term "community" implies. Communal antagonism began with the advent of modern representative politics in the early 20th century. Organized Hindu and Muslim interests competed for the limited political power that was available under the colonial constitutional scheme, but competition turned into violent confrontations in the 1920s. There had been earlier instances of Hindu-Muslim clashes but it is this later phase that saw the emergence of communal politics. Communalism is thus a modern phenomenon in the sense that political power has been the key factor motivating political leaders to rally the support of their co-religionists behind them.

The nationalist movement led by the Indian National Congress claimed to be a secular movement, despite groups within it that were inclined towards the idea of Hindu resurgence. Muslims who rallied under the banner of the Muslim League feared that the triumph of Indian nationalism and eventual independence from colonial rule would ultimately result in the marginalization of the Muslims who were, in undivided India, roughly one-fourth of the total population. The Muslim League alleged that the Congress was a political party of the majority community, i.e. the Hindus.

Communal polarization sharpened towards the later phases of the nationalist movement and the Congress could not win over a majority of the Muslims. This paved the way for the birth of two nations at independence in 1947 - India and Pakistan. The partition was accompanied by horrible communal carnage and massive migration of populations of the two communities took place across the India-Pakistan borders in Punjab and Bengal.

However, a substantial Muslim population chose to remain in India because the Indian state was defined as a secular state. Until the mid-1960s communal riots, which had become an endemic feature before independence, were rare. But from then onwards communal riots have been on the upswing, with short periods of amity. Also, a change in the pattern of communal riots is discernible. While in the 1960s they were mostly sparked off by local factors, they have become more political and organized as a consequence of which there is greater destruction of life and property. Earlier, communal riots were sparked off by local factors such as disputes about which route a religious procession would take, or over playing music outside mosques, etc. Now, in their more organized forms there are chain reactions to single riots and the issues involved have wider political dimensions.

The 1980s have also seen a sharpening of communal politics between the Sikhs and the Hindus. Religion is being given fundamentalist political interpretations among Hindus, Sikhs and Muslims, the cumulative effect of which is that the government finds it difficult to de-escalate communal tension. Even though the Indian state continues to be based on secular principles, Muslims and Sikhs who constitute a small minority (85 percent Hindus to 11 percent Muslims and 2 percent Sikhs) feel insecure in the current phase of heightened communal polarization. However, communalism is neither the central characteristic of Indian politics, nor does it have an obvious presence in the daily life of Indians. The countryside has been more or less spared communal conflict. Over 75 percent of the Indian people therefore live in considerable communal harmony. It is possible that, with economic opportunities opening up for Indians as a whole, communalism will take a back seat, though it is difficult to be too optimistic as conflict of this kind tends not to disappear easily.

INDIA IN THE SPACE AGE

In comparison with most other post-colonial nations, India can be said to have emerged from colonialism with a reasonable level of industrialization, which, though inadequate, provided a basic infrastructure. After independence, great emphasis was given to industrialization and technological development through the planning process and by the expansion of the public sector. Yet enough room was left for private enterprise. A sizable industrial and technological infrastructure has already been built as India goes through her seventh Five Year Plan, even though there is acute awareness of the fact that India has slipped behind in industrial growth when compared with some of the other newly industrialized countries.

But one of India's achievements has been that the need for basic self-reliance was recognized early and the development of indigenous technology was attempted through governmental effort; research into atomic power, outer-space exploration and space technology, deep-sea exploration and mining, oceanography etc., was undertaken by institutions that were developed within the country. Active collaboration with other countries, cutting across the global ideological divide, have also been encouraged in respect of these matters. India's first man in space was Squadron Leader Rakesh Sharma when he took off aboard the Soyuz T II spaceship from Baikonour in the former U.S.S.R., along with two Soviet cosmonauts, in 1984.

The India Space Research Organization (ISRO) at Bangalore is responsible for the planning, execution and management of space research activities. It now has six major establishments: the Vikram Sarabhai Space Centre at Trivandrum; the ISRO Satellite Centre at Bangalore; the SHAR Centre at Sriharikota island in Andhra Pradesh; the Space Applications Centre at Ahmedabad; the Auxiliary Propulsion System Unit at Bangalore and Trivandrum; and the Developmental and Educational Communication Unit located at Ahmedabad.

India's first space mission was the launch of the experimental satellite "Aryabhatta" (1975). In 1980 India's first satellite launch vehicle (SALV-3) was successfully launched from ISRO's SHAR center at Sriharikota. India's two Augmented Satellite Launch Vehicle (ASLV) missions have not been successful, but ISRO's future plans include the manufacture of a polar SLV. The space program has been crucial to the development of the Indian National Satellite System (INSAT). The INSAT-1B and I1C are being used by India for TV services, communication and the collection of important meteorological data. India's Remote Sensing Satellite was launched into space on 17 March 1988 from a Soviet cosmodrome, making India the first developing nation to have its own remote sensing satellite in space. India successfully launched an IRBM in May 1989. Spokesmen claim that if required India can produce ICBMs, too.

Modern India has an advanced nuclear establishment which is geared to power generation for peaceful purposes, but her firm refusal to sign the Non-Proliferation Treaty and the successful implosion at Pokhran in 1974 have given rise to the suspicion that India has a covert weapons program. India has also been able to develop her own fast breeder technology at the Reactor Research Center at Kalpakkam near Madras.

In the sphere of Ocean Research the country has been accorded Pioneer Investor Status by the Third U.N. Conference on the Law of the Sea in 1982. Moreover there were seven Indian expeditions to the Antarctic between 1981 and 1987. Two permanent research bases, "Gangotri" and "Maitree" have been installed in the Antarctic.

MEN OF GOD

In India, a very common sight is that of *sadhus* (recluses, ascetics) with shaven heads, or with long beards and matted hair, wandering with begging bowls in their hands. What is also common is the respect and attention accorded to them. Their number is greater in pilgrim centers; their dress and appearance may vary. In the last three decades, particularly, some *gurus* have caught the imagination of westerners, of people in search of an alternate world-view, and have emerged as cult figures.

There are a lot of *ashrams* all over India, which range from the secluded forest hermitage to highly organized institutions which run schools, universities and hospitals, and conduct a variety of social service activities. Visitors are allowed to stay at the *ashram* and benefit from the presence of the *guru*, or his teachings as they are passed on by his devotees. Gurus have long been synonymous with India. They were integral to traditional Indian society, in which their role encompassed more than that of the spiritual mentor. Their teachings are relevant today as well, and can be specially meaningful in our attempts to cope with those pressures which seem inseparable from contemporary life.

The presence of such men of god arises from the Indian view of life cherished for over 2000 years. The Vedic seers realized that the root cause of all human suffering is materialistic desire. It was written: "As man thinks in terms of objects, he develops an attachment to them, from which springs forth the desire for possession. From desire arise anger, hatred, envy.... These upset his sobriety, and result in the loss of the faculty of cognition. In the end he loses his own self".

Buddhist and Jain seers, too, believed that the way to eradicate human suffering is to control desire and discipline one's senses, and that the best way to achieve this lies in the observance of detachment from everything worldly. In the Jain faith there exists an old custom of fasting unto death, considered the supreme mode. But this is to be undertaken only when there is no desire even for death; it should not be resorted to as an escape from life. In the ultimate analysis, it was counseled that one should be detached even from the otherworldly. It would come as a surprise to many that a society as rooted in the caste system as the Indian one believes ultimately in a casteless state. Once the *sadhus* have embraced a life of renunciation they cast aside the limitations of family, territory, caste and creed, and rise to the boundless realm of universal consciousness, becoming still centers radiating tranquillity. This poised and disciplined state of mind evokes veneration, all the more so since it can be attained only by continued efforts and awareness, and a sense of detachment.

In the process of this realization, such men are believed sometimes to acquire supernatural powers that can cure mental and physical afflictions. But the traditions and sacred texts prescribe that such miraculous powers should be used only for ameliorating the sufferings of others; if used for the acquisition of fame or wealth for oneself, those powers are lost.

This is the ideal of men of God, cherished since Vedic times. There is no lack of unscrupulous men, who exploit the faith placed by society on this ideal and enrich themselves under various guises. Even as early as 1500 years ago, men were already aware of the existence of such pseudo-*sadhus*.

A verse ascribed to Sankara states: "The wearing of saffron robes or silken garments, the shaven heads or the matted locks are only various adornments for filling the belly. The true pursuers of reality are one in a million." But the truly realized persons - maybe one in a million - do exist, and they serve as beacons of illuminating knowledge.

THE SACRED COW

The unique veneration of the cow in India can be traced back almost 3,500 years, to the Aryans, who were initially peasants. It was also the time when Vedic sacrifice, which involved offerings and the recitation of sacred hymns, was an essential part of daily life. The recitation and the rituals of the sacrifice were performed by the Brahmins, but the sacrificial offering, which consisted mainly of melted butter prepared from cow's milk, was made by all people.

The cow occupied as important a position in the Vedic way of life as the Vedic fire and the Brahmin poet. Of the domesticated animals, the cow was remarkably useful and the most loved animal, and it could also be easily looked after by the Brahmin. Every product of the cow was useful - milk, curd (yogurt), butter, *ghee* (clarified butter), cow-dung and even urine (cow's urine could cure many diseases). The cow therefore became a cherished item of wealth, worthy of possession by the Brahmins.

The cow was Kamadhenu, the fulfiller of all desires. Feeding and caring for a cow was an act of devotion. In course of time the cow came to be regarded as a symbol of divinity, in which all gods reside. To make a gift of a cow (*Godana*) to a Brahmin was considered a pious act, for he would love the cow and thereby propitiate all the gods, who in turn would bestow spiritual merit on the donor and also the community. The sanctity attached to the Brahmin priest was also associated with the cow.

One of the Vedic legends, of a fight between the Brahmin sage Vasishta and the king Visvamitra, illustrates the veneration the Vedic people had for the cow. Vasishta owned the cow Kamadhenu, the fulfiller of all wishes. King Visvamitra wanted to posses the cow but was unable to do so despite his might and power. He realized that the Brahminical power symbolized by the cow was far superior to the martial power of a king. He did severe penance, and after several failures was recognized as a Brahmin sage.

There is another legend about the sage Chyavana performing severe penance underwater, at the confluence of the Ganga and the Yamuna. Fisherman came by and cast their net and were perturbed to find the sage in their haul of fish. The sage reassured them that they had caused no offence. But he requested them to tell the king that he, too, like the fish, should fetch a price. The king rushed to the spot. He offered vast amounts of money, then half his kingdom, and then, in despair, his entire realm. But each time the sage refused. Finally the king offered a cow as the value of the sage, at which Chyavana nodded his approval.

The five products of the cow - milk, curd, *ghee*, urine and cow-dung are essentials in temple worship, especially in libation. In the temple, when the doors of the *sanctum sanctorum* are opened early in the morning, a cow is stationed before them so that when the deity opens his eyes to the universe his sight falls first on the back of the cow. This ritual, considered most auspicious, is called *Vis-va-rupa Darsana*, the sight of cosmic form, and ensures limitless blessings on the people. Similarly, in the past when a king woke up in the morning he was shown a few sacred objects, including a cow, to ensure his well being.

There are 16 gifts, which include the cow, that a king or a rich person could make on an auspicious occasion. Similarly, in death ceremonies, the gift of a cow is a must for the fulfilment of rites. Saivites often wear sacred ash (on their forehead and body) prepared from cow-dung. Krishna, the great God, was a cowherd fond of cow's milk and butter, and is specially propitiated with offerings of these. With such a vital role in the daily life of the Hindus, it is no wonder that the cow is venerated in India.

THE VEDIC PANTHEON

Vedic hymns were often inspired by the awesome manifestations of nature encountered by the Aryans. Every aspect of nature was personified and endowed with supernatural powers. In the course of successive centuries, these personifications were transmuted into the Hindu gods, who are considered the different forms of a single Divine Being and worshiped to this day. A total of 33 Vedic gods are praised and grouped into deities of three spheres, terrestrial, aerial and heavenly. All the Vedic gods were personified and propitiated by offerings of butter and *soma* juice, and the chanting of hymns. While most of the deities were males, some goddesses such as Ushas (dawn) and the river Sarasvati, were also extolled; as were some abstract ideas.

Agni (fire), is an important god of the Vedic people. Agni is derived from the Indo-European word and occurs as *Igni* in Latin and *Ogni* in Slavonic. Agni's rising flames are likened to hairs and to tongues with which he receives the oblations and carries them to all the other gods. He is nourished three times a day and is called the domestic priest. Indra is the most powerful god of the Vedic people. He is the personification of the thunderstorm, which vanquishes drought and darkness. The clouds are likened to moving fortresses, attacked by Indra; and so he is called the destroyer and was often invoked by the Aryans during warfare. The all-encompassing sky is personified as Varuna, the great Lord, next only to Indra in importance, steadying heaven and earth, keeping them apart, which is called the great law. Originally the storm in its baleful aspect, seen in the destructive agency of lightning, Rudra, was considered young and unaging.

Rudra shines like a radiant sun. Rudra is the bountiful and auspicious Siva. He is also terrible like a beast and mortals are afraid of his wrath. He possesses cooling remedies and is praised as the physician of physicians. Rudra is often identical with Agni, fire. From this position, Rudra rose to be Siva. Vishnu, the shining one, is also a Vedic god. He is the brightness of the sun, and so takes three strides, corresponding to the three courses of the sun - earth, air and heaven. Vishnu is said to have measured the world with these three strides.

The other god of interest, who assumed importance in the later period is Brahma, the creator, who is identical with Brahaspati of the Vedas. The word originally meant the lord of prayer, associated with singers. The three gods – Rudra, Vishnu and Brahma – occupied a secondary position in the early Vedic period, but the powerful imagery later created around them brought them to the forefront of the Hindu pantheon. Siva is the deity of contrasts, of unified polarities within his nature. This unifying feature characterizes the fearsome and auspicious Siva (Siva means auspicious) most distinctly. In the traditional Hindu trinity of gods Brahma is called the Creator, and Vishnu the Preserver, whereas Siva is known as the Destroyer of the Universe at the end of time, emphasizing his ferocious aspects as the deliverer of universal death. But just as Vishnu plays all three divine roles for his devotees, Siva is also regarded by his believers as Creator and Preserver. Vishnu is worshiped as the Preserver of the Created World during the periods of time between each successive emergence and dissolution of the universe. He is called the All-Preserver, but he is also said to be the primal person and the first-born of creation, who has neither beginning nor end.

The multiple powers attributed to the deities are symbolized by multiple arms and the epithets of various deities are also applied to one and the same deity. The unity and diversity of the Hindu pantheon have been beautifully captured in the poetic imagery of the Vedic hymns.

Nelles Maps ...the maps that get you going.

NEPAL

NELLES VERLAG

KENYA

NELLES VERLAG

THAILAND

NELLES VERLAG

India 1
NORTHERN INDIA

NELLES VERLAG

Road Atlas
INDONESIA

NELLES VERLAG

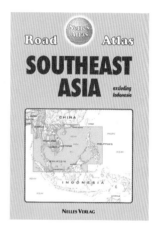

Road Atlas
SOUTHEAST ASIA excluding Indonesia

NELLES VERLAG

- Afghanistan
- Australia
- Bangkok
- Burma
- Caribbean Islands 1 / Bermuda, Bahamas, Greater Antilles
- Caribbean Islands 2 / Lesser Antilles
- China 1 / North-Eastern China
- China 2 / Northern China
- China 3 / Central China
- China 4 / Southern China
- Crete
- Egypt
- Hawaiian Islands
- Hawaiian Islands 1 / Kauai
- Hawaiian Islands 2 / Honolulu, Oahu

Nelles Maps

- Hawaiian Islands 3 / Maui, Molokai, Lanai
- Hawaiian Islands 4 / Hawaii
- Himalaya
- Hong Kong
- Indian Subcontinent
- India 1 / Northern India
- India 2 / Western India
- India 3 / Eastern India
- India 4 / Southern India
- India 5 / North-Eastern India
- Indonesia
- Indonesia 1 / Sumatra
- Indonesia 2 / Java + Nusa Tenggara
- Indonesia 3 / Bali
- Indonesia 4 / Kalimantan
- Indonesia 5 / Java + Bali
- Indonesia 6 / Sulawesi

- Indonesia 7 / Irian Jaya + Maluku
- Jakarta
- Japan
- Kenya
- Korea
- Malaysia
- West Malaysia
- Manila
- Mexico
- Nepal
- New Zealand
- Pakistan
- Philippines
- Singapore
- South East Asia
- Sri Lanka
- Taiwan
- Thailand
- Vietnam, Laos Cambodia

TABLE OF CONTENTS

TRAVELING TO INDIA

This section provides general information on travel to India, as well as helpful tips for traveling within the country. For more detailed enquiries you should contact the Government of India Tourist Offices (GITOs).

Arriving in India

Air: Nearly 50 international carriers operate over 150 flights a week to India's four major cities - Delhi, Bombay, Calcutta, Madras. Choose an entry point to suit your travel plans in India (Madras is only serviced by bi-weekly British Airways flights from London). Some chartered services fly directly to Goa.

Sea: Several ports dot India's sprawling coastline - Bombay, Cochin, Madras, Visakhapatanam and Calcutta. However, these ports are mainly used by cargo ships. The only passenger liner servicing India is the Queen Elizabeth II.

Arrival Formalities

Immigration/Visas: A valid national passport and a visa (obtained from Indian missions abroad) are a must. If the visa is for 90 days or less registration on arrival is unnecessary. If otherwise, you must personally obtain a Registration Certificate and Residential Permit, within a week of arrival, from the nearest Foreigner's Registration Office. Four photographs are required and change of address and absence for more than 15 days has to be reported. Visas can be *collective* (issued to groups sponsored by a GOI recognized travel agency, it allows splitting up, visiting different places and reassembling before departure), *transit* (advance application to the Ministry of External Affairs, Delhi, required) or multiple-entry 90 day *tourist* visas.

Other types are issued if the purpose of visit is to conduct business, study, attend a conference, undertake media activity (e.g. make a film), participate in adventure sports (trekking, river-rafting, etc.) or study Indian culture (learn yoga or dance, for instance). Exit visas are unnecessary if you leave within the validity period of the visa (six months from the date of issue). Extension can be sought for a stay of up to six months.

Climate

Temperatures in India can vary from sub-zero to over 50° C. Though October to March is the recommended travel season, visits timed otherwise can be as rewarding. In summer, when the plains are hot and dry, there are nearly 30 hill resorts to choose from.

A western bugbear is the Indian monsoon. This is a wandering phenomenon and follows a regular path around the country each year. Rain-bearing clouds arrive from June to September and since they do not expend themselves everywhere at once, they are just as easy to avoid as to seek!

In winter, some high altitude tourist destinations suffer inclement weather or are altogether inaccessible. The option is to head for the Indian coastline - studded with innumerable beaches. Except for humidity in the rainy season, these enjoy glowing weather round the year.

Clothing

Your itinerary and its timing will determine this. Two pullovers, one light and the other heavy, are a must in winter. In some areas heavy woolens would also be required. For daywear light clothing will suffice; this will be suitable for the coastline destinations as well. Dispense with synthetics.

Ideal footwear would be open sandals in summer and walking shoes in winter. Except for the beaches, it would be wise for women to dress conservatively.

Currency and Exchange

Currency: Coinage in India is decimal based with 100 paise to every rupee. Coins are available in denominations of 5, 10, 20, 25 and 50 paise and one and two rupees, while notes come in 1, 2, 5, 10, 20, 50 and 100 rupee denominations. It is illegal to export or import Indian currency. Rupee traveler's checks issued abroad are an exception.

Banks: Foreign and nationalized Indian banks conduct business from 10 am to 2 pm. Monday through Friday, and from 10 am to 12 noon on Saturdays. A few are open in the evening and on Sundays. Banks close on national holidays, June 30 and December 31.

Exchange: You can bring in any amount of foreign exchange in the shape of coins, bank notes and traveler's checks provided these are declared on arrival in the CD form (up to US$ 1000 or equivalent need not be declared, unless it is a currency draft). All encashments and exchange must be recorded and receipts maintained (including hotel bills and airline tickets) to facilitate reconversion of unspent money on departure. This is doubly useful for income tax exemption, in case your visit exceeds 90 days. Money should be exchanged only by authorized banks/money changers. Major credit cards are accepted by established hotels, shops and restaurants.

Customs

Red and green channels exist for clearance. A random check of baggage may be conducted. Duty free imports include personal effects (jewelry too), a camera with five film rolls, binoculars, portable typewriter, radio, a tape-recorder, camping equipment, skis, etc; also up to 200 cigarettes and 95 ml alcohol. Vehicles can be brought in under a triptyque/carnet issued by any internationally recognized automobile association. Both pro-

fessional equipment and high value articles must be declared. Import of the following articles is prohibited – dangerous drugs, live plants, gold and silver bullion, unlicensed weapons. These rules extend to unaccompanied baggage. Prohibited articles of export are antiques (over 100 years old), skins, gold jewelry exceeding Rs. 20,000 in value, other jewelry (including precious stones) valued at over Rs. 10,000.

Departure

Reservations for departure must be reconfirmed well in advance. Also allow two hours for check-in as security checks can be intensive. All passengers (including infants) have to pay a **Foreign Travel Tax** (at the airport/seaport) of Rs. 300 prior to check in. Those headed for Afghanistan, Bangladesh, Bhutan, Burma, Nepal, Pakistan and Sri Lanka pay half the fee.

Health (Regulations and Precautions)

A vaccination certificate is essential only if you have traveled through yellow fever endemic countries (mostly in Africa and South America), ten days prior to reaching India. Otherwise, you could face six days in quarantine.

No other certificate is required but it is advisable to get vaccinations for cholera, typhoid and tetanus. You will find a medical kit containing the following handy in India: anti-malaria, anti-emetic, anti-diarrhoeal pills, antibiotics, anti-allergens, an insect repellent, suntan lotion (for high altitudes), an antiseptic cream, band-aids and salt pills (necessary only in summer). These are available at medical stores in all towns and cities. Chemists attached to major hospitals are open 24 hours. Boiled water, soda, mineral water or aerated drinks are recommended. Scrupulously avoid salads, peeled fruit and ice in smaller towns and establishments. Fresh food straight off the fire is comparatively safe.

Statistics on India

Area: 3,287,263 sq. km; Population: (1986): 761070100; No. of States: 25; No. of Union Territories: 8; Religion: Hindus - 82.64%; Muslims - 11.35%; Christians - 2.43%; Sikhs - 1.96%; Buddhists - 0.71%, Jains - 0.48%; Others - 0.42%.

TRAVELING IN INDIA

Accommodation

India offers accommodation to suit budgets and preferences ranging from luxury resorts and hotels to modestly priced travelers' lodges. If you want home comforts, stick to luxury hotels (a list can be obtained from your nearest GITO) which require prior booking specially during the tourist season (October-March). With the major hotel chains, reservations are centralized and options are offered. Accommodation is available at the four city airports as well as at most railway stations. The YWCA, YMCA, Youth Hostels and State Tourism outlets are cheap and comfortable. In smaller towns, the local district authorities can be contacted at least six weeks in advance for reservation of Inspection Houses and Dak-Bungalows, which are primarily meant for bureaucrats. Paying guest accommodation can be arranged by GITO. Camping sites exist in some areas.

Domestic Airlines

The two domestic carriers are *Indian Airlines* (Air India handles outbound traffic) and *Vayudoot*. IA services over 61 domestic destinations and also operates to Afghanistan, Bangladesh, the Maldives, Nepal, Pakistan, Singapore, Sri Lanka and Thailand. Booking is compu-

terized in Bangalore, Bombay, Calcutta, Delhi, Hyderabad and Madras. During the tourist season (October to March) please confirm reservations well in advance. Also, check in an hour before departure. A reliable coach service connects various hotels to the airport.

IA offers packages (available only against foreign currency) which can also be purchased outside of India: *Discover India* (US 400) permits unlimited travel within India for 21 days (with some routing restrictions) and the *India Wonderfare* (US$ 200) allows unlimited travel for a week in a region (north/south/east/west) of your choice (US$ 100 extra for those who opt to visit Port Blair from Calcutta or Madras). Further incentives are discount tickets for yougsters (25% discount for students/those under 30) and tourists heading south (30% off US dollar tariff on select sectors). *Vayudoot*, a feeder airline, has a number of tourist packages. A big draw is the *Air-Trek* over the Himalayas. *Air-Trek* services are available from Delhi or Dehra Dun.

Electricity

A 220 volts (alternate current) 50 cycle system is in operation throughout the country. Good hotels provide step-down transformers to alter voltage to suit individual electric appliances. Confirm with the hotel information.

Etiquette

It is essential to remove footwear (socks are acceptable) and to cover the head (this is insisted upon in *gurdwaras*) when visiting shrines (these include temples, mosques and memorials, and in Kerala, churches). Some religious places take exception to leather goods while others prohibit photography. You should carefully read the rules displayed and act accordingly. Indians are generally very warm and hospitable and will be pleased

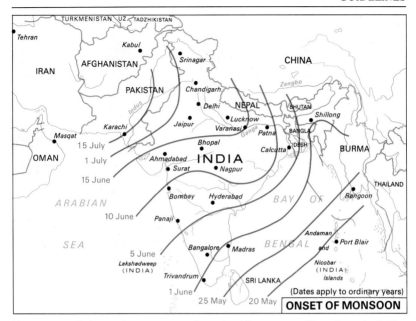

ONSET OF MONSOON

(Dates apply to ordinary years)

if you return their greeting, *namaste*, offered with folded hands. A handshake will be a nice gesture only with men. Indian women do not customarily shake hands even with their own men.

Festivals and Holidays

Since most festivals are determined by the lunar calendar it is advisable to get a list of holidays for the current year from the GITO. Certain holidays have fixed dates: Republic Day - January 26; Independence Day - August 15; Gandhi Jayanti - October 2; Christmas - December 25. (See Guideposts for the important festivals of each state.) On Republic Day, Independence Day and Gandhi Jayanti even shopping centers remain closed.

Guides

English and other foreign language speaking tourist guides can be hired at all the major tourist centers. This can be arranged by a travel agent or GITO. Guides

should carry a certificate from the Indian Department of Tourism. Unapproved guides are not permitted to enter protected monuments. At some monuments guide books from the Archeological Survey of India are available.

Liquor

Prohibition is in force in some states where permits are required; consult GITO to obtain one. Public holidays and certain days of the month are observed as dry days. While bars in hotels offer a wide array of drinks most city restaurants are not licensed to serve liquor. Liquor should be bought only from shops, displaying "English Wine" or "Indian Made Foreign Liquor" (IMFL) signs. Others sell country brews, best avoided.

Local Transport

Next to rail, motor transport is widely used by locals as well as tourists to travel within and between cities.

241

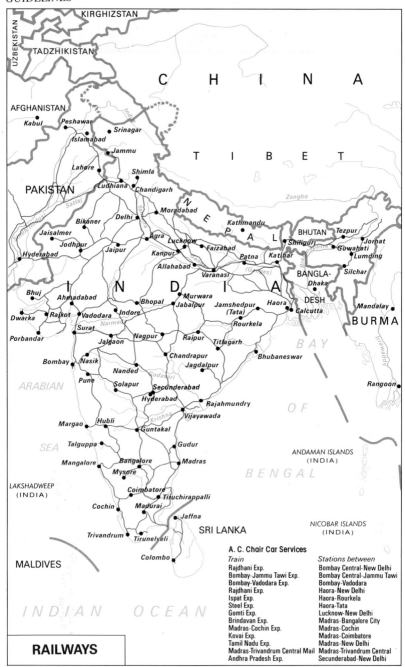

A. C. Chair Car Services

Train	Stations between
Rajdhani Exp.	Bombay Central-New Delhi
Bombay-Jammu Tawi Exp.	Bombay Central-Jammu Tawi
Bombay-Vadodara Exp.	Bombay-Vadodara
Rajdhani Exp.	Haora-New Delhi
Ispat Exp.	Haora-Rourkela
Steel Exp.	Haora-Tata
Gomti Exp.	Lucknow-New Delhi
Brindavan Exp.	Madras-Bangalore City
Madras-Cochin Exp.	Madras-Cochin
Kovai Exp.	Madras-Coimbatore
Tamil Nadu Exp.	Madras-New Delhi
Madras-Trivandrum Central Mail	Madras-Trivandrum Central
Andhra Pradesh Exp.	Secunderabad-New Delhi

RAILWAYS

Taxis: These are metered yellow and black, and non-metered tourist cars run by private tour operators. The latter can be air-conditioned or non-air-conditioned, of Indian or foreign make. Charges vary from state to state, nowhere exceeding Rs. 5 per km. The metered three wheel auto-rickshaw accommodates three passengers without extra charge. Due to frequent rises in fuel prices, meters often do not indicate the revised rates. Ask the driver to show the fare chart which indicates revised rates or pay 6 percent to 10 percent more than what the meter shows. Night charges are extra. From airports taxi numbers are noted as well as the name and destination of the passenger. International airports also have prepaid taxi services. For the convenience of passengers in transit, international airports have regular coach services to the domestic airport. It is in your own interest to make sure that the meter is zeroed to the minimum fare before your journey. Fare structure/rules vary from location to location.

Buses: These should be avoided during rush hours within the city. Inter-city connections are offered by several road transport companies who operate regular, deluxe and ordinary coaches. The deluxe occasionally have an additional feature - video films.

Museums and Art Galleries

There is a select group of national museums which presents a comprehensive picture of the principal periods and styles of the 4000-year-old Indian civilization, and 21 on-site museums. Some are devoted exclusively to specialized areas like folk/tribal art or textiles.

Most museums remain open on Sundays and close on another day of the week as well as on public holidays. Entry fees to museums are incredibly low. Art galleries in larger cities periodically hold exhibitions-cum-sales of paintings, photographs, etchings, lithos, woodcuts, sculpture, ceramics and pottery (see Guideposts).

Newspapers and Periodicals

The large number of English and vernacular publications reflect the great interest Indians have in current affairs. Leading English dailies include *The Times of India*, the *Hindustan Times*, *The Hindu*, *The Telegraph* and the *Indian Express*. Among magazines, *India Today* (a fortnightly) and *Sunday* (a weekly) cover both national and international events. The *Illustrated Weekly* is a general features magazine, *The India Magazine*, *Imprint* and *Marg* cater to specialized interests. *Destination Traveller* is specific to travel and tourism.

Photography

Photography is permitted in most places. Wherever there are restrictions such as at defense installations, bridges, certain monuments and areas, large notices inform you of this. Films are available and processing (barring Kodachrome) is possible. However, it is advisable to buy films from large stores.

Postal Services

Mail services are generally reliable. So are poste restante facilities which are available at major post offices in the cities. Instead of posting (personally or through a bell boy) letters bearing high denomination stamps in a mail box, present them at any post office counter for immediate defacing (see Guideposts for each region).

Railways

Covering 62,000 km (38,500 mi), the Indian Railway is the longest rail system in Asia and the fourth longest in the

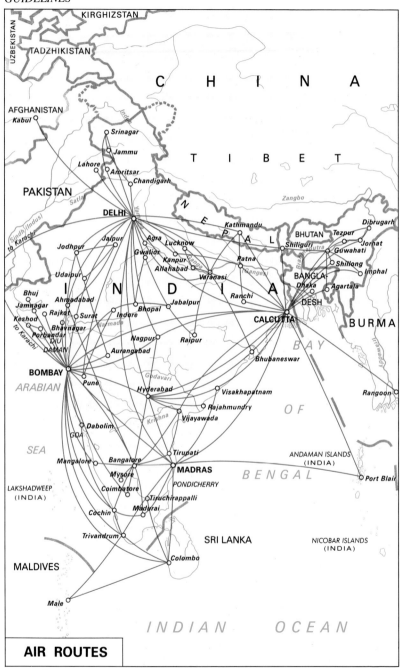

AIR ROUTES

world, and recommended for a first-hand encounter with the diversity of India. Of the five categories of accommodation available, restrict yourself to air-conditioned first class, first class, two-tier air-conditioned sleeper and air-conditioned chair car. You can ask for bed rolls and extra blankets while purchasing the ticket. If possible, stay with the express trains. Food to suit western tastes is served in dining cars attached to all important trains. There are Tourist Information Centers at stations in Bombay, Delhi and Calcutta. Certain trains set apart a foreign tourist quota which gets you priority in reservations.

Indrail Passes, which cost between US$ 95 and US$ 690, for the categories advised, are now available from Asra-Orient, Kaiserstrasse 50, D-60329 Frankfurt, and Hari World Travel 13, Rockefeller Plaza, Shop No. 21, Mezzanine North, New York NY 10112. These are valid from a week to 90 days. However, these do not entitle reserved accommodation. Ask the agent instead for details on the *Indrail Rovers* scheme. Especially designed to cover tourist circuits, 32 itineraries ensure confirmed availability of train accommodation if booked 90 days in advance. For railway buffs there are still many delights like steam locomotives, narrow gauge lines and "toy trains" in the hill areas.

Palace on Wheels: The luxuriously appointed saloons - belonging to erstwhile Indian princes and British Viceroys - which this holiday train comprises justify its name. It leaves Delhi every Wednesday (only between October and March) to cover Jaipur, Udaipur, Jaisalmer, Jodhpur, Bharatpur, Fatehpur Sikri and Agra in a week long tour. Most distances are covered overnight, leaving the day for sightseeing. The fare, ranging from US$ 100 to US$ 200, includes cost of travel, all meals, conducted tours, guide and entrance fee at monuments, elephant, camel, boat rides, and cultural entertainment. Details can be obtained from your travel agent, GITO or the Rajasthan Tourism Development Corporation, Palace on Wheels, Chandralok Building, 36 Janpath, New Delhi. Telex: 031-63142. Tel: 3321820.

Restaurants

Restaurants offering a choice of Continental, Chinese and Indian cuisine are many, and in the big cities those attached to luxury hotels further specialize in Italian, Cantonese/Szechwan, Japanese, Spanish and Thai food. There are any number of 24-hour coffee shops and fast food joints. Chilled beer and wine to go with the meal are, however, served only at select restaurants confined to the cities. Be cautious about eating at the ubiquitous wayside eateries called *dhabas.*

Shopping

India has a long tradition of crafts, and even objects of everyday utility are fashioned with artistic skill. The range of handwoven textiles and ready to wear clothes is equally stupendous. If you fear you are being charged a "touristy price" for your acquisition, make purchases exclusively from government emporiums (and other approved establishments listed with the GITO and mentioned in the Guideposts).

Tours

Conducted tours are run by nearly every state tourism department. They charge moderately for a day of sightseeing within a city and its immediate environs. There are also package tours, from a week to ten days, which link destinations within a state. If you have a special interest, wildlife, museums, ethnic groups or adventure sports like hang gliding, trekking and river running, approach any of the following private agencies to chart a suitable itinerary: Shikkar Travels; Wildlife Adventure Tours; Alpine Travels & Tours; High Points Expedition & Tours; Thomas Cook; Sita World Travel; and Travel Corporation of India. Most of these are located in Delhi. Some of these agencies have branch offices in Bombay, Calcutta and Madras.

Travel Restrictions

Some destinations or trekking routes can fall in the category of areas protected/restricted/closed to foreigners.

These include areas in Assam, Meghalaya, Tripura, Nagaland, Sikkim, Arunachal Pradesh, Manipur, Mizoram, West Bengal, Pubjab, Rajasthan, Jammu and Kashmir, the Andaman, Nicobar and Lakshadweep islands.

Ascertain details from your travel agent or GITO and accordingly apply (six weeks notice essential) to the Indian diplomatic mission or the Under Secretary, Ministry of Home Affairs, Foreigners Section, Lok Nayak Bhavan, Khan Market, New Delhi 110003, Tel: 619709, for a Restricted Area Permit. This can also be collected after arrival from any of the Foreigners Regional Registration offices at Delhi, Bombay, Calcutta and Madras. In some cases, immigration authorities grant permission on the spot. Seek details from the Mission GITO. The restriction can be on individual travel or the duration of stay (see Guideposts).

Telecommunication

Facilities for making local, inland and international calls are available at certain Public Call Offices (PCOs) at airports, railway stations and post offices.

Other national and international calls can either be dialed direct or booked through the operator. Service is available on demand for 70 destinations in India and for the U.K. Collect calls (outgoing) can be made to 20 countries. International calls can take anything from 15 minutes to 24 hours. Telex and Fax facilities are available in select cities at a few post and telegraph offices. Some private operators offer Fax facilities (see Guideposts).

Time

Despite the country's vastness, a single time zone exists. Indian Standard Time (IST) is 5 1/2 hours ahead of GMT and 9 1/2 hours vis-a-vis U.S., E.S.T. (Delhi: 12:00 hrs. corresponds to Bonn: 07:30 hrs).

Tourist Offices

The Department of Tourism, Government of India, has 18 overseas and 21 inland information bureaus (see Guideposts). These are equipped to handle queries on all aspects of tourist activity - visa requirements, liquor permits, health and export regulations. They also dispense free tourist literature on each destination/region.

You may find directories (of services) particularly useful as these list categories of accommodation and their tariff, taxi fares, distances between locations and facts under headings like local transport, shopping, banks and money-changers, "eateries" etc. Addresses (with telex numbers) are provided should you wish to book rooms in advance. GITOs as well as other state tourist information outlets in India do not make any travel arrangements. For this see a travel agent (listed with the GITO).

Weights and Measures

India uses the metric system for both weights and measures. Gold jewelry and certain articles in silver are sold by weight, and weighed at many establishments in *tola*, a traditional measure equal to 11.5 gm. Gems are sold by the carat (0.2 gm). Indians frequently use *lakh* (one hundred thousand) and *crore* (one hundred *lakhs* or ten million) while quoting figures.

Airlines

Air France. *Bombay*: Maker Chambers, V, Nariman Point, Tel: 2025021. **Air India**. *Bombay:* Air India Bldg, Nariman Point, Tel: 2023747, 2024142. *Madras:* 19 Marshalls Rd. Egmore, Tel: 847799, 848899. **Air Lanka**. *Bombay:* Mittal Towers 'C', Nariman Point, Tel: 223299. *Madras:* Connemara Hotel, Mount Road. Tel: 86315. **Alitalia**. *Bombay:* Dalamal House, 206 Nariman Point, Tel: 220795. *Madras:* 738 Anna Salai, Tel: 811306, 810936. **British Airways**. *Bombay:* Vulcan Insurance Bldg. 202 B Vir Nariman Rd., Tel: 221314, 220888. *Madras:* Fadun Mansions, 26 CMC Rd. Egmore, Tel: 474272/559/388. **Indian Airlines**. *Bombay*: Air India Bldg., Nariman Point, Tel: 2023031. *Madras:* Raja Annamalai Bldg. Meenambakkam, Tel: 477098/478333. **Japan Airlines**. *Bombay:* GSA Onkar Travels, 2 Raheja Chambers, Nariman Point, Tel: 233312/36. *Madras:* GSA Global Travels, 733 Mount Rd., Tel: 867957. **KLM Royal Dutch Airlines**. *Bombay:* 198 J. Tata Road, Churchgate, Tel: 221013/1185, 2965. **Lufthansa**. *Bombay:* Express Towers, Nariman Point, Tel: 2023430, 0887. *Madras:* 189 Anna Salai, Tel: 869095/ 9197/9296. **Pakistan Intl. Airlines**. *Bombay:* Oberoi Towers, Nariman Point, Tel: 2021455. *Madras:* GSA Bap Travels, Wellington Estate, 24 CMC Rd. Tel: 422611, 869985. **Royal Nepal Airlines**. *Bombay:* GSA Stic Travels & Tours, 6 Maker Arcade, Cuffe Parade, Tel: 2181431, 2181440. *Madras:* GSA Stic Travels & Tours, 142 Nungambakkam High Rd., Tel: 471195. **Swissair**. *Bombay:* Maker Chamber VI, 220 Nariman Point, Tel: 2870122/3461. **Vayudoot**. *Bombay:* Air India Bldg Nariman Pt., Tel: 2024142, 2028585.

Embassies / High Commissions Consulates

Australia. *Bombay:* Maker Tower 'E', 16th Floor, Cuffe Parade, Colaba, Tel: 2181071. *Delhi:* 1/50 G Shantipath, Tel: 601112, 601238. **Austria**. *Bombay:* Taj Bldg. (3rd floor), 210D. Naoroji Rd., Tel: 2042044, 2044580. *Delhi:* EP-13 Chandra Gupta Mg. Chanakyapuri, Tel: 611512, 601238. *Madras:* Kothari Bldg. Nungambakkam High Rd., Tel: 476036. *Calcutta:* 96/1 Sarat Bose Rd., Tel: 472795. **Bangladesh**. *Calcutta:* 9 Circus Ave, Tel: 444458. *Delhi:* 56 Ring Rd. Lajpat Nagar III., Tel: 615668,699209. **Belgium**. *Bombay:* Morena, 11 M.L. Dahanukar Marg, Tel: 4939261, 4929202. *Delhi:* 50N Shantipath, Tel:608295. *Calcutta:* 5/1A Hungerford St., Tel: 443886. *Madras:* 23 Spurtank Rd. Chetpur, Tel: 665495. **Bhutan**. *Calcutta:* 48 Tivoli Court, Pramothesh Barua Sarani, Tel: 441301/2. *Delhi:* Chandragupta Marg, Tel: 609217, 609112; **Canada**. *Bombay*: 1 Walchand Hirachand Mg., Tel: 265219. *Delhi:*7/8 Shantipath, Chanakyapuri, Tel: 608161. **China**. *Delhi:* 50D Shantipath, Chanakyapuri, Tel: 690349. **Denmark**. *Bombay:* L&T House, Narottam Morarjee Mg. Ballard Estate, Tel: 2618181, 2614462. *Delhi:* 2 Golf Links, Tel: 616273. *Calcutta:* 'Mcleod House' 3 Netaji Subhas Road, Tel: 287476/78. *Madras:* 292 Mowbrays Road, Tel:83141. **Germany.** *Bombay:* Hoechst House, 10th Floor, Nariman Point, Tel: 232422, 232517. *Delhi:* 6 Shantipath, Chanakyapuri, Tel: 604861. *Calcutta:* 1 Hasting Park Road. Alipore, Tel:459141/43, 454866. *Madras:* 14 Bishop's Garden, Greenways Road, Adyar, Tel: 76013. **France**. *Bombay:* Datta Prasad, Pedder Rd., Bombay 26, Tel: 4949808. *Calcutta*: 23 Park Mansions, Tel: 298314. *Delhi:* 2 Aurangzeb Rd., Tel: 3014682. *Madras:* Kothari Building, Nungambakkam High Rd., Tel: 811469. **Ireland**. *Bombay:* Royal Bombay Yacht Club Chambers, Tel: 2872045. *Delhi:* 13 Jor Bagh, Tel: 617435. **Italy**. *Bombay:* Consulate General of Italy, Vaswani Mansions, 120 Dinsha Wachha Road, Churchgate, Reclamation, Tel: 2874773, 2874777. *Calcutta:* 3 Raja Santosh Road, Alipore, Tel: 451411/2. *Delhi:* 13 Golf Links, Tel 618311/2. *Madras:* 738 Mount Road., Tel: 83780. **Japan**: *Bombay*: 1 M.L. Dahanukar Marg, Cumballa Hill, Tel: 4933857/4934610. *Calcutta:* 12 Pretoria St., Tel: 442441/45. *Delhi:* 4-5 Block 50G Shantipath, Chanakyapuri, Tel: 604071. *Madras:* 60 Spur Tank Rd., Tel: 665594. **Nepal**. *Delhi:* Barakhamba Rd., Tel: 3329969. *Calcutta:* 19 Woodlands, Alipore, Tel: 452024. **Netherlands**. *Bombay:* 'The International' 16 Maharshi Karve Rd, P.O. Box 1135, Tel: 296840. *Calcutta:* 18A Brabourne Road, Tel: 262160/64. *Delhi:* 6/50F Shantipath, Chanakyapuri, Tel: 609571/4. *Madras:* Chordia Mansion, 739 Anna Salai, Tel: 86411/13. **Pakistan**. *Delhi:* 2/50 Shantipath, Chanakyapuri, Tel: 600603. **Spain**. *Bombay:* Ador House, 6 K. Dubash Marg, Tel: 244664. *Calcutta:* No.1 Taratolla Rd. Garden Reach, Tel: 235539. *Delhi:* 12 Prithviraj Rd., Tel: 3015892. *Madras:* Lawdale, 8 Nimmo Rd, San Thome, Tel: 72008. **Sri Lanka**. *Bombay:* 'Sri Lanka House', 34 Homi Modi St., Tel: 2045861/ 8503. *Delhi:* 27 Kautilya Marg, Chanakyapuri, Tel: 3010201/2/3. **Sweden**. *85,* Sayari Rd., Bhubesh Gupta Bhavan, Prabhadevi, Bombay 25, Tel: 4360493. *Calcutta:* 6 Poonam Building, 5/2 Russell Street, Tel: 213621. *Delhi:* Nyaya Marg, Chanakyapuri, Tel: 604011. *Madras:* 41 First Main Road, Raja Annamalaipuram. **Switzerland**. *Bombay:* Manek Mahal, 7th Floor, 90 Vir Nariman Road, Tel: 2043003, 2043550, 2042591. *Delhi:* Nyaya Marg, Chanakyapuri, Tel: 604225/6. **U.K.** *Bombay:* Maker Chamber IV, 2nd floor, Nariman Pt., Tel: 233682, 232330. *Calcutta:* 1 Ho Chi Minh Sarani, Tel: 445171. *Delhi:*

Shantipath, Chanakyapuri, Tel: 601371. *Madras:* 24 Anderson Rd., Tel: 473136. **U.S.A.** *Bombay:* Lincoln House, 78 Bhulabhai Desai Rd., Tel: 3633611, 3633618. *Calcutta:* 5/1 Ho Chi Minh Sarani, Tel: 443611. *Delhi:* Shantipath, Chanakyapuri, Tel: 600651. *Madras:* 220 Mount Rd., Tel:83041.

Govt. of India Tourist Offices Outside India

Australia: Levell, c/o H.C.I. 17, Castlereagh Street, Sydney NSW 2000, Tel: 0061-2-232-1600/17961. **Canada**: 60 Bloor Street, West Suite No. 1003, Toronto, Ontario M4W 338, Tel: 416-962-3787/88. **France**: 8 Boulevard de la Madeleine, 75009 Paris 9, Tel: 4265-83-86. **Germany**: Kaiserstrasse 77-111, D-60329 Frankfurt, Tel: (069) 235423/24. **Italy:** Via Albricci 9, 20122 Milan, Tel: 804952, 8053506. **Japan**: Pearl Building, 9-18 Ginza, 7 Chome Chuo ku, Tokyo 104, Tel: (03) 571-5062/63. **Malaysia**: Wisma HLS, 2nd Floor, Lot No. 203, Jalan Raja Chulan, 50200 Kuala Lumpur, Tel: 2425301. **Singapore**: 20, Kramat Lane, 01-01 A. United House, Tanglin Rd, Singapore 1024, Tel: 2353800. **Spain**: c/o Indian Embassy, Avenida 31-32 PIO XII., Madrid Tel: 28016, 3457339. **Sweden**: Sveavagen 9-11 Stockholm S-11157, Tel: 08-215-081. **Switzerland**: 1-3 Rue de Chantepoulet, 1201 Geneva, Tel: 022-21-813, 4677. **Thailand**: Singapore Airline Bldg., 3rd Floor, 62/5 Thaniya Road, Bangkok, Tel: 2352585. **U.A.E.**: P.O. Box, 12856, Nasa Building, Al Makhtoum Road, Deira, Dubai, Tel: 274848, 274199. **U.K.**: 7 Cork St, London WIX 2AB, Tel: 01-437-3677/78. **USA**: 230 North Michigan Avenue, Chicago IL 60601. Los Angeles: 3550 Wilshire Blvd, Suite 204, Los Angeles CA 90010, Tel: (213) 380-8855. New York: 30 Rockfeller Plaza, Suite 15, North Mezzanine, New York NY 10112, Tel: 212-586-4901/2/3.

USEFUL HINDI PHRASES

Hindi is spoken by 50 percent of the population and is the predominant language of the north. In all there are 14 major Indian languages and over 200 dialects. English is widely spoken and understood, so the following Hindi words and phrases will more likely be used to enjoy the feel of another language.

Hello/Goodbye . . . . *Namaste*
What is your name? . . . . *Aap ka shubh naam?*
My name is ___. . . . . *Mera naam ___ hai.*
My home is in ___. . . . . *Mera ghar ___ mein hain.*
Where is the ___? . . . . *___ kidhar hai?*
How far is ___? . . . . *___ kitni door hai?*
How do I get to ___? . . . . *___ kaise pahunch sakte hain?*
How much does this cost? . . . . *Iski keemat kya hai?*
This is expensive. . . . . *Ye bahut mehenga hai.*
May I see the menu?. . . . . *Mujhe menu dikhaiye.*
Do not add ice. . . . . *Baraf nahin daaliye.*
I want something to drink. . . . . *Mujhe kuch peene hai.*
May I have the bill ?. . . . . *Bill laayiye.*
I am here for ___ days. . . . . *Mein ___ din ke liye yahan hoon.*
Where do you live? . . . . *Aap kidhar rehte hain?*
What is this?. . . . . *Ye kya hai?*
What is he doing?. . . . . *Vo kya kar rahe hain?*
I am feeling unwell. . . . . *Meri tabeyat thik naahin hai.*
What is the time? . . . . *Kya bajaa hai?*

I . . . . *mai*	night . . . . *raat*	1 . . . . *ek*
less . . . . *kum*	tea . . . . *chai*	2 . . . . *doe*
you . . . . aap	week . . . . *hafta*	3 . . . . *teen*
more . . . . *zyada*	milk . . . . *doodh*	4 . . . . *char*
we . . . . *hum*	month . . . . *mahina*	5 . . . . *paanch*
come . . . . *aaiye*	yogurt . . . . *dahi*	6 . . . . *chche*
okay- . . . . *achha*	year . . . . *saal*	7 . . . . *saat*
go . . . . *jaaiye*	rice . . . . *chawal*	8 . . . . *aath*
yes . . . . *han*	clean . . . . *saaf*	9 . . . . *nau*
price . . . da*am/keem*at	sugar . . . . *chini*	10 . . . . *das*
no . . . . *nahin*	dirty . . . . *gandaa*	20 . . . . *bees*
shop . . . . *dukaan*	salt . . . . *namak*	30 . . . . *tees*
big . . . . *baraa*	hot . . . . *garam*	40 . . . . *chalis*
medicine . . . . . *dawaa*	butter . . . . . . *makkhan*	50 . . . . *pachaas*
small . . . . *chhotaa*	cold . . . . *thanda*	60 . . . . *saath*
market . . . . *bazaar*	food . . . . *khanaa*	70 . . . . *sattar*
today . . . . *aaj*	breakfast . . . . . *nashtaa*	80 . . . . *assi*
room . . . . *kamra*	please . . *meherbani se*	90 . . . . *nabbe*
noon . . . . *dopahar*	thank you . . . *shukriya,*	100 . . . . *sau*
vegetable . . . . *sabzi*	. . . . *dhanyavaad*	1000 . . . . *hazaar*
evening . . . . *shaam*		100,000 . . . . *lakh*
water . . . . *pani*		10,000,000 . . . . . *crore*

AUTHORS

Shalini Saran is a well-known travel writer and photographer whose profession has emerged from her desire to explore, understand and share the beauty of India. Widely traveled in India, her articles and photographs have appeared in *The India Magazine, Namaste, Swagat, Namaskaar, Udit, The Taj Magazine* and *Soma*, published from India, and *Orientations, Discovery* and *Sawasdee* published from Hong Kong. She has also contributed to the APA *Rajasthan Insight Guide* and written the section on India for the APA *South Asia Insight Guide*. She has received two awards in the "Fotofest" organized by the Government of India for the Festival of India in Russia, and participated in "Pratibimba", an exhibition of Indian photography which has traveled to Russia and Britain. Based in New Delhi, Shalini has also worked as an editor with a publishing house.

Ravinder Kumar is a social historian in the history of Indian civilization. He is currently Director of the Nehru Memorial Museum and Library, New Delhi. Prior to this he was Professor of History at the University of New South Wales, Sydney, and the University of Allahabad. His published works include *Western India in the 19th Century* (London, 1968); (Ed.) *Essays in Gandhian Politics* (Oxford, 1971); *Essays in the Social History of Modern India* (Oxford, 1983); (Ed.) *Philosophical Theory and Social Reality* (New Delhi, 1984); and *The Making of a Nation* (New Delhi, 1989). He has also published essays in scholarly journals in India and overseas.

Nirmal Ghosh is a New Delhi-based photo-journalist specializing in wildlife and ecology, travel and socioeconomic affairs. He is a well-known wildlife conservationist, and regularly holds photographic exhibitions on the subject. He has received the Travel Agents Association of India's Best Travel Writer Award twice running, in 1986 and 1987. He is widely traveled and successfully combines his photography, writing and wildlife conservation activities with his present assignment at *The Times of India* (India's largest publishing house) marketing and coordinating Special Features on foreign countries.

Sumita Paul spent many years in Uttar Pradesh before coming to New Delhi. She has worked as a freelance writer and is now the editor of *Udit*, a magazine published by the International Airports Authority of India. *Udit* features various aspects of India's art and culture.

Bill Aitken was born in Scotland in 1934. He took his M.A. in Comparative Religion at Leeds University and hitch-hiked overland to India in 1959. He has lived in Himalayan ashrams, worked as a teacher and been the private secretary to a maharani. He spends the summer in the Himalaya chasing wild blue sheep and the winter chasing vintage steam locomotives in the plains. He became a naturalized Indian citizen in 1972.

Hamdi Bey, a true Calcuttan, has written on diverse topics for several newspapers from 1935 to 1975. The last newspaper he worked for was *The Statesman*, for which he still reviews books.

Zothanpari Hrahsel belongs to the Lusei tribe living in Mizoram. She took an M.Phil. from Jawaharlal Nehru University, New Delhi, the subject of her dissertation being the tribes of Mizoram. She is presently Director, Northeastern Cell, of the Indian National Trust for Art and Cultural Heritage (INTACH). Zothanpari also writes regularly on the tribes of the northeast and has been acknowledged for her contribution towards creating an awareness of the area.

Varsha Das is busy as an editor in charge of Adult Literacy publications, National Book Trust, New Delhi. She is a scholar of Sanskrit and Hindi and a regular contributor to several national dailies and periodicals in Gujarati, Hindi and English on subjects of artistic, cultural and literary interest. She has published books in Gujarati and Hindi, and being fluent in several Indian languages she has worked on translations as well. She belongs to Gujarat and travels widely in connection with her work.

Probir Sen is an officer of the Indian Administrative Service. After graduation in History he joined the Madhya Pradesh cadre and apart from other posts held, has been Director of Archaeology and Museums, Director of Tourism and Managing Director of the Tourism Development Corporation of Madhya Pradesh. Seventeen years of service in the state has nurtured his knowledge of, and love for it.

Ashis Banerjee took his M.A. in Political Science from Allahabad University where he has also taught for a number of years. He went on a Rhodes Scholarship to Balliol College, Oxford, where he took an M.Litt. He has been Visiting Fellow at the Centre for Policy Research, New Delhi, where he worked on problems related to the subject of national integration. He is presently a Fellow at the Nehru Memorial Museum and Library, New Delhi. All his publications are related to Indian politics and society.

After a distinguished career in archeology, **Dr. R. Nagaswamy** retired as Director, Department of Archeology, Tamil Nadu. He is a leading scholar of Sanskrit, with a deep knowledge and understanding of south Indian art and culture. An internationally renowned expert on Indian bronzes, he has been responsible for bringing to light many hitherto unnoticed images, and also establishing their chronology. He has published over 20 books in Tamil and English, and more than 300 research papers. At present he is Director of a project on the Brihadesvara Temple, Tanjore, sponsored by the Indira Gandhi National Centre for Arts. He is also on several national committees related to art and culture. Dr. Nagaswamy is a poet, and composes dance-dramas in the classical tradition as well.

Poonam Kulsoom has worked with the India Tourism Development Corporation in an editorial capacity for over six years. She has accomplished the painstaking task of gathering information for all the Guideposts with meticulous care.

PHOTOGRAPHERS

Arya, Aditya:	18, 28, 29, 44, 115, 157, 159L, 159R, 170 ,188, 198, 202 / 203, 207, 210
Banerjee, Jyoti /Fotomedia:	74
Chwaszcza, Joachim:	98 / 99, 107, 108, 204
Dilwali, Ashok:	21, 90, 120
Ghosh, Nirmal:	121, 227
Höbel, Robert:	8 / 9, 16 / 17, 37, 65, 82, 92, 216
Israni, Prakash:	10 / 11, 66 / 67, 71, 81, 132
Kaempf, Bernhard:	179, 228 / 229,
Kiedrowski, Rainer:	80
Klein,Wilhelm:	2, 24, 25, 32, 38, 41, 43, 45, 49, 61, 68, 84, 89, 114, 138L, 138R, 144, 150 / 151, 162 / 163, 164, 166, 171, 157, 176, 180, 181, 187, 196, 200 / 201, 211, 220, 222
Mazzoni, Leandro:	39
Mitra, Santanu:	27, 135, 140, 142, 147, 148
Sahai, Kamal:	62, 91, 124 / 125, 194
Saran, Shalini:	1, 12, 34, 47, 48, 52, 54, 59, 177
Scharf, Werner	cover
Sharma, Satish:	30, 53, 131, 189, 190